MW00566037

FOOD&**WINE**

Wine Guide
2010

WINE GUIDE 2010

editor in chief **Dana Cowin**
wine editor **Ray Isle**
volume editor **Kristen Wolfe Bieler**
senior editor **Christine Quinlan**
copy editor **Amy K. Hughes**
tastings coordinator **Colleen McKinney**
tastings assistants **Roxanne Downer, Stephanie McKinnon McDade,
Katherine Ramos, Scott Rosenbaum**
chief researcher **Janice Huang**
researchers **Jenny Choi, Annie Lok, Lawrence Marcus, Paola Singer**
indexer **Andrea Chesman**

produced for FOOD & WINE magazine by gonzalez defino, ny
www.gonzalezdefino.com
principals **Joseph Gonzalez, Perri DeFino**

designer **Patricia Sanchez**
map illustrations **Ethan Cornell**

cover photography **David Prince**
food stylist **Melissa Rubel**
prop stylist **Alistair Turnbull**

AMERICAN EXPRESS PUBLISHING CORPORATION
president/ceo **Ed Kelly**
senior vice president/chief marketing officer **Mark V. Stanich**
cfo/senior vice president/corporate development & operations **Paul B. Francis**
vice presidents/general managers **Frank Bland, Keith Strohmeier**

vice president, books & products/publisher **Marshall Corey**
director, book programs **Bruce Spanier**
senior marketing manager, branded books **Eric Lucie**
assistant marketing manager **Lizabeth Clark**
director of fulfillment & premium value **Philip Black**
manager of customer experience & product development **Charles Graver**
director of finance **Thomas Noonan**
associate business manager **Desiree Bernardez**
operations director **Anthony White**

FOOD&WINE

Wine Guide 2010

by Anthony Giglio

FOOD&WINE
BOOKS

American Express Publishing Corporation
New York

contents

old world

new world

old & new worlds

foreword

With the United States becoming a nation of wine drinkers, our annual FOOD & WINE Wine Guide is more valuable than ever. Americans are opening almost 4 billion bottles of wine a year—and choosing those bottles from the approximately 13,000 different wines for sale in restaurants, wine shops and supermarkets. Making an intelligent choice requires information—and information is what this guide provides.

There's an extraordinary amount of expert advice packed into our 12th annual edition, from insights into the latest wine trends to lists of star producers in top regions to substantial tasting notes on more than 1,100 recommended wines. These represent a distilled selection of the 4,000-plus wines that New York–based writer Anthony Giglio sampled over the course of the year.

Also included are a cheat sheet on pairing wine and food, a hit list of F&W's favorite wine websites and regional reports from some of the top experts in the wine world. Sommelier David Lynch weighs in on Piedmont's terrific 2005 and 2006 vintages; Champagne guru Tom Stevenson notes the great bargains to be found this year in the world's most prestigious region for sparkling wine; and journalist Victor de la Serna reports on one of the year's most unlikely trends, ice wines in Spain. Whether you're a beginner or an expert, within these pages you'll find all the information you need to help you navigate the ever-expanding world of wine.

Dana Cowin
Editor in Chief
FOOD & WINE

Ray Isle
Wine Editor
FOOD & WINE

acknowledgments

The author would like to thank the following people *not* named in the masthead, without whose help this seemingly small book would have been a far bigger task.

Deepest thanks to wine authority Jeffery Lindenmuth, for dropping everything to jump in when there were simply too many corks to pull, and for sharing his endless resourcefulness, generous spirit and deadpan wit.

A 21-gun salute to the Wine Guide Tasting Room's neighbors at The Hired Guns for grace under fire when the boxes of wine kept coming in waves, and the thousands of bottles seemed to engulf the overall décor of their beautiful office loft. Here's to you, Allison Hemming, Bart Codd, Jeffery Wernecke, Scott Benaglio, Daniella Kraut, Jessica Stone, Jennifer Pugh, Mary Matyas and Jude Sanjek. A special thank-you to concierge Eric Perkins for signing for all of those wine boxes over the course of five months.

My sincere appreciation goes to colleague and officemate Larry Smith of smithmag.net for keeping me focused—if not always calm—with his fresh-brewed Gorilla brand Ethiopia Harar coffee day after day.

A tip of my hat to Tony Nikolla, our "guy Friday" who did everything from assembling shelving in our Tasting Room and researching prices and winery information to hauling thousands of pounds of wine bottles around the office.

A toast to Maximilian Riedel, CEO of Riedel Crystal of America, for his generous donation of dozens of his gorgeous Vinum glasses to the Wine Guide Tasting Room.

To Neil Stolz and the staff at Central Avenue Wines in Jersey City for the ample supply of sturdy wine-case boxes used to keep bottles stacked and organized.

And finally, my wife, Antonia LoPresti Giglio, and our two greatest vintages, Sofia and Marco, for their patience during my long absences while writing this book.

how to use this book

All of the wines in this guide are for sale this year. For ease of reference, the wines are listed alphabetically by producer name, followed by the vintage year. The quality and price symbols used to rate each wine are described below.

You may note that certain wines have significantly older vintage dates than others. This is because some wines are released within months after harvest, while others are aged for years before release. Though most wines are thoroughly drinkable when they are put on the market, some will taste better if they've had a few more years to age in the bottle. These are usually wines that are heavy in tannins, such as Cabernet Sauvignon, Barolo and red wines from Bordeaux. There are no guarantees, however, that aging a wine in your cellar will improve it.

Certain producers have proven themselves capable of making excellent wines every year without fail. Wineries that are second to none in their categories are highlighted in the "Star Producers" sections in various chapters throughout the guide.

For more expert advice from FOOD & WINE magazine on bottles to buy and perfect food pairings, go to foodandwine.com/wine.

Key to Symbols

QUALITY

★★★★ **OUTSTANDING** Worth a search

★★★ **EXCELLENT** Top-notch of its type

★★ **VERY GOOD** Distinctive

★ **GOOD** Delicious everyday wine

PRICE

$$$$ **OVER $60**

$$$ **$31 TO $60**

$$ **$21 TO $30**

$ **$20 AND UNDER**

the year in wine

The Year of the Bargain Bottle

Americans continued to increase their wine consumption in 2008 and the first part of 2009, but they definitely cut back on the amount they were willing to spend per bottle. Demand for wines priced over $50 dropped precipitously both in restaurants and wine shops, while bottles priced at $10 or less soared in popularity—accounting for fully 66 percent of the U.S. wine market's estimated $30 billion in annual sales. In fact, according to one market study, the biggest jump over the last year was for wines priced between $3 and $5.99, followed by wines costing $2.99 or less. That "extreme-value" realm is the one in which Fred Franzia, one of the wine industry's more controversial figures, operates. Franzia was one wine purveyor who was not weeping at the otherwise bleak economy in 2009. Instead, he celebrated the sale of the 400 millionth bottle of Charles Shaw, better known as Two Buck Chuck, the original extreme-value brand.

Everything's Coming Up Rosé

After years as a moribund style—partly done in by an unfair association with sweet, soda pop–like white Zinfandel—rosés are enjoying a boom. Sales of imported rosés in the United States rose 42 percent in 2009. And in a victory on the side of quality, the European Union repealed a tentative decision that would have allowed rosés to be made by blending white and red wines. Many traditional rosé producers, who make their wines more labor-intensively, by crushing red grapes and letting them rest only a short while on their skins, had protested the change.

Eco Packaging

Anyone interested in being green while drinking their red found more and more eco-friendly options in wine this year. Australia's Wolf Blass launched its "Green Label" wines packaged in recyclable PET plastic bottles, and California brand Fog Mountain, owned by Boisset Family Estates, followed suit. These lightweight containers require less fuel for transportation, resulting in, Blass estimates, a 29 percent decrease in greenhouse gas emissions and a reduction in the overall carbon footprint. Other green-friendly packaging innovations include Tetra Paks (paper-based containers similar to juice boxes) from brands like Three Thieves and Yellow + Blue, as well as Mommessin's sleek aluminum bottle used for its reserve Beaujolais.

Washington's Riesling Crush

For years, Washington State winemakers have garnered critical acclaim for their Syrahs and Merlots. But recently, increasing demand for good Riesling has produced a noticeable shift toward that variety in the state's vineyards, and producers are making more with each passing vintage. In 2008, Washington State wineries crushed some 28,500 tons of Riesling—more than any other variety—and Riesling now accounts for almost 40 percent of the state's entire white wine production. Nor does the Riesling boom show any signs of slowing down: in 2009, two new American Viticultural Areas (AVAs) were approved in Washington State—Snipes Mountain and Lake Chelan—both of which produce Riesling.

Wine 2.0

Participation in wine-focused social media sites boomed during the past year, both on established platforms such as Facebook (where, for instance, there are now more than 500 different groups devoted to wine) and on wine-specific sites such as CellarTracker, Snooth and VinCellar. The trend generated some unlikely manifestations—nearly 1,000 YouTube-hosted videos were submitted by applicants for Murphy-Goode winery's opening for a social media–savvy "lifestyle correspondent"—as well as numbers that are extremely impressive: CellarTracker alone, for example, brings together more than 80,000 users commenting on some 10 million bottles.

food & wine's american wine awards 2009

To find the winners of FOOD & WINE magazine's annual American Wine Awards, F&W editors polled a select group of wine professionals including writers, retailers, restaurateurs, sommeliers and past award winners. Here are our picks for the year's top winemaker, best importer, most promising new winery and most outstanding American wines both under and over $20.

winemaker of the year

Charles Smith spent more than a decade managing rock bands in Scandinavia before moving to Washington State's Walla Walla region to make wine nine years ago. He named his Syrah-centric boutique winery "K Vintners" as a play on the Doris Day song "Que Sera, Sera," and while he earned a cultlike following for his small-batch, single-vineyard cuvées, his breakthrough wines were the Magnificent Wine Company's $10 House Red and House White. Smith's latest bottles include Kung Fu Girl Riesling, The Beautiful Syrah, The Boy Grenache-based blend and Charles & Charles Syrah-based rosé.

wine importer of the year

Vineyard Brands was founded by Robert Haas in 1971 and today represents over 25 growers of estate-bottled wines in Burgundy, Chablis, the Rhône and Loire valleys, Alsace and southern France, as well as some of the finest wines from around the world. Daniel Haas, Robert's son, continues the tradition of maintaining a close family relationship with the French proprietors. Its stringent selection process and commitment to quality have made Vineyard Brands one of the best specialty importers in the U.S.

most promising new winery

Anthill Farms Winery was created in 2004 by Webster Marquez, David Low and Anthony Filiberti, three friends who met while working harvest at Sonoma's esteemed Williams Selyem winery. The trio scraped together $9,000 to buy four tons of grapes and a couple of barrels, and secured rent-free space at Papapietro Perry winery in the Sonoma town of Healdsburg. Six years later, demand far exceeds supply of Anthill Farms' 1,900 cases of supremely elegant, single-vineyard Pinot Noirs, made with grapes from some of the finest parcels in Sonoma and Mendocino counties.

best wines under $20

Hanna | **2008** | SAUVIGNON BLANC

Luli | **2008** | CHARDONNAY

Sineann | **2008** | PINOT GRIS/PINOT GRIGIO

Siduri Sonoma County | **2007** | PINOT NOIR

Chateau Ste. Michelle Indian Wells | **2006** | MERLOT

Foxglove | **2007** | ZINFANDEL

Twenty Rows | **2006** | CABERNET SAUVIGNON

Copain Tous Ensemble | **2007** | SYRAH

best wines over $20

Spottswoode | **2007** | SAUVIGNON BLANC

Tandem Porter-Bass Vineyards | **2006** | CHARDONNAY

Tablas Creek Vineyard Esprit de Beaucastel Blanc | **2007** | RHÔNE-STYLE WHITE

Peay Scallop Shelf | **2006** | PINOT NOIR

Pride Mountain Vineyards | **2006** | MERLOT

Seghesio Family Vineyards Home Ranch | **2007** | ZINFANDEL

Hourglass Blueline Vineyard | **2006** | CABERNET SAUVIGNON

Arnot-Roberts Alder Springs Vineyard | **2007** | SYRAH

Domaine Carneros Brut | **2005** | SPARKLING WINE

wine tasting guide

Tasting wine is like any other acquired skill: the more you practice, the better you become. Most of us possess the necessary tools to taste wine. Our tastebuds can detect sweet, salty, bitter and sour sensations, plus "umami," the savory flavor found in mushrooms and meat. And our noses can differentiate between hundreds of aromas. The most important thing to learn is how to pay attention to the wine in your glass. Here are a few tips to help get your palate into tasting shape.

set the mood For each wine you want to taste, find a clear, stemmed glass that is comfortable to hold. Choose a well-lit place that's relatively odor-neutral. It is best not to wear perfume or scented lotion.

set the scene Pour just enough wine in the glass so it barely reaches the widest part of the bowl. This way you'll have room to swirl the wine without spilling it.

check the color A light color generally indicates a light-bodied wine; a darker color, a fuller-bodied wine. Also, white wines deepen in color with age; reds get lighter and take on an orangish or even brown hue. If you've poured more than one wine, compare the colors and guess which wine will taste more concentrated. Young wines that appear brown may be the result of poor winemaking or storage.

swirl & sniff Hold the glass by its stem and swirl it gently to release the wine's aromas. Sniff. What do you smell? Sniff again. Do you smell fruit? What sort? The wine might evoke herbs, flowers, spices, vanilla or wood. Some wines smell like bell pepper, leather, roasted meat or even manure. Don't worry about cataloguing every aroma. Just articulate what you smell. Doing so will help you tell the difference between one wine and another. Sharing your impressions will help you learn and remember. Noxious smells like sulfur or must might dissipate with air. If the wine smells bad, give it a few minutes and swirl the glass to bring more contact with oxygen. If the wine still has an unappealing odor, move on to another one. If a wine smells like wet, moldy cork or cardboard, it may be "corked," meaning it has been infected by an unpleasant-smelling compound called TCA that can be found in corks. TCA is harmless, but it makes wine taste bad.

sip & swish Sip the wine and swish it around in your mouth. Try to suck air into your mouth while wine is still in it (this takes practice). This allows the wine to release more aromas. How does it feel? Does it coat your mouth? Is it light, prickly and refreshing? Does it taste bitter or sweet? Does it recall specific fruits or spices? Smell again. Does it smell like it tastes? Do you like it? There are no wrong answers; it's all about what you perceive.

to spit or swallow? If you're tasting more than a couple of wines at one sitting and want to be able to detect as much as possible from every glass (and remember your impressions tomorrow), it's important to spit.

taste in context In a horizontal tasting, you sample a range of wines that are alike in all but one way. This could be a group of wines from the same region and vintage, but made by different producers, or a group of wines from the same producer, same grape and same vintage, but from different vineyards. Comparing the differences among such similar wines will expand your knowledge. In a vertical tasting, you sample the same wine from the same producer made in different years. It's a great demonstration of how vintage can make a difference, as well as how age can change a wine's look and taste.

wine terms

You won't find much fussy wine jargon in this guide, but some of the terms commonly used to describe the taste of wine might be unfamiliar or used in an unfamiliar way. Many tasting notes mention specific flavors or describe a wine's texture. These references to flavors and textures other than "grape" are meant to serve as analogies: all the wines in this guide are made from grapes, but grapes have the ability to suggest the flavors of other fruits, herbs or minerals. A wine said to taste like raspberries, for example, isn't infused with raspberries. Rather, it evokes flavors similar to those of raspberries. Here's a mini-glossary to help you become comfortable with the language of wine.

acidity The tart, tangy or zesty sensations in wine. Ideally, acidity brightens a wine's flavors like a squeeze of lemon brightens fish. Wines lacking acidity taste "flabby."

balance The harmony between acidity, tannin, alcohol and sweetness in a wine.

body How heavy or thick a wine feels in the mouth. Full-bodied or heavy wines are often described as "big."

corked Wines that taste like wet cork or newspaper are said to be "corked." The cause is trichloroanisole (TCA), a contaminant sometimes transmitted by cork.

crisp A term used to describe well-balanced, light-bodied wines that are high in acidity.

dry A wine without perceptible sweetness. A dry wine, however, can have powerful fruit flavors. "Off-dry" describes a wine that has a touch of sweetness.

earthy An earthy wine evokes flavors like mushrooms, leather, damp straw or even manure.

finish The length of time a wine's flavors linger on the palate. A long finish is the hallmark of a more complex wine.

fruity Wine with an abundance of fruit flavors. Sometimes fruity wines can give the impression of sweetness, though they are not actually sweet.

herbaceous Calling a wine "herbaceous" or "herbal" can be positive or negative. Wines that evoke herb flavors can be delicious. However, wines with green pepper flavors are less than ideal, and are also referred to as "vegetal."

mineral Flavors that reflect the minerals found in the soil in which the grapes were grown. The terms "steely," "flinty" and "chalky" are also used to describe these flavors.

nose How a wine smells; its bouquet, or aroma.

oaky Wines that transmit the flavors of the oak barrels in which they were aged. Some oak can impart "toast" flavors.

oxidized Wines that have a tarnished quality due to exposure to air are said to be oxidized. When intended, as in the case of Sherry (see p. 267), oxidation can add fascinating dimensions to a wine. When unintentional, oxidation can make a wine taste tired and unappealing.

palate The various sensations a wine gives in the mouth, including sweetness, flavors, texture and alcohol. The term "mid-palate" refers to the way these characteristics evolve with time in the mouth.

powerful Wine that is full of flavor, tannin and/or alcohol.

rustic Wine that is a bit rough, though often charming.

tannin A component of grape skins, seeds and stems, tannin is most commonly found in red wines. It imparts a puckery sensation similar to over-steeped tea. Tannin also gives a wine its structure and enables some wines to age well.

terroir A French term that refers to the particular attributes a wine acquires from the specific environment of a vineyard, i.e., the climate, soil type, elevation and aspect.

wine buying guide

Buying wine should be fun and easy, yet too often it isn't. Thankfully, there are several ways to gain confidence and make wine buying enjoyable no matter where you shop.

in shops

scope out the shops Visit local wine shops and determine which has the most helpful salespeople, the best selection and the lowest prices. Ask about case discounts, and whether mixing and matching your own assorted case is allowed. Expect at least a 10 percent discount; some stores will offer 20 percent. As wine shoppers have become more value-conscious, many retailers have increased their discounts and are offering one-liter bottles and three-liter wine boxes that deliver more wine for the money. Finally, pay attention to store temperature: the warmer the store, the more likely the wines are to have problems.

ask questions Most wine-savvy salespeople are eager to share their knowledge and recommend some of their favorite wines. Let them know your likes, your budget and anything else that might help them select a wine you'll love.

become a regular The better the store's salespeople know you, the better they can suggest wines that will please you. They may also alert you to sales in advance.

online

know your options The two most common ways to buy wine online are via online retailers or directly from wineries. Retailers may offer bulk discounts if you buy a case and shipping discounts if you spend a certain amount. Wineries don't often discount, but their wines can be impossible to find elsewhere. A great advantage of online shopping is price comparison: websites like wine-searcher.com allow you to compare prices at retailers around the world.

know the rules The difference between browsing for wine online and actually purchasing it has everything to do with where you live and how "liberal" your state is about interstate wine shipments. The laws governing direct-to-consumer interstate shipments differ from state to state. If you're considering buying wine from an out-of-state vendor, find out first whether it can ship to your state.

in restaurants

check out the list Most good lists feature wines in all price ranges. A poor list might be limited in selection, have too many wines from one producer or fail to list vintages. When faced with a bad wine list, order the least expensive bottle that you recognize as being reasonably good.

ask questions Treat the wine list as you would a food menu. You should ask how the Bordeaux tastes in comparison to the California Cabernet as readily as you'd ask the difference between two fish dishes. The first question should always be "May I speak to the wine director?" Then, tell that person the type of wine you're looking for—the price range, the flavor profile—as well as the dishes you will be having. With this information, the wine director should be able to recommend several options.

taste the wine When the bottle arrives, make sure it's exactly what you ordered—check the vintage, the producer, the blend or variety. If it's not, speak up. If the listed wine is out of stock, you might prefer to choose something else. You may be presented with the cork. Ignore it. Instead, sniff the wine in your glass. If it smells like sulfur, cabbage or skunk, tell your server that you think the wine might be flawed and request a second opinion from the wine director or the manager. If there's something truly wrong, they should offer you a new bottle or a new choice.

france

When it comes to wine, France is synonymous with greatness, representing quality, tradition and prestige. Missing from that list, perhaps, is innovation, as France has been slow to respond to New World competition. But a transition long under way in France is finally bringing change, as a rule-breaking younger generation of winemakers is crafting wines that are better than ever.

Principal Wine Region

Paris ☆
• Reims
Strasbourg •
Champagne
Alsace
Orléans •
Loire Valley
• Dijon
• Nantes
Burgundy
Atlantic Ocean
• Limoges
• Lyon
Bordeaux •
Rhône Valley
Bordeaux
• Avignon
Nîmes •
• Nice
Southwest
Provence
Languedoc-Roussillon
Marseille
Mediterranean Sea

France: An Overview

There's a debate about whether Italy or Spain makes more wine than France, but there is no question that France makes more *fine* wine than any other country on earth. Thanks to France's varied topography and climate, coupled with centuries of experimentation, the French produce excellent wines in nearly every category. Most are made in five major wine regions. Red wines are concentrated in Bordeaux, Burgundy (renowned for white and red wines alike) and the Rhône Valley. The remaining two principal regions, Alsace and the Loire Valley, both specialize in white wine.

France has maintained its long-standing position as the epicenter of the wine universe partly because the majority of the world's most esteemed grape varieties are French, including Chardonnay, Cabernet Sauvignon, Merlot, Pinot Noir, Syrah and Sauvignon Blanc. But while the French care about grape varieties—and strictly regulate where and how different grapes are planted—what really matters to them is a wine's *terroir*. The idea of *terroir,* a term that refers to all the distinguishing elements of a place, such as climate, sun exposure, soil makeup and surrounding flora, is fundamental to French winemaking philosophy. It is the belief that nature and geography make the wine, not man. Perhaps that is why, surprisingly, there is no French word for winemaker; someone who makes wine is called a *vigneron*—literally, a vine grower.

French Wine Labels

Most French labels list appellation (i.e., region or subregion) but not the grape variety used to make the wine. (Alsace labels are an exception; see p. 23.) A wine bearing its appellation name is required to satisfy certain regulations designed to guarantee quality and authenticity. The system governing these regulations is known as the *Appellation d'Origine Contrôlée* (AOC), or "controlled region of origin." The AOC hierarchy from top to bottom is:

• **AOC** This category encompasses the majority of French wines imported to the U.S. and ensures that the wines meet regional requirements. While standards vary from region to region, they typically spell out permitted grapes, winemaking practices, minimum alcohol levels (higher alcohol levels mean riper grapes, which in theory yield more flavorful wines) and harvest size (overly large grape harvests yield dilute wines). There are AOC regions *within* larger AOC regions as well, and generally, the more specific the subregion, the higher the standards. In Burgundy, for example, a wine bearing a district name like Côte de Nuits Villages must meet more stringent requirements than those labeled with the region-wide appellation Bourgogne. Wines from the Vosne-Romanée, a village within the Côte de Nuits, must conform to stricter standards. Those from Vosne-Romanée Les Suchots, a *Premier Cru* denomination of Vosne-Romanée, must meet even higher standards.

• **VIN DÉLIMITÉ DE QUALITÉ SUPÉRIEURE (VDQS)** Wines designated VDQS meet standards that are often less rigid than those required of AOC wines and are considered minor players within the French wine hierarchy. But if a particular VDQS region produces enough wines of sufficiently high quality, the region might be promoted to AOC status.

• **VIN DE PAYS** Translated as "country wines," Vins de Pays are subject to lower standards than AOC or VDQS wines, but they are allowed to list the wine's region and grape. Most Vins de Pays are forgettable, but there are a growing number of innovative winemakers who wish to work beyond the restraints of AOC requirements, and many are producing exemplary wines with this designation.

• **VIN DE TABLE** The lowest rung on the quality ladder of wines that fail to meet AOC requirements, Vins de Table (literally, "table wines") are not permitted to mention vintages or grape varieties on their labels, or give a place of origin more specific than "France." Most are dull, but certain iconoclasts who have chosen to ignore some of the AOC demands (which they believe inhibit quality production) are currently making some great Vins de Table.

alsace

It is easy to mistake wines from Alsace for their German counterparts: they share the same slim, tapered bottles, German surnames and even a history, as Alsace changed hands between France and Germany at various times between the 17th and 20th centuries.

Alsace Grapes & Styles

In Alsace, German winemaking practices influence everything from the grape varieties to the labeling—by variety, not region. Two of the area's most noble grapes are German: Riesling and Gewurztraminer. However, while many German Rieslings are sweet, Alsatian examples are generally dry. French Pinot Blanc, Pinot Gris, Muscat and Auxerrois make up the bulk of Alsace's other white varieties and are all widely planted. Pinot Noir is the region's only red variety. Alsace is also known for its wonderful dessert wines (see p. 273) and for Crémant d'Alsace, a Champagne-style sparkling wine (see p. 261).

Alsace Wine Labels

Unlike other French regions, Alsace labels its wines by grape variety. While European Union standards require that the listed grape compose at least 85 percent of the bottle's contents, Alsatian standards insist that it make up 100 percent. (Pinot Blanc is an exception; see p. 24.) Most Alsace wines fall into one of three categories: regular, reserve or late-harvest. Blended white wines are called *Edelzwicker* or *Gentil,* or they may be named after the vineyard from which the grapes came. Wines labeled *Réserve,* a term used fairly liberally in Alsace, may also list a place name. Alsace vineyards officially designated superior to all others can add *Grand Cru* to their labels. The integrity of this designation, however, is a matter of debate, and some wineries with Grand Cru sites prefer to use only the vineyard name, or proprietary names like Hugel & Fils "Cuvée Les Amours" Pinot Blanc. These names have no legal meaning but are mostly applied to premium wines.

ALSACE

pinot blanc & pinot gris

As their names imply, Pinot Blanc and Pinot Gris are indeed related, yet they can produce radically different wines. Pinot Blanc is softer, yielding subtle pear, citrus and nut flavors, while Pinot Gris is headier, with vibrant apricot and orange peel aromas. And although Pinot Gris is technically the same grape as the high-acid Pinot Grigio of Italy, the wines the two yield are very different in style, with Italian versions much lighter in body. Curiously, many Alsace wines labeled "Pinot Blanc" are blended with (and sometimes even made entirely from) the white grape Auxerrois. Until recently the region's Pinot Gris was labeled "Tokay d'Alsace," but to avoid confusion with the wines from Hungary's Tokaj region (made from Furmint), regulations now demand that it be called simply "Pinot Gris."

pinot blanc recommendations

Domaine Mittnacht Freres | 2007 |
★ ★ ★ $ This boutique biodynamic vintner makes tiny amounts of largely undiscovered wines. Seek this one out for its heavenly mix of vibrant lemon-lime flavors and chalky minerals on a medium-bodied, nicely textured palate.

Domaine Weinbach Clos des Capucins Réserve | 2007 |
★ ★ ★ $ $ In Alsace, 2007 was a benchmark vintage featuring the longest maturation period in 25 years. This always-excellent Pinot Blanc is especially rich and ripe, with waxy flavors of spiced applesauce and a pleasing tartness on the finish.

Josmeyer Mise du Printemps | 2006 |
★ ★ $ $ Josmeyer was founded in 1854 and achieved organic certification in 2004. This beautifully expressive white balances its subtly sweet flavors of plums, grapes and honey-coated green apples with a serious kick of spice.

Trimbach | 2006 |
★ $ This steely, mineral-laden Pinot Blanc is somewhat leaner than many but still offers generous flavors of lemon rind and orange zest and a powerful undercurrent of wet stone.

pinot gris recommendations

Domaine Ostertag Fronholz | 2006 |
★ ★ ★ $ $ $ André Ostertag likes to experiment with winemaking techniques not traditional to the region, such as the judicious use of new oak barrels for some of his whites. A master of Riesling, he also crafts stunning Pinot Gris. Infused with citrus oil and star anise flavors, with highlights of cinnamon and almonds, this medium-weight white is beautifully complex.

Domaine Paul Blanck | 2007 |
★ ★ $ For this Pinot Gris, winemaker Philippe Blanck uses natural yeasts to kick-start fermentation, a process that can take up to ten weeks. The result is a luscious, medium-bodied wine with slightly sweet flavors of ripe melon, white peach and lemon rind on a somewhat oily palate.

Lucien Albrecht Cuvée Romanus | 2007 |
★ ★ $ $ The Albrecht family has been making wine since 1425 and Romanus was the name of its first winegrower. Honeyed flavors of lemon tart and lime zest have a velvety, almost syruplike quality in this lovely Pinot Gris.

Pierre Sparr Réserve | 2008 |
★ ★ $ $ The Sparr family's history in the wine business dates back three centuries, yet their high-tech, computerized winery is entirely modern, as are their clean, pure wines. This excellent white displays lush, ginger-infused apple strudel flavors that come across remarkably fresh and dry on the finish.

ALSACE

riesling & gewurztraminer

Of Alsace's two preeminent grape varieties, Riesling is the more popular, thanks to its elegance, versatility and grace. Generally crafted in a medium-bodied and dry style, Alsace Rieslings possess zesty citrus and peach flavors and a flintiness that is unique to the region's terroir. While many wine drinkers appreciate the exotic, intensely flavored exuberance of Gewurztraminer, it is not for everyone. Big and brash, Gewurztraminer yields wines exploding with ripe lychee aromas and a wonderful spicy quality (*Gewürz* means "spice" in German).

riesling recommendations

Domaine Mittnacht Freres | 2007 |
★ ★ $ $ Youthful, floral and entirely dry, this Riesling shows an impressive purity of flavors in the form of flowers, apples and notes of cracked black pepper.

Domaine Paul Blanck | 2007 |
★ $ The dense mineral quality of this likable wine speaks to its origins in sandy, gravelly vineyard soils. Light and fresh, it has a nice mid-palate weight.

Domaine Weinbach Clos des Capucins Grand Cru Schlossberg | 2007 |
★ ★ ★ $ $ $ One of the finest producers in Alsace, Weinbach was founded in 1612 by monks and is now run by Colette Faller and her daughters. This exceptional Riesling is racy, fresh and youthful, with a bright lemon-lime acidity, clean citrus flavors and accents of cloves on the finish.

Paul Zinck Eichberg Grand Cru | 2005 |
★ ★ $ $ Founded in 1964, Paul Zinck is a relative newcomer by Alsatian standards. This Riesling tastes remarkably fresh for a 2005, with lemony acidity supporting flavors of apples and citrus and a hint of honey; it has a slightly oily mouthfeel.

Trimbach | 2006 |
★ $ Trimbach wines are consistently high quality and well distributed; the 2006 Riesling is zippy, fresh and mouthwatering, with lemon zest and green apple flavors underscored by a chalky minerality.

gewurztraminer recommendations

Domaines Schlumberger Les Princes Abbés | 2006 |
★ ★ $ $ This traditionalist vintner still uses horses to plow the steep terraces of its estate vineyard, indicative of a respect for the past that is reflected in Schlumberger's outstanding wines. This is thick, dense Gewurztraminer, featuring an explosion of spice, candied ginger, roses and apricots and a clean, off-dry finish that goes on and on.

Hugel & Fils Hugel | 2007 |
★ ★ $ Intensely floral, this medium-bodied, dry wine balances its hint of sweetness well: there is a subtle petrol aroma amid delicious flavors of honeysuckle, pear and lychee and a cleansing acidity on the well-integrated palate.

Léon Beyer | 2006 |

★ **$ $** This longtime Alsace producer fashions a more austere style of Gewurztraminer, with a firm coating of chalky minerals wrapped around ripe flavors of quince, pear and lemon.

Lucien Albrecht Cuvée Marie | 2005 |

★ ★ **$ $** Named for one of Jean Albrecht's daughters, this concentrated wine was fermented for a full three months and aged *sur lie* (on lees, see p. 53), adding a lemon curd–like creaminess to off-dry flavors of candied citrus rind, spice and quince.

Pierre Sparr Mambourg Grand Cru | 2007 |

★ ★ ★ **$ $ $** This wonderfully expressive wine delivers an intoxicating mix of apricot nectar, candied orange peel and a kick of ginger on the palate. Though it is viscous and rich, a lively acidity keeps it vibrant and balanced.

star producers
alsace

Domaine Marcel Deiss

Jean-Michel Deiss is a committed terroirist, cultivating single-vineyard field blends like his Bergheim Burg and Grand Cru Mambourg.

Domaine Ostertag

Vintner André Ostertag, an alumnus of the famous Beaune wine school, has applied his technical expertise to the production of biodynamic wine since 1998.

Domaines Schlumberger

Founded in 1810, Schlumberger is one of Alsace's largest and finest wineries, now managed by Séverine Beydon-Schlumberger and her uncle, Alain Beydon-Schlumberger.

Domaine Weinbach

The widow and daughters of legendary Alsace advocate Theo Faller honor his dedication to excellence by crafting some of the region's most spectacular wines.

Hugel & Fils Hugel

This family winery has been in business for 12 generations, thanks to strict adherence to its central philosophy: "The wine is already in the grape."

Josmeyer

Josmeyer is located in a dry microclimate, which makes the production of biodynamic wine difficult. Still, the vintner has been meeting the challenge with great success since 2004.

other alsace whites

Alsace is France's only major region that champions its single-variety wines, yet many excellent blended wines, sometimes called Edelzwicker or Gentil, are made here, too. Blends usually contain Sylvaner, Auxerrois or Chasselas—good, if unexceptional, varieties. Superior blends contain noble grapes such as Riesling, Gewurztraminer or Pinot Gris. The two kinds of Muscat grown in Alsace are usually blended with each other, not with other grape varieties, and tend to deliver aromatic honeysuckle and citrus flavors.

other alsace white recommendations

Domaine Marcel Deiss Engelgarten | 2005 |
★ ★ ★ ★ $ $ $ An early adopter of natural winemaking, Jean-Michel Deiss is also a huge believer in the process of blending. This field blend of Riesling, Pinot Gris and Muscat, among others, displays an enticing whiff of petrol, followed by ripe peach flavors and a healthy dose of clean, dry minerals.

Josmeyer "H" Vieilles Vignes Pinot Auxerrois | 2005 |
★ ★ ★ $ $ $ This sublime wine makes a big first impression with rich, mouth-coating flavors of almond paste, candied apricots and lychees; though it gives the impression of sweetness with its concentrated, nectarlike consistency, it is completely dry.

Pierre Sparr One | 2008 |
★ ★ $ An expressive blend of Muscat, Sylvaner, Riesling, Pinot Blanc, Gewurztraminer and other grapes, this fresh and zingy white wine is intensely floral on the nose and has an appealing hint of sweet cotton candy on the palate.

bordeaux

Bordeaux is easily the most recognized wine region in the world, and its legendary reputation is predominantly based on its formidable, long-lived reds, many of them made by celebrated châteaux. Elegant, earthy and substantial, the best wines of Bordeaux are crafted from a blend of noble grapes, led by Cabernet Sauvignon and Merlot.

Bordeaux Grapes & Styles

When most people think of Bordeaux, they think of red wine, but many excellent whites are made here, too, with Sauvignon Blanc, Sémillon, Muscadelle or some combination thereof. Some of the best whites, made in the Graves and Médoc districts, are dry, with stone fruit flavors. Those from the vast Entre-Deux-Mers area are light and citrusy. The greatest Bordeaux blancs are the sweet wines from Sauternes and its satellite regions (see p. 272). Bordeaux's iconic red wines are made from some combination of Cabernet Sauvignon, Merlot, Cabernet Franc, Malbec, Petit Verdot and/or Carmenère. Cabernet Sauvignon excels on the Left Bank of the Gironde; Merlot is at its best on the Right Bank, though blending is vital in all Bordeaux regions.

Bordeaux Wine Labels

Bordeaux wines are labeled by region, and, generally, the more specific the regional designation, the better the wine. Wines labeled simply "Bordeaux" can be made anywhere in Bordeaux. The next level up is *Bordeaux Supérieur*; these wines are required to be higher in alcohol, which implies they were made from riper grapes—often a measure of better quality. Wines from Bordeaux's districts—such as Médoc, Graves and St-Émilion—are required to meet even higher standards. And within the districts are communes— Pauillac and Margaux in Médoc, for example—which must meet more stringent requirements still. Bordeaux's system for ranking wines was established with the famous 1855 classification, which created a hierarchy of wineries (or châteaux) considered superior based on the prices their wines commanded over time. Known as the *Cru Classé* system, the ranking grouped 61 superior wineries by *cru* (growth), from first (*Premier Cru*) on top to fifth. Châteaux that didn't make the cut, but were still considered good, received the rank *Cru Bourgeois*. The 1855 system is limited to châteaux in Médoc and Sauternes, and one in Graves. In 1955 a similar system was set up to rank wines from St-Émilion, but it is subject to revision every decade or so. The famed wines of Pomerol are not ranked.

bordeaux whites

The best white Bordeaux—such as the highly regarded examples from the Pessac-Léognan subregion of Graves—are worth seeking out for their flavors of citrus, peach, grass and stone. The vast majority of Bordeaux whites come from the district of Entre-Deux-Mers; while they display similar flavors, and many are quite fine and affordable, most tend to be less impressive.

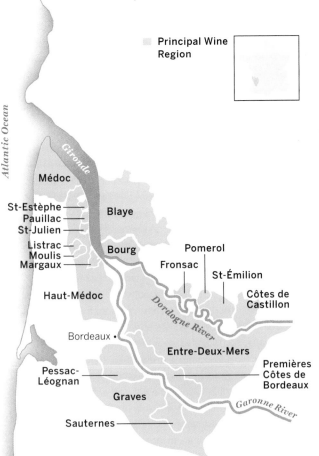

Principal Wine Region

bordeaux white recommendations

Château Bonnet | 2008 | **ENTRE-DEUX-MERS**
★ $ From the André Lurton wine empire comes this nicely refreshing, lemon-flavored quaffer, made with 50 percent Sauvignon Blanc, 40 percent Sémillon and 10 percent Muscadelle, all grown in limestone-clay soils. Four months spent on its lees gives it a softer, rounder texture than many other whites from the region.

Château Haut Rian | 2007 | **BORDEAUX**
★ $ Michel Dietrich left his native Alsace to become the owner of Haut Rian, where he specializes in Sémillon-dominated wines like this white. Notes of honey infuse a core of bright lemon flavors and add a lush, viscous quality.

Château Lafont Fourcat | 2007 | **BORDEAUX**
★ ★ $ Muscadelle is typically used as a blending variety but goes it alone here, yielding a floral, elegant wine marked by lemon and pear notes highlighted by minerals and a zesty kick of spice.

Château Lamothe de Haux | 2008 | **BORDEAUX**
★ ★ ★ $ This outstanding white—a blend of Sauvignon Blanc, Sémillon and Muscadelle—offers a generous dose of vibrant, fresh, lemon-saturated floral flavors for a low price. With a racy acidity, it would make a great aperitif as well as a good match for many foods.

Château Nicot | 2007 | **ENTRE-DEUX-MERS**
★ ★ $ This is lovely, light-bodied refreshment in the form of clean, pure citrus and flower flavors held up by a lively acidity.

Les Arums de Lagrange | 2007 | **BORDEAUX**
★ ★ $ $ Lagrange dates back to the early 17th century, yet has been making this white only since the late 1990s. Time spent in new and old oak adds a baked pear–flavored richness to enticing flavors of fresh hay, honey and citrus.

Michel Lynch Sauvignon Blanc | 2007 | **BORDEAUX**
★ $ Created by Pauillac's legendary Lynch-Bages estate in honor of its founder, Michel Lynch, this brand is all about great wine at very affordable prices. This pleasing, straightforward Sauvignon Blanc is full of grassy, chalky, mineral-infused lemon flavors.

Real Stones Sauvignon Blanc | 2007 | **BORDEAUX**
★ $ Sauvignon Blanc shows its mineral side—rounded out by notes of grapefruit—in this wine, which takes its name from Bordeaux's famously gravelly soils.

bordeaux reds

Nearly 90 percent of Bordeaux wines are red, made mostly with Cabernet Sauvignon and Merlot, plus Cabernet Franc, Petit Verdot and Malbec. Each subregion yields wines with distinctive characteristics: those from Pauillac are tannic and full-bodied; those from St-Julien are more taut. The wines of Margaux are delicate, while those from St-Émilion are plush. Most share a common earthiness and finesse.

bordeaux red recommendations

Château Angélus Grand Cru | 2006 | ST-ÉMILION
★★★★ $ $ $ $ This outstanding Merlot-dominated red, filled out with Cabernet Franc, wafts blueberry pie served with a bracing shot of espresso. The soft, supple texture nicely offsets powerful tannins that are sweet and approachable.

Château Boutisse Grand Cru | 2005 | ST-ÉMILION
★★ $ $ Merlot thrives in the clay soils of St-Émilion's St-Christophe-des-Bardes commune, producing wines with firm acidity and bold flavors, like this blend full of plum, berry, spice and vanilla.

Château Brane-Cantenac Grand Cru | 2006 | MARGAUX
★★★ $ $ $ A classified second-growth estate, Brane-Cantenac is on a par with many first growths. In this powerful, complex red, cherry and red currant flavors are woven with sweet tobacco, earth, eucalyptus and cigar box notes and balanced by a refreshing streak of acidity, all leading to a fabulous finish.

Château Cantemerle Grand Cru | 2006 | HAUT-MÉDOC
★★★ $ $ Cantemerle is a go-to Bordeaux bargain. The 2006 has all the classic hallmarks of the region, including dried berry and cherry flavors, a medium body and present but not overwhelming tannins.

Château Carbonnieux Grand Cru | 2006 | PESSAC-LÉOGNAN
★★★ $ $ $ With leafy tobacco and sweet cherry aromas reminiscent of Burgundy, this elegant, mouthwatering red is a standout, well worth seeking out along with its more famous white sibling.

Château Clinet | 2006 | POMEROL
★★★★ $ $ $ $ For under $80—a relative bargain by Bordeaux standards—this huge, powerful wine delivers a stunning mix of smoke, dried meat and blackberry flavors framed by huge tannins that will enable it to age for years.

Château Cordeillan-Bages | 2006 | PAUILLAC

★ ★ ★ $ $ $ $ Opulent ripe fruit, velvety tannins, medium acidity and a long finish make for a deliciously decadent Left Bank blend. It will evolve beautifully as it ages; cellar for ten years.

Château de Bel-Air | 2006 | LALANDE-DE-POMEROL

★ ★ ★ $ $ Michel Rolland, the renowned wine consultant, is the man behind the curtain at Bel-Air, crafting this plummy, vanilla-spiced wine. Touches of lead pencil, cedar and herbs are held up by ripe tannins on a long, rich finish.

Château d'Issan Grand Cru | 2006 | MARGAUX

★ ★ ★ ★ $ $ $ Chateau d'Issan has been a favorite of critics since the early 1700s. The 2006 vintage is exceptional now but will delight for decades. Notes of black currant, lead pencil, wet leaves and licorice are balanced by bold acidity and powerful, fine-grained tannins.

star producers
bordeaux reds

Château Angélus

Angélus was an underachieving vineyard just 20 years ago, but today—with an impressive number of legendary vintages under its belt—it has earned star producer status.

Château d'Issan

This 15th-century château was reborn in 1945, when the Cruse family took it over and began quality improvements that continue to this day.

Château Haut-Brion

In great and mediocre vintages alike, this first-growth vintner is considered one of the most consistent producers of world-class wines.

Château Latour

Located in the famed Pauillac appellation, Latour is known for being dependably great. It dates back to medieval times, but today boasts an ultra-modern winemaking facility.

Château Lynch-Bages

The Cazes family has run this legendary Pauillac estate since 1934, and is responsible for the impeccable reputation the winery enjoys today.

Château Margaux

Under longtime owner Corinne Mentzelopoulos and manager Paul Pontallier, this first-growth producer represents the pinnacle of quality.

Château Figeac Grand Cru | 2006 | ST-ÉMILION

★ ★ ★ ★ $ $ $ $ Black currant, dried black cherry and eucalyptus aromas leap from the glass, followed by ripe, generous flavors of extracted fruit. This Figeac vintage is uncharacteristically soft and plush, and instantly approachable.

Château Fonplégade Grand Cru | 2006 | ST-ÉMILION

★ ★ ★ $ $ $ $ Owned by American businessman Stephen Adams, Fonplégade produces a well-balanced St-Émilion, fragrant with ripe red berry, sweet spice, violets, lead pencil and earth and framed by bold tannins. The finish is juicy and long.

Château Haut Selve | 2005 | GRAVES

★ ★ ★ $ $ The owners of Château de Laubade Armagnac, the Lesgourges family, also produce this amazingly well-priced, complex Bordeaux. Firm tannins support the rich black fruit flavors, which show hints of lead pencil, violet and sweet spice on the finish.

news from a wine insider

bordeaux by Fiona Morrison, Bordeaux-based Master of Wine and international journalist

In the News

The mood in Bordeaux is somber these days. The region is heavily influenced by the world economy and has been hit hard by the global recession. As feared, the 2007 wines offered as futures were far too expensive and sold poorly. The financial crisis has also sparked rumors of châteaux changing hands, and Bordeaux is buzzing with the gossip that a host of properties are up for sale.

The World Market

British wine merchants are taking advantage of fluctuating exchange rates to offload their stocks of Bordeaux wines.

Christie's auction house closed its wine department in South Kensington, London, but is expanding its Hong Kong wine department to make the most of this burgeoning market. (Hong Kong became a destination for large quantities of expensive Bordeaux when it did away with its import duty on wine in 2008.)

Vintage Note

A series of bad vintages—2006 and 2007—hasn't helped this struggling region. The good news, however, is that the 2008 wines may be of higher quality than those from 2007, though yields were very low.

Château Lafite-Rothschild | 2006 | PAUILLAC
★ ★ ★ ★ $ $ $ $ This vintage from the first-growth superstar might actually be as good as its legendary predecessor, the 2005—at a fraction of the price (though still not cheap). Full-bodied and heady, with aromas of truffles, slate, earth and tobacco, it is packed with layers of black fruit and plush tannins.

Château Lynch-Bages Grand Cru | 2006 | PAUILLAC
★ ★ ★ ★ $ $ $ $ Vintage after vintage, Lynch-Bages offers first-growth quality in spite of its fifth-growth status and price. This 2006 offers a gorgeous mix of licorice and cassis flavors, earthy tobacco nuances and muscular tannins that promise longevity.

Château Pichon Longueville Comtesse de Lalande Grand Cru | 2006 | PAUILLAC
★ ★ ★ ★ $ $ $ $ Coffee and cocoa aromas introduce this spectacular wine, which is flavored with juicy prune, black currant, cedar and spice, held up by formidable tannins that are approachable now but ensure the ability to age. This is the estate's first vintage since it was purchased by the Louis Roederer Champagne firm.

Château Preuillac Cru Bourgeois | 2005 | MÉDOC
★ ★ ★ $ $ This harmonious wine from the gravelly soils of the Left Bank balances ripe, fine-grained tannins with lush black fruit, sweet spices, violets and a medium to full body. The finish lingers with rich fruit and spice.

Château Rauzan-Segla Grand Cru | 2006 | MARGAUX
★ ★ ★ ★ $ $ $ $ Though Cabernet Sauvignon only slightly dominates in this refined Margaux blend—filled out with nearly as much Merlot and a splash of Petit Verdot—it defines this wine, accounting for flavors of black currants, mushrooms and licorice as well as the supple tannins.

Château Saint-Sulpice | 2006 | BORDEAUX
★ ★ $ From the Entre-Deux-Mers region, where a lot of basic Bordeaux wine is produced, comes a blend that rises above the rest. Red and black currant, sweet tobacco and spice flavors are balanced by assertive tannins that will benefit from a few years of aging.

Château Tour de Ségur | 2005 | LUSSAC–ST-ÉMILION
★ ★ $ $ The satellite appellations of St-Émilion offer many wine bargains, like this 2005 marked by fresh plum and blackberry flavors and accents of minerals and lead pencil. Firm tannins and strong acidity round out the satisfying finish.

Château Trimoulet Grand Cru | 2005 | ST-ÉMILION
★ ★ $ $ $ After eight generations of producing wine at the Château Trimoulet estate, the Jean family has turned the reins over to its first female leader: Cécile Jean. She upholds the legacy well with this beautifully structured wine, characterized by complex layers of red fruit and earth flavors and a spicy finish.

Château Villa Bel-Air | 2004 | GRAVES
★ ★ ★ $ $ This red is an excellent value for its balance of vibrant acidity, fine-grained tannins and an array of flavors—cherry, mocha, spice, flowers and cigar box—that carry well into the finish.

Christian Moueix | 2006 | ST-ESTÈPHE
★ ★ ★ $ $ The Moueix name is attached to legendary wines like Pétrus that few can afford. But under his eponymous label, Christian Moueix offers good wine at earthly prices. The St-Estèphe is powerful, taut and beautifully layered with black fruit, cedar, pepper and spice.

Moulin de Duhart | 2005 | PAUILLAC
★ ★ ★ $ $ $ The second wine of Château Duhart-Milon, which is the second label of Château Lafite-Rothschild, Duhart offers the power and finesse of its superior sibling for a much gentler price. Black currant, pepper, pencil and cedar notes are balanced by firm acidity and elegant tannins on the long, complex finish.

Tertre Roteboeuf Grand Cru | 2004 | ST-ÉMILION
★ ★ ★ ★ $ $ $ $ The name isn't pretty—it translates as "hill of the belching beef"—but everything else about this wine is. Aromas of plum, black cherry, dried roses, cedar, mint and cocoa flood the glass, followed by an equally complex mix of flavors that are brilliantly structured and finish long.

burgundy

Burgundy is a small region with a reputation that far exceeds its size. Its ethereal, mineral-laden, smoky wines are among the most highly prized in the world. Yet, because Burgundy is one of the northernmost and coolest grape-growing regions in France, it can produce some highly variable (and often disappointing) vintages. In a good year—like 2005—a great *vigneron* can make white Burgundies that are extraordinarily complex and rich, and reds that are downright sensual.

Burgundy Grapes & Styles

Burgundy's fame is tied to two grape varieties: Chardonnay and Pinot Noir. Basically, all white wines here are made from Chardonnay, except for small yields of Sauvignon Blanc (grown in and around St-Bris) and Aligoté (mostly from the Côte Chalonnaise)—both of which are indicated on labels—and tiny amounts of Pinots Blanc and Gris. Pinot Noir is responsible for the lion's share of Burgundy reds, with the significant exception of Beaujolais wines, which are produced from the Gamay grape. Though considered part of the Burgundy region, Beaujolais has a distinctly different climate, terroir and style of wine. Another unique, if less important, appellation is Irancy; its reds are made from a blend of Pinot Noir and the local grape César.

Burgundy Wine Labels

All wine labels in Burgundy list region, some also list subregion, and a small number add the vineyard name. Generally, the more specific the place information on a label, the finer the wine, but the producer and vintage carry far greater weight when it comes to assessing quality in this region. Over the years, certain vineyards have achieved distinction for their consistently outstanding wines. But it's smart to research well in Burgundy, as a poor producer can make a disappointing wine from even the best grapes, while less-prestigious grapes can yield a terrific wine in a good year or in the hands of a dedicated producer.

• **REGION** The most basic wines of Burgundy are labeled with the name of the region, Bourgogne, and occasionally the grape variety. Though unassuming, some of these wines nonetheless offer good quality at an excellent price.

• **DISTRICT** A district appellation (such as Chablis) is the next step up in terms of quality. The grapes must be grown exclusively in that district. Wines labeled with the word "Villages" after the district name are theoretically superior.

• **VILLAGE** A wine may take the name of a specific village if all its grapes have been grown within that village's boundaries. This is often a good sign, as wines from the same terroir typically have similar characteristics.

• **PREMIER CRU** Certain vineyards with a history of producing superior wines have earned the distinction Premier Cru. These wines account for only about 10 percent of Burgundy's wines, and they must be made with grapes from these designated vineyards, which are sometimes included in the name (Meursault-Genevrières Premier Cru, for example). This is the second-highest distinction in Burgundy, after Grand Cru. (Confusingly, in Bordeaux it's the reverse: Premier Cru is the more prestigious rank.)

• **GRAND CRU** Burgundy's Grand Cru vineyards are so elite (fewer than 2 percent hold the honor), and the wines so famous, that some, like Montrachet, don't even include the "Grand Cru" title on their labels. These are the region's finest wines, requiring years of age to reach their full potential. So great is the prestige of these wines that some villages added the name of the local Grand Cru vineyard to their own names decades ago. Thus the wines from Chassagne, for example, became Chassagne-Montrachet; while many of them are superb, they're not true Montrachet.

BURGUNDY

chablis

For many connoisseurs, Chablis is one of the world's premier wines. Unfortunately, knockoff producers have tarnished its reputation by labeling inferior bottles with the Chablis name. Located in the north of Burgundy, Chablis has a cool climate and limestone-rich soils, perfect for yielding high-acid, mineral-laden wines. That, along with lively citrus flavors and an uncanny ability to age, makes Chablis one of France's most fascinating wines. Petit Chablis, made from grapes grown throughout the district, is technically not Chablis, but can be quite good.

chablis recommendations

Corinne et Jean-Pierre Grossot Les Fourneaux Premier Cru
| 2006 | CHABLIS
★★ $ $ $ Full malolactic fermentation softens this wine's acidity and imparts a round, soft mouthfeel. Minerals and lemons dominate the nose, while the palate offers green apple and stone.

Domaine Laroche St-Martin | 2006 | CHABLIS
★ $ $ Though golden-hued and creamy, this Chablis spends no time in oak, so its citrus and pear flavors are crisp and clean.

Gilbert Picq & Ses Fils Vosgros Premier Cru | 2007 | CHABLIS
★★★ $ $ $ This Chablis would make a fine pour alongside shellfish. Refreshing and mineral-laden, it displays an almost glacial purity of green apple, lime and pear flavors.

J. Moreau & Fils | 2006 | CHABLIS
★★ $ $ This delicious, well-priced white seduces with aromas of flower, mineral and citrus. Though matured entirely in stainless steel, which preserves the brightness of its apple and grapefruit flavors, it shows the richly textured palate common in oak-aged wines.

Joseph Drouhin Vaudésir | 2006 | CHABLIS GRAND CRU
★★★★ $ $ $ $ The Drouhins set up shop in Chablis in 1968 and currently make some of the region's finest wines. This single-vineyard Chablis is full-bodied and plush, with multiple layers of smoke, spice and stone fruit flavors.

Laurent Tribut Beauroy Premier Cru | 2007 | CHABLIS
★★★ $ $ $ A perfectly executed Chablis—refreshing, full and balanced—this showcases a mineral-dominated nose and palate, with subtle hints of apple and pear on the long finish.

Louis Michel & Fils Montmains Premier Cru | 2007 | CHABLIS
★★ $ $ $ This sixth-generation, family-owned estate has earned a reputation as one of the most consistent producers in the Chablis region. This waxy-textured wine is no exception, delivering juicy pear and citrus flavors.

William Fèvre Montmains Premier Cru | 2006 | CHABLIS
★★★★ $ $ $ Though the family sold this winery to Champagne producer Henriot in 1998, the winery continues its tradition of excellence. Persistent length, balanced acidity and a concentrated palate of tart citrus and mineral flavors summarize this outstanding wine.

BURGUNDY

côte d'or

The Côte d'Or (literally, "slope of gold") is Burgundy's premier winemaking region. The region is split into two halves: Côte de Nuits in the north and Côte de Beaune in the south. In the Côte de Nuits, such renowned villages as Nuits-St-Georges, Gevrey-Chambertin and Chambolle-Musigny produce some of the region's finest reds, bursting with cherry flavors underscored by a pronounced minerality. The Côte de Beaune is noted for its whites from villages such as Puligny-Montrachet and Meursault, though the villages of Pommard, Volnay and Aloxe-Corton are known for some excellent reds as well.

côte d'or recommendations

WHITES

Bouchard Aîné & Fils Cuvée Signature Morgeot Premier Cru | 2006 | CHASSAGNE-MONTRACHET

★ ★ ★ ★ $ $ $ $ *Négociants* since the 1750s, the Bouchard family landed a gold mine when they purchased this vineyard, named for its original steward, the Morgeot Abbey. The 2006 vintage displays superb balance, with its lively acidity countered by complex flavors that are creamy and soft.

Domaine Henri Clerc & Fils | 2006 | PULIGNY-MONTRACHET

★ ★ ★ $ $ $ The Clerc family made Puligny-Montrachet their home in the 16th century. Today Vincent Girardin is in charge of vineyards and winemaking at the estate, crafting top-notch wines like this example. Bright with citrus, apple and mango flavors, it is complemented by oak, almond, vanilla and spice notes.

Domaine Jobard-Morey Poruzot Premier Cru | 2005 | MEURSAULT

★ ★ ★ $ $ $ $ This Meursault is a sublime wine made by a small family estate with fruit from one of the region's top vineyard properties. The 2005 Jobard-Morey balances its round, creamy texture with vibrant flavors of citrus zest, green fruit, chalky minerals and notes of toasted walnuts.

Jean-Claude Boisset Les Charmes Premier Cru | 2006 | MEURSAULT

★ ★ ★ $ $ $ $ From old, organically farmed vines grown on some of Meursault's finest vineyard sites comes this full-bodied, mouth-filling wine, loaded with generous flavors of juicy mangoes, spice, butter and oak. It is smooth and creamy throughout, lingering on the palate long after the last sip.

JJ Vincent Chardonnay | 2007 | BOURGOGNE

★ ★ $ Jean Jacques Vincent's family has been in the Burgundy business since 1864. Carrying on the tradition, Vincent makes this everyday wine brimming with citrus flavors, a hint of oak, refreshing acidity and a crisp, clean finish.

Joseph Drouhin Laforet Chardonnay | 2007 | BOURGOGNE

★ ★ $ This may be designated "entry-level" Burgundy, but there's nothing basic about it. Lively acidity and a plethora of flavors—citrus, apple, ginger, white pepper and a whiff of butter—make for a charming expression of Chardonnay.

Louis Carillon & Fils | 2006 | PULIGNY-MONTRACHET
★★ $ $ $ The Carillon family's winemaking tradition stretches as far back as the 15th century, and their wines are built to last. This age-worthy example offers spicy oak aromas followed by tropical fruit, ginger and citrus flavors on the palate.

Louis Jadot | 2006 | CHASSAGNE-MONTRACHET
★★★ $ $ $ One of the biggest names in Burgundy, the Louis Jadot estate has crafted quality wines from the region since 1859. This vintage shows crisp apple and pear flavors with a hint of mushroom, bright acidity and a slightly creamy texture.

Marc Brocot Les Champs Salomon | 2006 | MARSANNAY
★★★ $ $ Red wine reigns in the Côte de Nuits, but this small estate in Marsannay produces intriguing whites like this 2006. Minerals and high acidity enliven flavors of mushroom, earth and stewed apple.

Olivier Leflaive | 2007 | CHASSAGNE-MONTRACHET
★★★ $ $ $ A descendant of the wine-producing Leflaive family, Olivier launched his own domaine with his brother Patrick in 1984 and soon earned a reputation for gorgeous Chardonnays. His silky-textured 2007 shows layers of fresh fruit, mushroom and cream, with notes of ginger and a piercing acidity.

Pierre et Jean-Baptiste Lebreuil Dessus des Gollardes
| 2005 | SAVIGNY-LÈS-BEAUNE
★★★ $ $ $ In this little village, the Lebreuil family turns out beautifully crafted Chardonnays at fair prices for the region. Sour green apple and mineral flavors dominate here, woven with hints of white pepper and nuts.

Pierre Morey | 2006 | MEURSAULT
★★★★ $ $ $ This fabulous Meursault is worth the splurge for its creamy, mouth-filling flavors of spice and fruit. Zesty acidity keeps it lively and refreshing throughout.

Thierry et Pascale Matrot | 2007 | MEURSAULT
★★★ $ $ $ A complex wine that will evolve with time, this Meursault alternates among waves of citrus, green fruit, ginger and yogurt, with underlying notes of mushroom and walnut.

Vincent Girardin Grand Cru | 2006 | CORTON-CHARLEMAGNE
★★★★ $ $ $ Vincent Girardin achieves grand harmony with this Grand Cru, striking a balance between pure flavors of citrus, gunflint, walnuts and yogurt, a mouthwatering acidity and a creamy texture. This drinks well now, and will age beautifully for ten years.

REDS

Chanson Père & Fils Pinot Noir | 2006 | **BOURGOGNE**
★ ★ **$ $** A vibrant, well-structured wine for the price, this offers bold raspberry and cherry flavors punctuated by hints of sweet spice and dried meat, all balanced by strong acidity and chalky tannins.

Domaine Arlaud Roncevie | 2007 | **BOURGOGNE**
★ ★ **$ $** Roncevie's vineyards are next door to Gevrey-Chambertin, and in character its wines are similar to those of its more prestigious neighbor. This red possesses a lovely depth of flavor in the form of earth, sweet tobacco, cinnamon, spice and red fruit.

Domaine Bernard Morey et Fils Clos St-Jean Premier Cru
| 2006 | **CHASSAGNE-MONTRACHET**
★ ★ ★ **$ $ $** The Morey family doesn't filter their red wines, which renders them beautifully pure and complex. The range of flavors—red berries, earth and wet leaves—creates a nice weight on the palate.

star producers
côte d'or

Domaine Bernard Morey et Fils
Few Morey vineyards are Grand Cru, yet the domaine's wines are as good as those from the best estates in the Côte d'Or.

Domaine Bouchard Père & Fils
A rarity among Burgundy *négociants,* Bouchard actually owns 321 acres, of which 180 acres rank as Premier Cru and 30 acres as Grand Cru.

Domaine de la Romanée-Conti
The prized wines produced in DRC's Grand Cru vineyards are considered among the most distinctive in Burgundy.

Domaine Georges Roumier
Christophe Roumier is the third generation of his winemaking family to craft some of the most highly coveted wines of Chambolle-Musigny.

Domaine Henri Gouges
This domaine's small Nuits-St-Georges vineyard yields tight, dense wines that take years to soften—but are worth the wait.

Joseph Drouhin
Since 1880 Drouhin has symbolized quality in Burgundy, especially with its Montrachet Marquis de Laguiche offering, a white wine of such power and complexity some call it a "red in disguise."

43

Domaine Bruno Clair Les Longeroies | 2006 | MARSANNAY
★★★ $ $ $ Bruno Clair and his excellent cellar master, Philippe Brun, combine their talents to craft Pinot Noirs that show rare structure and near-perfect balance. This delivers a stunning mix of black cherry and mineral flavors.

Domaine Charles Audoin Cuvée Des Demoiselles | 2005 | MARSANNAY
★★ $ $ $ Charles Audoin works with his wife and fellow oenologist, Marie-Françoise, to construct wines that incorporate equal parts structure, backbone, fruit and finesse. Together, they yield wines with great balance, like this cassis- and cherry-flavored example underscored by chalky, firming minerals.

Domaine Dupont-Tisserandot Pinot Noir | 2006 | BOURGOGNE
★★ $ $ As in many 2006 Burgundies, the fruit on the Dupont-Tisserandot is somewhat muted, giving center stage to notes of earth and mushroom. Soft, ripe tannins, medium acidity and a long length make for an all-around, delicious red.

Domaine Henri Gouges Les Chênes Carteaux Premier Cru | 2006 | NUITS-ST-GEORGES
★★★ $ $ $ $ Henri's grandsons, Pierre and Christian, now run the Gouges estate. Their 2006 combines fresh raspberry, candied cherry and baking spice aromas that take an earthier turn on the palate, which is supported by fine-grained tannins.

Domaine Jean Chauvenet | 2005 | NUITS-ST-GEORGES
★★★ $ $ $ This 2005 still possesses bright red berry aromas and zesty acidity yet demonstrates signs of maturity on the palate, with subtle notes of dried leaves, sweet spice and smoked meat all supported by ripe tannins.

Domaine Jean-Marc Bouley Clos des Chênes Premier Cru | 2006 | VOLNAY
★★★ $ $ $ $ Volnay is known for its delicate, refined red wines, and this Bouley is true to form, with its elegant layers of supple fruit, earth, spices and herbs balanced by firm acidity and soft tannins that finish smooth.

Domaine Jessiaume Las Cent Vignes Premier Cru | 2005 | BEAUNE
★★★ $ $ $ Jessiaume uses fruit from vines that are between 41 and 55 years old to make this wine. The result is a heady mix of blackberry, cherry and plum flavors on a silky-smooth palate, leading to a mouthwatering finish.

Domaine Potel Vieilles Vignes | 2007 | SAVIGNY-LÈS-BEAUNE
★★ $$$ Old vines impart a rare concentration of fruit here. Hints of vanilla, oak, minerals and wet leaves are also woven throughout this medium-bodied, lively 2007.

Jean-Claude Boisset Les Bressandes Premier Cru | 2006 |
BEAUNE
★★★ $$$ On the sandy, east-facing slopes of Les Bressandes, Pinot Noir grapes tend to grow thicker skins, which explains this wine's deep concentration of earth and wild raspberry flavors, firm tannins and high acidity.

Joseph Drouhin | 2006 | CHOREY-LÈS-BEAUNE
★★ $$ Bright berry flavors mingle with oak and earth aromas in this lively Burgundy. Firm, fine-grained tannins and medium acidity carry it through the earthy, berry-laced finish.

news from a wine insider
burgundy by Daniel Johnnes, wine director for the Daniel Boulud restaurant group

Vintage Note
Wines from the 2006 and 2007 vintages are best for drinking now rather than aging. In general, the 2006 whites are somewhat soft, thanks in part to grapes that ripened very quickly toward the end of the season. Producers who picked early created wines that are fruit-forward yet retain their fresh, vibrant acidity. Those who picked later produced heavier, and sometimes clumsy, wines. The 2007 whites have firmer acidity and a pronounced minerality; they resemble whites from the 2004 vintage, though with more flesh and body. The 2006 reds are elegant and pure, displaying the distinctive characteristics of their appellations and terroirs. Overall, the 2007 reds are ripe and tasty but probably won't benefit from long-term aging.

Significant Trends
Good news for Burgundy lovers who wish to replenish their cellars: global demand for fine wine has dropped because of the economy, and importers, distributors and retailers are struggling to move inventory, thus driving down prices. Many collectors are thinning out their cellars at auction, and real deals can be found.

Louis Jadot | 2006 | GEVREY-CHAMBERTIN
★ ★ ★ $ $ $ Rich and dense, with concentrated red berry flavors, this Jadot comes from one of the finer villages of the Côte de Nuits, and shows muscular tannins, refreshing acidity and mineral hints.

Thibault Liger-Belair Grand Cru | 2006 | CLOS DE VOUGEOT
★ ★ ★ ★ $ $ $ $ A spectacular effort from Thibault—who practices biodynamic winemaking—this powerful yet refined red is introduced by cured meat, black fruit and dusty herb aromas, which are augmented on the palate by wet stone and plush tannins that linger.

Vincent Girardin Les Santenots Premier Cru | 2006 |
VOLNAY
★ ★ ★ $ $ $ $ This Volnay is meant to be savored. Enticing aromas of raspberry and savory spices dance with earth, mushrooms, wet leaves and black pepper before giving way to rich, well-integrated flavors and a long, balanced finish.

BURGUNDY

côte chalonnaise

The Côte Chalonnaise region is often overlooked, but true Burgundy aficionados know that great values can be found here. The villages of Mercurey and Givry produce delicious, well-priced reds, while the Chardonnays of Montagny provide lower-priced alternatives to the more popular vineyards to the north. In addition to Chardonnay, the village of Rully makes a small amount of sparkling wine, while Bouzeron offers Aligoté—Burgundy's "other" white grape.

côte chalonnaise recommendations

WHITES

Danjean-Berthoux La Plante Premier Cru | 2006 | GIVRY
★ ★ $ $ At the request of his American importer, Pascal Danjean-Berthoux no longer filters his Givry, which results in wines like this rich, buttery gem brimming with apple flavors and chalky minerality.

Domaine Faiveley Clos Rochette | 2007 | MERCUREY
★ ★ ★ $ $ $ This Mercurey producer has vines dating back as far as 1960. Soft aromas of butter and acacia flowers up front lead to layers of green apple and citrusy acidity and a crisp, clean finish.

Domaine Jacques Dury La Chaume | 2006 | RULLY
★ ★ $ $ Dury and his son now grow grapes on eight parcels of vineyards, three of which are Rully Premiers Crus. This floral, minerally Chardonnay is buoyant and lively, with green apple and toasted nut nuances and just a hint of creamy oak in the finish.

J.M. Boillot Le Meix Cadot Premier Cru | 2007 | RULLY
★ ★ $ $ $ Jean-Marc Boillot left his family's Henri Boillot winery in Volnay to strike out on his own as both a Burgundy *négociant* and a vineyard owner in Côte Chalonnaise, where he makes tasty, well-built wines like this rich, delicious Chardonnay.

REDS

Danjean-Berthoux La Plante Premier Cru | 2006 | GIVRY
★ ★ ★ $ $ $ Earthy and complex, this unfiltered Premier Cru Pinot Noir deftly balances sweet, fresh cherry flavors with dark, chewy tannins and nuances of wet leaves.

Domaine Faiveley Clos des Myglands Premier Cru | 2007 | MERCUREY
★ ★ ★ $ $ $ Faiveley's Clos des Myglands estate, where the vine age averages 41 years, was elevated to Premier Cru status in 1989, thanks to its long tradition of excellence. The 2007 is beautifully perfumed with flowers and cherries, while the cherry- and berry-infused palate is lifted by bright acidity and soft, elegant chalk notes.

Guillemette et Xavier Besson Le Haut Colombier | 2006 | GIVRY
★ ★ $ $ At Domaine Xavier Besson, old vines yield delicious, dependable Pinot Noirs with spicy flavors. This mouthwatering example contrasts up-front cherry flavors with dusty sage accents.

BURGUNDY

mâconnais

The Mâconnais produces mostly simple, fresh whites, though some subregions are more ambitious. Pouilly-Fuissé is the region's most acclaimed appellation, as well as its most expensive, while St-Véran offers similar quality at a lower price. The best values can be found in wines with the Mâcon designation (listed here in ascending order of quality): Mâcon, Mâcon Supérieur, Mâcon-Villages or Mâcon followed by a particular village name, such as Mâcon-Viré.

mâconnais recommendations

Chanson Père & Fils | 2006 | VIRÉ-CLESSÉ
★ ★ $ $ Introduced by earthy, nutty aromas, this full-bodied white moves on to apple, baking spice, vanilla and butter flavors, which finish wonderfully crisp.

Domaine Chataigneraie-Laborier Bélemnites | 2007 | POUILLY-FUISSÉ
★ ★ ★ $ $ $ With a quiet elegance, this Pouilly-Fuissé conjures a well-integrated mix of subtle white fruit and slate aromas, which are followed by fresh-baked brioche flavors on a creamy palate.

Domaine Jean Touzot Vieilles Vignes Chardonnay | 2007 | MÂCON-VILLAGES
★ ★ $ A solid value, this Chardonnay boasts fresh aromas of pineapple, apple and melon. The palate is juicy and tropical, without losing its Burgundian character, while an understated acidity holds it together through the floral finish.

Domaine Talmard | 2007 | MÂCON-CHARDONNAY
★ $ Produced with no oak, this polished white is defined by clean, crisp apple flavors, a fleshy texture and refreshing acidity; beautifully structured, it is a quaffable wine for everyday drinking.

Domaine Thomas Tradition | 2007 | ST-VÉRAN
★ ★ $ $ Made from 40- to 50-year-old vines, this unoaked white is focused and utterly charming. Bright apple, pear and citrus on the nose and palate conclude in a dry, mineral-rich finish.

Joseph Burrier Château de Beauregard Classique | 2006 | POUILLY-FUISSÉ
★ ★ ★ $ $ Fresh-cut apple aromas are balanced with hints of limestone in this medium-bodied wine. Its elegant, mouthwatering flavors of citrus, apple and minerals make this a great aperitif.

L'Ancestra | 1998 | MÂCON-CHAINTRÉ
★ ★ ★ $ $ This unusual wine is as delicious as it is original. Released unfiltered after more than three years of fermentation and more than five of maturation, it offers unctuous honey, saffron and apple aromas and subtly oxidized flavors of peach, apricot, wildflower and citrus.

Louis Jadot | 2007 | POUILLY-FUISSÉ
★ ★ $ $ Widely distributed and highly enjoyable, this toast-accented white balances its oak nicely amid flavors of vanilla, cantaloupe, ripe apple, cedar and minerals.

BURGUNDY

beaujolais

As Burgundy's southernmost region, Beaujolais is distinctly different from its neighbors to the north. To begin with, wines here are made exclusively with Gamay (instead of Pinot Noir), and the region has its own ranking system for quality. Beaujolais produces an abundance of mostly inexpensive, simple-but-satisfying red wines, as well as a number of high-quality bottles that can satisfy the palate of a Burgundy lover at a mere fraction of the cost. A handful of Chardonnay-based whites are also made here.

• **BEAUJOLAIS NOUVEAU** Designed for consumption within weeks of harvest, Beaujolais Nouveau is as light and simple as red wine gets. By law, it is released the third Thursday of every November, conveniently coinciding with the American holiday season.

• **BEAUJOLAIS** Wines made from grapes grown anywhere within the designated region earn the moniker Beaujolais. These reds are marked by distinctive light, fruity flavors and are a bit more substantial than Beaujolais Nouveau.

• **BEAUJOLAIS-VILLAGES** The title of Beaujolais-Villages is given to any wine made from grapes grown within the 39 villages occupying the rolling hills at the center of the region. These wines are typically made with more care and precision, producing bright fruit flavors as well as an added depth of mineral and spice.

• **CRU BEAUJOLAIS** The region's greatest wines come from ten hillside villages in the northern part of Beaujolais. Called Cru Beaujolais, these wines show an even heavier concentration of berry, mineral and spice flavors than Beaujolais-Villages, plus ample tannins, which allow them to age, unlike other Beaujolais. These wines are so well regarded that many vintners don't even put "Beaujolais" on their Cru Beaujolais labels, listing instead just the name of the village where the grapes were grown: Brouilly, Chénas, Chiroubles, Côte de Brouilly, Fleurie, Juliénas, Morgon, Moulin-à-Vent, Régnié or St-Amour.

beaujolais recommendations

WHITES

Jean-Paul Brun Terres Dorées Chardonnay | 2008 |
BEAUJOLAIS

★ ★ $ When fermenting his wines, Brun eschews industrial yeast in favor of those growing naturally nearby. The choice benefits this sumptuous, mineral-laden white, marked by gorgeous baked apple, acacia and honeysuckle flavors.

REDS

David Gobet | 2007 | BEAUJOLAIS-VILLAGES

★ ★ $ A perfect Beaujolais (chilled) for everyday sipping, this couples black cherry and blackberry flavors with a chalky, mouth-watering finish, which makes it easy to pair with just about any food.

Domaine Georges Viornery | 2007 | CÔTE DE BROUILLY

★ ★ ★ $ $ The aromas and flavors of this savory red are dominated by blueberry, with sage, spice and fruit pie nuances on the dense, intensely fruity palate.

G. Descombes | 2007 | RÉGNIÉ

★ ★ $ $ In the cru Beaujolais hierarchy Régnié is one of the more powerful regions, and its wines are often compared to those from Burgundy "proper" to the north. This well-built example features chewy tannins that prop up the pure berry flavors.

Jean Foillard Côte du Py | 2007 | MORGON

★ ★ ★ $ $ Foillard is a champion of the natural wine movement, and this Morgon layers pure blueberry and coffee aromas with spice, cured meat and supple tannins on the palate—a profile that renders this more like a pricier Burgundy than a Beaujolais.

Louis Jadot Château des Lumières Côte du Py | 2006 |
MORGON

★ ★ ★ $ $ $ Named for the seminal filmmakers who for a time inhabited this property's original château, this delicious Morgon is somewhat New World–like, with flavors of toast, violets and berries and a plush mouthfeel.

Paul Janin et Fils Clos Du Tremblay | 2007 | MOULIN-À-VENT

★ ★ ★ $ $ Paul Janin's grandparents planted these Gamay vines over 60 years ago, which explains this red's unexpected complexity. Brown butter and pencil shavings on the nose culminate in full-bodied blackberry flavors and soft, dusty tannins on the finish.

loire valley

Stretching some 300 miles along the Loire River, the fertile Loire Valley is one of the largest and most diverse wine regions of France—and one of its most underappreciated. The wines made here range from dry, still reds, whites and rosés to sparklers and dessert bottles. Almost all Loire wines, however, possess relatively high acidity.

Loire Valley Grapes & Styles

The Loire Valley is home to a vast array of grapes. Of the whites, Muscadet, known locally as Melon de Bourgogne, makes crisp dry wines, while Chenin Blanc produces dry, sweet and sparkling wines. Chardonnay and Sauvignon Blanc are also grown in much of the valley, with the latter grape responsible for the well-known whites of Sancerre and Pouilly-Fumé. The valley's dominant red grape is Cabernet Franc, though Pinot Noir is also grown in the eastern part of the region. Blending is permitted in certain appellations, such as Valençay, where whites may be made from a combination of Sauvignon Blanc and Chardonnay.

Loire Valley Wine Labels

Loire Valley wines are identified by appellation, and since blending of grapes is rare, the appellation is usually enough to determine the variety. Wines made from grapes not tied to a region will list both the grape and the region name.

loire valley whites

The Loire Valley's broad range of white wines, from simple aperitifs to profoundly earthy wines designed for aging, are made from three primary grapes: Melon de Bourgogne, Sauvignon Blanc and Chenin Blanc. Melon (Muscadet) produces light, lively wines that partner well with shellfish. Sauvignon Blanc yields similarly vibrant wines, with expressive citrus, mineral and herb notes. The wines from the distinctive Chenin Blanc grape vary greatly across the quality spectrum, but the gems are well worth seeking out.

LOIRE VALLEY WHITES

chenin blanc

Chenin Blanc is the Loire Valley's most versatile grape, capable of producing some truly impressive and unusual wines. Styles can range from dry to sparkling to exquisitely sweet, but almost all are high in acidity, which gives them the ability to age beautifully. Though the Loire's most famous Chenin Blancs are probably the off-dry versions from the Vouvray appellation, there are also dry bottlings; the same is true for Montlouis, across the river. For higher-quality Chenins capable of long-term aging, look to Savennières, as well as to Saumur and Anjou, where the best Chenin Blancs display marvelous honey, citrus, truffle and smoke flavors.

chenin blanc recommendations

Château de Chamboureau | 2005 | SAVENNIÈRES
★★★ $ $ Château de Chamboureau's vineyards were well on their way to organic certification (officially received in 2006) when this wine's grapes were harvested. A rich, hand-crafted Chenin, it offers fresh-baked brioche, buttered almond and apricot aromas offset by elegant minerals.

Domaine des Baumard | 2005 | SAVENNIÈRES
★★ $ $ A classic Savennières from an estate established in 1634, this is brimming with sweet pear and unctuous quince aromas. The mineral-laden palate has a chalky texture, which cushions flavors of ripe melon, citrus and cream.

Domaine du Vieux Pressoir Elégance | 2006 | SAUMUR
★★ $ The French have a phrase for easy-drinking wines like this that are typical of many parts of the Loire: *sec tendre,* which means tender and not too dry. This wine is round, with lush flavors of honeyed peach and brioche. It is also a good bargain.

Domaine Vincent Carême Le Peu Morier | 2006 | VOUVRAY
★★ $ $ Quince is the calling card of many great Loire whites, and this off-dry Vouvray fills the bill. Unctuous quince flavors are complemented by lime zest and honeysuckle straight through the elegant, formidable finish.

Jean-Maurice Raffault | 2007 | CHINON
★★ $ $ Jean-Maurice's talented son Rodolphe now heads up this famed estate in Chinon. Here he's crafted a fresh, bright, minerally wine, with mouthwatering pear and peach flavors and citrus-zest acidity on the finish.

Sauvion | 2007 | VOUVRAY
★★ $ This wine, made entirely with Chenin Blanc, is a spot-on, mouthwatering Vouvray. Flavors of green apple, lime and melon are pure and refreshing.

LOIRE VALLEY WHITES

melon de bourgogne/ muscadet

Basic Muscadets are relatively neutral white wines that are light-bodied, with pleasant citrus flavors. Muscadets labeled *"sur lie"* (on lees), however, can achieve considerably more flavor intensity by remaining in contact with the "lees" (a sediment consisting of yeast cells, grape seeds, pulp, stem and skin fragments that is left behind after the fermentation process). The most interesting Muscadets hail from Sèvre et Maine and are at their best a year or two after vintage, though some well-made versions have the ability to age a decade or more.

muscadet recommendations

Château de la Ragotière (Black Label) sur Lie | 2006 |
MUSCADET SÈVRE ET MAINE
★★ $ If ever a wine were created exclusively for fresh-shucked oysters, this briny, citrus-scented and -flavored wine would be it. Mineral-rich and steely, it finishes with pronounced acidity.

Domaine La Haute Févrie Le Fief du Pégatine sur Lie | 2006 |
MUSCADET SÈVRE ET MAINE
★★★ $ Domaine La Haute Févrie is a member of "Vini Vitis," a highly respected French association whose label is a guarantee of sustainable agricultural practices. This Muscadet stands out for its rich, ripe, biscuit-laden palate propped up by refreshing acidity and a subtle stone-accented finish.

Domaine Les Hautes Noëlles Serge Batard sur Lie | 2007 |
MUSCADET CÔTES DE GRANDLIEU
★ $ A great value that does exactly what a Muscadet is supposed to
do: deliver fresh, citrusy acidity, clean mineral notes, a hint of quince
paste and a chalky, satisfying finish.

Marc Pesnot La Bohème | 2007 | **VIN DE TABLE**
★ ★ $ One of the few organic winemakers in this area, Pesnot sources
grapes from vines that are between 30 and 50 years old, and they
endow this wine with incredibly concentrated fruit flavors balanced
by bracing acidity and minerals.

LOIRE VALLEY WHITES

sauvignon blanc

From Sancerre and Pouilly-Fumé, at the eastern reaches of
the Loire Valley, come the finest Sauvignon Blancs the
region has to offer. Filled with grapefruit, gooseberry and
grass flavors, the wines typically possess a refreshing acidity plus a distinctive "gunflint" aroma. Sancerre tends to be
fuller-bodied, while Pouilly-Fumé is lighter and more perfumed. Similar wines can be found in neighboring Quincy,
Menetou-Salon and Reuilly.

sauvignon blanc recommendations

Comte Lafond | 2006 | **SANCERRE**
★ ★ ★ $ $ This delicately floral Sancerre—crafted by a family with a
winemaking history that dates back to 1787—wafts springtime aromas of hibiscus, acacia, elderflower and a hint of straw. The palate
turns to bright citrus and wet stone, with grass notes on the finish.

de Ladoucette Château du Nozet Baron de L | 2005 |
POUILLY-FUMÉ
★ ★ ★ $ $ $ $ This traditional white shows Sauvignon Blanc at its
best. With fragrant and complex flavors of gooseberry, pear, mineral
and fresh herbs, it has a silky texture and perfectly balanced acidity.

Domaine Baron Les Vieilles Vignes | 2007 | **TOURAINE**
★ $ The fresh aromas in this Touraine are intensely green—lime,
grass and bell pepper. However, the palate is somewhat New World–
like, with bold flavors and assertive acidity that make it a good choice
for creamy seafood dishes.

Domaine de Chatenoy | 2007 | MENETOU-SALON
★★★ $ $ This Menetou-Salon vintner crafts white wines that are remarkably rich in style. Zesty grapefruit, lemon and lime aromas are augmented on the palate by earth, smoke and walnut notes.

Domaine du Tremblay | 2007 | QUINCY
★★ $ Located west of Sancerre, this tiny appellation can yield wines with the same profile as its better-known neighbor for much less money. Tremblay's version starts off with limestone and sea air aromas, which are rounded out by flavors of ripe citrus, gooseberry and a hint of musk.

Domaine Michel Thomas Silex | 2006 | SANCERRE
★★★ $ $ Three generations of sons have tended the vines here since 1946. This unfiltered white is a ripe, concentrated expression of Sancerre, defined by generous citrus, apple, stone fruit and mineral flavors highlighted by nuances of smoke, almond and thyme.

Domaine Vacheron | 2007 | SANCERRE
★★★ $ $ This is a lively, aromatic Sancerre with enticing aromas of lemon, grapefruit, green apple, orange blossom and limestone. The palate offers a full range of invigorating citrus flavors, with dry minerals and a touch of saline.

Les Deux Tours | 2006 | TOURAINE
★★ $ From a vintner known for consistent quality and value, this Touraine displays aromas of peach, dried apricot and flowers. The palate shows surprising depth and richness, with green apple, flint and citrusy acidity.

loire valley reds

A crucial blending grape in Bordeaux, Cabernet Franc performs even better in the Loire Valley. The grape's range is impressive, producing fruity, peppery wines meant to be enjoyed in their youth, as well as fuller-bodied, smoky, tannic reds suitable for considerable aging. The wines of Chinon and Saumur-Champigny are especially noteworthy. Pinot Noir, grown in the eastern part of the region, especially in Sancerre and Menetou-Salon, yields wines that tend to be light-bodied, with bright cherry flavors and high acidity. They're enjoyable, but rarely better than basic Burgundy. Gamay and other minor grapes are also grown in the Loire, though they are generally unremarkable.

loire valley red recommendations

Alphonse Mellot La Moussière | 2007 | SANCERRE

★ ★ ★ $ $ $ $ Alphonse Mellot is a 19th-generation winemaker who is also a renowned champion of biodynamic practices. His Pinot Noir is tenacious, with silky tannins, a long finish and flavors of smoke, earth and cherry that will benefit from aging.

Clos Cristal Hospices de Saumur | 2006 | SAUMUR-CHAMPIGNY

★ ★ $ $ This Cabernet Franc offers generous flavors of plum, spice and wild raspberry framed by remarkably firm tannins. It is unusually full-bodied for a red from this appellation.

Domaine du Mortier Graviers | 2007 | ST-NICOLAS-DE-BOURGUEIL

★ $ With a modest alcohol content of 11.7 percent, this light-bodied red tastes best with a slight chill. Aromas of bell pepper, mineral and blackberry precede the clean, fruit-driven palate.

Jean-Maurice Raffault Clos des Capucins | 2006 | CHINON

★ ★ ★ $ $ Though Chinon is the northernmost French red wine appellation, Cabernet Franc flourishes here. This well-built, complex example has dark fruit, spice and smoke enveloped by soft tannins.

Les Cailloux du Paradis Racines | 2005 | VIN DE TABLE

★ ★ $ $ $ Tart red berry flavors dominate the palate in this wine, softened by notes of candied cherry and pomegranate. Its bracing acidity is pleasantly uplifting.

Les Sablonnettes Les Copines Aussi Gamay Vendanges | 2007 | VIN DE TABLE

★ $ Though made from Gamay, this wine shows an earthier, spicier character than its Beaujolais counterparts. Serve it slightly chilled to better showcase its robust blueberry flavors and vibrant acidity.

Olivier Cousin Anjou Pur Breton | 2006 | VIN DE TABLE

★ ★ $ $ This biodynamically produced Cabernet Franc is introduced by pronounced aromas of barnyard, earth and raspberry, which are followed by ripe red berry flavors and firm tannins.

Olivier Cousin Le Cousin Vieilles Vignes Grolleau | 2007 | VIN DE TABLE

★ ★ $ $ Packaged in a playful bottle (the label features a mosquito carrying a corkscrew), this wine is entirely serious. Black fruit flavors are layered with earth and chewy tannins that linger on the palate.

rhône valley

The Rhône Valley of France has ascended to greatness relatively recently. Once dismissed as sturdy, second-class and often quite coarse, the wines of the Rhône Valley have the potential to express unbridled power, spiciness and an appealing earthiness that makes them unique among the fine wines of France. While many of the region's wines are still somewhat simple, vintners today are creating an increasing number of world-class reds that are just as profound as those from Burgundy or Bordeaux, yet with their own distinctive character.

Rhône Valley: An Overview

The Rhône River flows from the Swiss Alps down into France's Jura mountains and on to the Mediterranean. The Rhône Valley wine region is divided into northern and southern parts, which differ greatly in terms of grapes, wine philosophies, soils and microclimates. The Rhône Valley ranks second in total wine production among major French regions, and while every style of wine is made here, red wines represent approximately 90 percent of the region's AOC production.

RHÔNE VALLEY

northern rhône

The northern Rhône, bookended by the appellations of Côte-Rôtie in the north and Cornas and St-Péray in the south, is a narrow 50-mile or so stretch of terraced hills; some of the area's most coveted wines hail from its steepest vineyard sites. The region lies between cooler-climate Burgundy to the north and the warm, sunny Mediterranean-influenced southern Rhône, and its wines reflect this geographical and climatic diversity in their combination of elegance and robust flavors. The northern Rhône has recently been blessed with a string of standout vintages, including the excellent 2003, 2005 and 2007.

Northern Rhône Grapes & Styles

Though Viognier produces the Rhône Valley's most celebrated white wines, two other grapes play significant roles in the north: Marsanne and Roussanne. Viognier is synonymous with the whites of Condrieu and the tiny neighboring appellation of Château Grillet. Brawny Marsanne is customarily blended with elegant Roussanne to create the full-bodied, nutty, baked pear–scented whites of Hermitage, Crozes-Hermitage, St-Péray and St-Joseph. These wines

Côte-Rôtie
Condrieu
• Vienne

■ Principal Wine Region

Northern Rhône

St-Joseph

Crozes-Hermitage

Hermitage — • Tain-L'Hermitage

Cornas

St-Péray • Valence

—20 miles

Montélimar • **Coteaux du Tricastin**

Côtes-du-Rhône & Côtes-du-Rhône Villages
• Orange
Gigondas
—Vacqueyras
Lirac
Beaumes-de-Venise
Tavel — **Châteauneuf-du-Pape**

• Avignon

Rhône River

Southern Rhône

are not especially high in acidity, yet many have the ability to age for a decade or more. The only red grape permitted in the production of northern Rhône red wines is Syrah, which in certain appellations was traditionally blended with a small amount of the region's aromatic white grapes—for example, up to 20 percent Viognier is permitted in Côte-Rôtie. Very few winemakers today, however, take this approach. Of the appellation-specific red wines, St-Joseph tends to be the lightest in body and the least tannic, followed in order of ascending strength by Crozes-Hermitage, Côte-Rôtie, Hermitage and, finally, Cornas. Known for their power and longevity, the wines of Cornas must be made from Syrah alone, with no added white grapes. The total production of the northern Rhône is small, accounting for less than 5 percent of all Rhône Valley wine; of that amount, well over half comes from Crozes-Hermitage.

northern rhône recommendations

WHITES

Domaine Romaneaux-Destezet | 2007 |
VIN DE PAYS DE L'ARDÈCHE
★ ★ $ $ $ Big and creamy, with loads of toasted oak, this full-bodied white delivers a heady mix of pineapple and pear flavors punctuated by hazelnut, brioche and vanilla. A rigid, brisk acidity provides necessary balance, uplifting the oak-infused finish.

E. Guigal | 2007 | CONDRIEU
★ ★ ★ $ $ $ Made from 30-year-old vines, this Viognier shows Old World reserve, tending toward flavors of minerals, flowers and green fruit. The oily texture and full-bodied palate is expertly balanced by snappy acidity and a touch of vanilla on the finish.

M. Chapoutier Les Meysonniers | 2007 | CROZES-HERMITAGE
★ ★ $ $ $ This Marsanne-based wine exhibits minerals, ripe pear and herbs on the nose. It has lively acidity and waxy fruit flavors.

Paul Jaboulet Aîné Les Cassines | 2007 | CONDRIEU
★ ★ ★ $ $ $ *Cassines* refers to the fishermen's houses along this unique stretch of the Rhône River. Jaboulet's 2007 Viognier is equally distinctive, with ripe stone fruit, apple and summer flower aromatics, which are met by minerals and peach on the generous, round palate.

REDS

Delas Les Launes | 2006 | CROZES-HERMITAGE
★★ $ $ Made from 100 percent Syrah, this displays enticing aromas of smoky sausage, red pepper, dark plum and hints of iron. The tart acidity, bright pomegranate flavors and supple tannins make this medium-bodied red refreshing.

Domaine Courbis | 2005 | ST-JOSEPH
★★ $ $ Most of the Courbis family's vineyard holdings are located in St-Joseph, and they are experts at bringing out the best in the appellation's terroir. This wine is saturated with cassis and cherry flavors, punctuated by sausage, cigar and loam notes; chewy tannins and dry notes of stony earth give it a nice rustic quality.

E. Guigal Brune et Blonde de Guigal | 2005 | CÔTE-RÔTIE
★★★ $ $ $ $ A classic blend of Syrah and Viognier, this wine is opaque black, with rigid graphite and iron notes infusing a core of fresh black fruit and dark plum flavors. Elegant tannins and a kick of black pepper mark the lingering finish.

Gilles Robin Albéric Bouvet | 2006 | CROZES-HERMITAGE
★★ $ $ $ Sultry, smooth and polished throughout, this Crozes-Hermitage offers up classic aromas of violet, smoke, tar and warm black fruit that are met by red fruit, refreshing acidity and fine-grained tannins on the palate.

Hervé Souhaut Syrah | 2007 | VIN DE PAYS DE L'ARDÈCHE
★★ $ $ $ Though it has Vin de Pays status, this Syrah displays tremendous character in the form of expressive sassafras, spice, herb and tea leaf aromas, beautiful acidity on the palate and an intriguing raspberry tea–accented finish.

Jean-Luc Colombo La Louvée Syrah | 2006 | CORNAS
★★★ $ $ $ $ Made with grapes from vines 70-plus years old, this Cornas is tightly wound and incredibly refined, with a lively nose of earth, herbs, black fruit and violets. The sweet, ripe fruit flavors are silky on the palate, with some black olive nuances, firm tannic structure and acidic verve.

J. Vidal-Fleury Brune & Blonde de Vidal-Fleury | 2007 |
CÔTE-RÔTIE
★★★ $ $ $ $ Ripe raspberry and dried fig aromas introduce this well-built Côte-Rôtie. Sweet blackberry flavors are offset by notes of earth, black licorice and stony minerals on the palate and held together with firm tannins.

M. Chapoutier Petite Ruche | 2007 | CROZES-HERMITAGE
★ ★ $ $ Crafted in a simple, youthful, fruit-driven style, Chapoutier's *petite rouge* is made from 100 percent Syrah and shows pretty, ripe plum flavors with notes of clove, vanilla and smoke peeking through. Velvety tannins carry the plush, licorice-tinged palate through the medium-long finish.

Pierre Gaillard | 2007 | ST-JOSEPH
★ ★ ★ $ $ $ With a résumé that includes stints at esteemed wineries such as Guigal and Vidal-Fleury, Gaillard crafts this well-priced wine under his own label. Seductive ripe fruit, wood smoke, peppery spice and earth aromas slowly emerge from the glass, giving way to a pleasingly tart palate of cranberry, pomegranate and blackberry flavors that are framed by fine tannins.

star producers
northern rhône

Domaine Auguste Clape
The leading estate in Cornas for decades, Domaine Auguste Clape sets a high benchmark with its fine wines, some of which are made with grapes from 100-year-old vines.

Domaine Jean-Michel Gerin
Gerin's impressive energy, eye toward innovation and focus on quality peg him as one of the most dynamic winemakers in the northern Rhône.

Domaine Pierre Gaillard
Having discovered his passion for winemaking at the age of 12, Pierre Gaillard later founded his own vineyard in the medieval village of Malleval.

Jean-Luc Colombo
Colombo is renowned for his intense, dark Cornas reds, but as a trailblazer in one of the most traditional wine regions, he makes a standout range of wines all over the Rhône.

J. Vidal-Fleury
The Guigal family, whose patriarch began his career working for Vidal-Fleury, now owns this esteemed winery, which produces some of the Rhône's finest offerings.

M. Chapoutier
An early adopter of biodynamic winemaking, Michel Chapoutier creates wines that have a distinctive sense of place.

RHÔNE VALLEY

southern rhône

About 30 miles south of the northern Rhône, the milder, sunnier southern Rhône begins. Its rolling hills and wide-open vistas are home to vineyards that yield about 95 percent of the entire Rhône Valley's production.

Southern Rhône Grapes & Styles

There are 22 grape varieties permitted in the southern Rhône, but not all are allowed in each appellation. The most important white grapes include Grenache Blanc, Clairette and Bourboulenc, plus the classic northern Rhône varieties Marsanne, Roussanne and Viognier. They are typically blended and result in medium-bodied wines ranging in flavor from ripe peach and citrus to herbal and nutty. Of the permitted grape varieties used to make the southern Rhône's dark, fruity, earth-driven red wines, the principal one is Grenache, usually blended with Cinsault, Syrah, Mourvèdre and/or Carignan. Rosés and good sweet wines are also made here.

Southern Rhône Wine Labels

As in the northern Rhône, southern Rhône wines are labeled by appellation. Côtes-du-Rhône is the most basic category, and can be used for any Rhône Valley wine, though most wines so labeled are from the south. Wines made in the dozens of designated villages that satisfy stricter requirements are labeled "Côtes-du-Rhône Villages." Eighteen villages that make wines of consistent high quality have earned the right to add their name to the label, for example, Côtes-du-Rhône Villages Cairanne. The best villages—Châteauneuf-du-Pape, Gigondas, Tavel, Lirac and Vacqueyras—are permitted to use the village name alone. Satellite regions such as Côtes du Luberon, Côtes du Ventoux, Coteaux du Tricastin and Costières de Nîmes produce wines similar in style and taste profile to the basic Côtes-du-Rhône and are often nicely priced.

southern rhône recommendations

WHITES

Château de Beaucastel | 2006 | CHÂTEAUNEUF-DU-PAPE

★ ★ ★ ★ $ $ $ $ From a Châteauneuf master comes this exquisite blend of 80 percent Roussanne and 20 percent Grenache Blanc, Picardan, Bourboulenc and Clairette. Plush and dense, it has gorgeous aromas of apple, pear and flowers, which are augmented by spice, vanilla, butter and notes of almond on the creamy palate.

Château de la Tuilerie Grenache Blanc/Viognier | 2008 | COSTIÈRES DE NÎMES

★ ★ $ Château de la Tuilerie sources grapes from north-facing slopes, which explains the lively acidity in this white blend. Bold, aromatic Viognier shines here, with expressive summer flower and peach on the nose and flavors of vanilla, orange Creamsicle and juicy citrus.

Château Mont-Redon | 2007 | CHÂTEAUNEUF-DU-PAPE

★ ★ $ $ Grenache Blanc leads in this blend of five Rhône white grapes, imparting flavors of minerals, green apple and white peach that are crisp, firm and pure.

La Vieille Ferme | 2008 | CÔTES DU LUBERON

★ ★ $ Consistently a fantastic value, this white is tasty and fresh, replete with peach and floral aromas. The round, juicy body is packed with green apple and banana flavors and a hint of oak.

Les Vignerons d'Estézargues From the Tank Vin Blanc | 2007 | CÔTES-DU-RHÔNE

★ ★ $ $ (3 L) This producer is notable for both its penchant for natural winemaking and its progressive packaging. A three-liter box holds a nice white wine defined by peach, bubblegum and mint aromas, citrusy tangerine flavors and a vanilla finish.

ROSÉS

Château d'Aqueria | 2008 | TAVEL

★ ★ $ With its bright, vivid hue, this Tavel rosé offers a charming mix of flowers, cherries and wild strawberries on the nose. Hints of bubblegum accent the medium-bodied palate, filled out with raspberry flavors, crisp, bone-dry acidity and a touch of spice.

Domaine de la Berthète Sensation | 2008 | CÔTES-DU-RHÔNE

★ $ Created in 1950, this estate owns vines averaging 32 years of age. They yield fruity wines like this rosé, packed with flavors of raspberry, candied berry and banana that finish dry.

La Vieille Ferme | 2008 | CÔTES DU VENTOUX
★ ★ $ Another low-priced gem from La Vieille Ferme, this blend of 50 percent Cinsault, 40 percent Grenache and 10 percent Syrah is driven by aromas and flavors of fresh strawberries and raspberries, with hints of clove, anise and mineral on the fresh, delicious palate.

M. Chapoutier Belleruche | 2007 | CÔTES-DU-RHÔNE
★ ★ $ Chapoutier can claim a Rhône empire, with vineyards throughout the finest appellations, and still impress with a humble rosé. With juicy flavors of watermelon, strawberry and roses, it is nimble and refreshing, without any overt sweetness and just a touch of tannins.

REDS

Cave de Rasteau Ortas Tradition | 2006 |
CÔTES-DU-RHÔNE VILLAGES RASTEAU
★ $ Simple, sweet raspberry flavors show good weight on the palate of this simple yet tasty blend of 70 percent Grenache, 20 percent Syrah and 10 percent Mourvèdre. Lively acidity and slightly rustic tannins render it balanced and interesting.

Château de Beaucastel | 2006 | CHÂTEAUNEUF-DU-PAPE
★ ★ ★ ★ $ $ $ $ This benchmark Châteauneuf-du-Pape is known for its inclusion of all 13 grape varieties permitted in the region, led by Mour-vèdre. Sweet black cherry, tobacco and pronounced graphite aromas emerge from the dense, tightly wrapped nose; the palate is incredibly rich and concentrated, with flavors of sweet kirsch, blackberry, fig and dusty cherry, all supported by fine tannins.

Château de Domazan | 2006 | CÔTES-DU-RHÔNE
★ $ A slightly funky, earthy nose meets tart red berry flavors in this classically styled Rhône blend. A sweet and juicy low-priced quaffer, it is balanced by ample acidity and moderate tannins.

Château de la Tuilerie Syrah/Grenache | 2007 |
COSTIÈRES DE NÎMES
★ ★ $ Formerly classified as part of Languedoc, the Costières de Nîmes AOC joined the ranks of the Rhône in 1998, and justifiably so, since its wines have a more Rhône-like taste. This savory, smoky example displays a hint of beef layered with ripe cassis, berry and black licorice flavors.

Château des Tours Réserve | 2005 | CÔTES-DU-RHÔNE
★ ★ ★ $ $ Crafted by Emmanuel Reynaud, also of Château Rayas, this is a refreshing wine with inviting red currant and fig flavors and a touch of licorice; generous acidity beautifully brightens the palate.

Château Mont-Redon | 2006 | CÔTES-DU-RHÔNE
★ ★ $ In this lightly oaked wine, pretty, ripe fruit-forward flavors of cherry and kirsch—laced with tobacco leaf and earth—meet dark plummy fruit and powdery tannins on the palate.

Delas | 2007 | CÔTES DU VENTOUX
★ ★ $ Now under the helm of Champagne house Louis Roederer, Delas crafts this inky, violet-hued red brimming with cassis and crushed berry flavors, balanced by fine tannins and minerals on the long, rich finish.

Domaine de Châteaumar Cuvée Bastien | 2007 | CÔTES-DU-RHÔNE
★ ★ $ Made from grapes grown in a single vineyard of old-vine Grenache, this red displays aromas of smoked meat, clove and cinnamon; the dark fruit palate is woven with pepper and rustic tannins.

star producers
southern rhône

Château de Beaucastel
Before the Perrin clan took over, the vines at Château de Beaucastel were threatened by phylloxera infestation. Now Beaucastel crafts some of the finest Châteauneuf-du-Papes.

Château La Nerthe
One of Châteauneuf-du-Pape's larger properties, Château La Nerthe has been practically reborn under the direction of the talented Alain Dugas.

Domaine La Garrigue
The Bernard family planted their Vacqueyras vineyards in the 1940s and named their famous "Cuvée Romaine" in honor of the land's early Roman presence.

Domaine La Millière
Winemaker Michel Arnaud is a champion of Grenache. His vineyards in Cabrières are some of the best in all Châteauneuf-du-Pape.

E. Guigal
Philippe Guigal continues the organic traditions established by his grandfather nearly 60 years ago. Today Guigal makes prestigious boutique bottlings as well as great-value wines.

Perrin & Fils
Though founded in the early 1900s, Perrin & Fils is in tune with the times, regularly posting news about its stellar vineyard and winery on the company blog.

65

Domaine Fincham Red Note | 2006 | COSTIÈRES DE NÎMES

★ ★ $ Super-ripe, juicy and full-bodied, this has sweet berry aromas that build in the mouth, complemented by smoky herbs, graphite highlights and a spiciness that imparts a plum pudding quality.

Domaine Jérôme Gradassi | 2006 | CHÂTEAUNEUF-DU-PAPE

★ ★ ★ $ $ $ Gradassi holds the distinction of earning a Michelin star at his own restaurant before turning to winemaking. His exquisite 2006 is bright and jammy, with strawberries, graphite and violets. The solid structure and firm tannins contribute to a long finish.

Domaine Les Clapas Fesquier Grenache | 2007 |
VIN DE PAYS DES COTEAUX DE L'ARDÈCHE

★ $ Effusive smoked meat and herb aromas jump out of the glass, leading to a palate full of succulent, ripe fruit and figs. The finely tuned acidity is invigorating and brings harmony to this entry-level gem.

Domaine Patrice Magni | 2005 | CHÂTEAUNEUF-DU-PAPE

★ ★ ★ $ $ This small family estate includes about 17 acres of vineyard land in Châteauneuf, which yields the grapes for this gorgeous red. Ruby-colored and spicy, it shows round, sumptuous flavors of black cherry, flowers, earth and plum that finish fresh.

Domaine Rabasse Charavin | 2005 |
CÔTES-DU-RHÔNE VILLAGES RASTEAU

★ ★ $ $ Rasteau wines are known for their power. This figgy, smoky wine is a classic example: flavors of cassis and dried fruit are underscored by coffee and chocolate and held together with dry tannins.

E. Guigal | 2004 | CHÂTEAUNEUF-DU-PAPE

★ ★ ★ $ $ $ Matured for two years in oversize oak barrels, this Grenache-dominated blend is fragrant with flowers, dried cherries and earth. Round, juicy and satisfying in the mouth, it has refined tannins to see it through the mineral- and licorice-laden finish.

Féraud-Brunel | 2006 | CÔTES-DU-RHÔNE VILLAGES RASTEAU

★ ★ $ $ An alliance between Laurence Féraud and André Brunel of Les Cailloux, this winery crafts wines that are concentrated yet balanced. The 2006 is so ripe it's reminiscent of a raspberry jelly doughnut; fine tannins and a burst of acidity keep it fresh.

Font-Sane Tradition | 2006 | GIGONDAS

★ ★ $ $ Font-Sane strikes an impressive balance between power and elegance in this Gigondas. Crushed berry, lavender and rose petal aromas introduce a pleasing mix of black fruit flavors filled out with ripe tannins and notes of tobacco and stone.

In Fine | 2007 | CÔTES DU VENTOUX
★ $ A well-priced wine from an underappreciated appellation, In Fine is a blend of 90 percent Grenache and 10 percent Syrah. It delivers an intriguing mix of raspberry flavors that are up-front yet balanced.

J. Vidal-Fleury | 2007 | CÔTES-DU-RHÔNE
★ ★ $ This tasty value made by a Guigal-owned property is distinguished by intensely sappy, spicy aromas of dark fruit and mocha. The dense flavors of dark, sweet berries and cocoa bring to mind a chocolate-topped sundae.

Le Clos du Caillou Cuvée Unique Vieilles Vignes | 2006 | CÔTES-DU-RHÔNE
★ ★ $ $ This wine's refinement reflects its proximity to Châteauneuf-du-Pape. A bouquet of blueberry, blackberry and mulberry reveals lovely floral and spice notes; modest tannins frame sweet fruit, toast and mocha flavors through the dried fruit finish.

Les Vignerons d'Estézargues Les Grandes Vignes | 2007 | CÔTES-DU-RHÔNE
★ $ Fresh from the start, this fragrant Côtes-du-Rhône is dominated by tart flavors of pomegranate, boysenberry and cranberry that are further energized by a pronounced acidity.

Mas du Goudareau | 2006 | CÔTES-DU-RHÔNE
★ ★ $ Although this is only the second vintage from Mas du Goudareau (founded in 1999), it shows impressive complexity in the form of spice, herb, floral and fresh cherry flavors that are delicately laced with vanilla and ripe tannins in perfect balance.

M. Chapoutier | 2006 | GIGONDAS
★ ★ ★ $ $ $ A blend of mostly Grenache with Cinsault, Syrah and Mourvèdre, this wine is robust and brooding, marked by smoky char and bitter dark chocolate aromas filled out on the palate by decadent ripe plum flavors.

Paul Jaboulet Aîné Parallèle 45 | 2006 | CÔTES-DU-RHÔNE
★ $ A blend of Grenache and Syrah, this wine is named for the 45th north parallel, which runs very close to Jaboulet's winery. It is fresh and saturated with black cherries, herbs and subtle spice notes.

Perrin & Fils Les Sinards | 2005 | CHÂTEAUNEUF-DU-PAPE
★ ★ ★ $ $ $ From the family behind the benchmark Beaucastel, this Châteauneuf-du-Pape is rich and dark, with ripe red fruit aromas and a palate of cherry, kirsch, mocha and spice cake supported by silky tannins on the long finish.

southern france

The wine regions of France's south (Provence, Languedoc and Roussillon) and southwest encompass a vast swath of land. Until very recently, the south was known mainly for quantity, not quality. But in the 1990s, global demand for affordable wines brought the area renewed attention, inspiring bold vintners to experiment with nontraditional grapes.

Southern France: An Overview

Le Midi, the storied south of France, includes the regions of Languedoc, Roussillon and Provence (the first two are often referred to as a single hyphenated entity, Languedoc-Roussillon, or just Languedoc). This area is blessed with so much Mediterranean sunlight that it's possible to make wines of every imaginable style here. The lands of the French Southwest, *le Sud-Ouest,* are under the combined influences of the Atlantic and the Pyrenees mountains.

SOUTHERN FRANCE

languedoc-roussillon

In addition to being France's most prolific region, producing by some estimates more wine than the entire U.S., Languedoc-Roussillon has also become the most dynamic. In the last decade, vintners here have aggressively pursued quality winemaking, often by ignoring rigid government regulations on grape-growing and vinification processes. The resulting wines are widely regarded as some of the finest ever from the region, even though they must still be classified as merely Vins de Pays or Vins de Table.

Languedoc Grapes & Styles

The formidable Languedoc grows a wide range of grapes, some indigenous to the region, others (such as Cabernet Sauvignon) from different French regions. Red grapes dominate, especially Carignan, which is capable of delicious berry- and spice-flavored wines; excellent examples can be found in Corbières. Syrah, Grenache and Mourvèdre are blended to create the·hearty, often rustic wines of Minervois and Fitou, as well as those of the Roussillon appellation Collioure near Spain. Cabernet Sauvignon and Merlot— imported from Bordeaux and increasingly planted here— are used mostly for inexpensive wines destined for export (the wines from Cabernet champion Mas de Daumas Gassac are a notable exception). White varieties Grenache Blanc, Maccabéo, Muscat, Picpoul Blanc and Rolle create fresh, interesting wines, while Viognier yields richer, more complex whites similar in some cases to examples from the northern Rhône, yet available at a fraction of the cost. Chardonnays from Limoux are worth exploring, too. Roussillon is also famed for its dessert wines (see p. 278).

Languedoc Wine Labels

Languedoc labels list region and sometimes grape. Most of the simplest wines are designated *Vins de Pays d'Oc,* meaning they can be made from grapes grown anywhere in Languedoc. Vins de Pays made in specific areas will indicate this on their labels and are subject to greater restrictions. The appellations Languedoc (including the area known until 2007 as Coteaux du Languedoc) and Côtes du Roussillon are umbrellas for smaller ones. Within them, the appellations Minervois, Fitou and Corbières often produce wines showing distinct characteristics, as do Faugères, St-Chinian, Montpeyroux, Pic-St-Loup and Collioure.

languedoc recommendations

WHITES

Arrogant Frog Lily Pad White Chardonnay/Viognier | 2007 |
VIN DE PAYS D'OC
★ $ This lightly oaked white blend brings together aromas of buttered popcorn and sweet apple and vanilla flavors enhanced by honeysuckle and a touch of mineral on the finish.

Domaine de Lancyre Roussanne | 2007 |
VIN DE PAYS DE MONTFERRAND
★★ $ $ Thanks to this subregion's extra-long growing season, this gorgeous wine develops a range of enticing aromas, from acacia flower and honeysuckle to minerals, sweet pear and apple.

Domaines Barons de Rothschild (Lafite) Aussières Blanc
| 2007 | VIN DE PAYS D'OC
★ $ Domaines Barons de Rothschild revitalized the centuries-old vineyards that yielded the grapes for this 100 percent Chardonnay. It shows sweet ripe apple flavors upheld by soft acidity and a kick of spice in the finish.

French Rabbit Chardonnay | 2007 | VIN DE PAYS D'OC
★ $ (1 L) Boisset, the French company with wineries around the world, decided to ditch the bottle for this wine, packaging it in environmentally friendly Tetra Pak cartons. Inside is a nice everyday Chardonnay, replete with tropical fruit flavors and hints of spicy vanilla.

Jean-Luc Colombo La Violette Viognier | 2007 |
VIN DE PAYS D'OC
★ $ Jean-Luc Colombo, the so-called king of Cornas (the Rhône AOC), is known primarily for his intense reds, yet he succeeds with whites as well, as this light, value-priced Viognier demonstrates. Peach flavors are offset by notes of fresh-cut herbs and vanilla.

Zette | 2007 | VIN DE PAYS D'OC
★ $ Domaine de Lagrézette specializes in Malbec, yet this white blend is a lovely, low-priced addition to its portfolio. Zette is made with Chardonnay and Viognier and offers a mix of guava, mango and pineapple flavors, a creamy mouthfeel and a spicy finish.

ROSÉS

Château de Lancyre Pic St-Loup | 2008 |
COTEAUX DU LANGUEDOC
★★ $ Château de Lancyre is committed to expressing terroir in its wines. This rich blend of Syrah, Grenache and Cinsault displays an enticing mix of lavender, rosemary, thyme and raspberry flavors and a lively, refreshing finish.

Domaine de Nizas | 2008 | COTEAUX DU LANGUEDOC
★★ $ A blend of Syrah, Grenache and Mourvèdre, this addictive rosé is made by an estate owned by John Goelet (of California's Clos Du Val, among others). Aromas of fresh berries and peaches lead to rich fruit flavors with just enough minerals and spice for balance.

Domaine des Schistes Le Bosc | 2007 |
VIN DE PAYS DES CÔTES CATALANES
★★ $ The northwesterly tramontane wind blows across this Syrah vineyard, resulting in grapes that yield particularly intense flavors of spicy ripe plum and raspberry in this well-structured rosé.

REDS

Château de Jau | 2005 | CÔTES DU ROUSSILLON VILLAGES
★ ★ $ Primarily known for the lighthearted Le Jaja de Jau (Syrah-Grenache blends), the Dauré family also makes this Côtes du Roussillon red. A blend of Syrah, Mourvèdre, Carignan and Grenache, it brims with juicy red fruit and mineral flavors.

Château du Donjon Grande Tradition | 2007 | MINERVOIS
★ ★ $ Red berry and red plum flavors dominate in this soft, medium-bodied blend of Syrah, Grenache and Carignan. Fresh-cut herbs and earth notes mark the finish.

Domaine Cabirau Serge & Tony Grenache | 2007 |
VIN DE PAYS DES CÔTES CATALANES
★ ★ ★ $ Named for Serge, who grows the grapes, and Tony, who vinifies them, this outstanding Grenache is mouth-filling and luscious. Flavors of *salumi* (cured meats), coffee, mocha, mint and blackberry culminate in a long finish with nicely integrated tannins.

Domaine de Nidolères La Pierroune | 2007 |
CÔTES DU ROUSSILLON
★ ★ $ There is a bold cocoa powder presence on the nose of this Syrah-Mourvèdre-Grenache blend. Raspberry and dark cherry flavors join chocolate nuances in the mouth and are wrapped up in ripe tannins on the chewy, satisfying finish.

Domaine de Nizas | 2005 | COTEAUX DU LANGUEDOC
★ ★ $ Despite the fact that this winery is young (established in 1998), this wine has a charming Old World character. Generous apple, plum and black cherry flavors are framed by chewy, textured tannins.

Domaine Mas de Martin Cuvée Roi Patriote | 2006 |
VIN DE PAYS DU VAL DE MONTFERRAND
★ ★ $ $ This complex "kitchen sink" blend of six different grapes—Syrah, Cabernet Sauvignon, Tannat, Grenache, Merlot and Cabernet Franc—bears tart red cherry and raspberry aromas, which yield to black cherry, mocha and earth flavors on the palate.

Domaines Barons de Rothschild (Lafite) Château d'Aussières | 2006 | CORBIÈRES
★ ★ ★ $ $ Château d'Aussières was saved by the Church from wartime destruction in the Middle Ages and then saved again by the Rothschilds from languishing in disrepair in the 20th century. This lucky château crafts a delicious Syrah-Grenache blend with meat, berry and tobacco aromas, generous cherry flavors and supple tannins.

Domaines François Lurton Les Salices Pinot Noir | 2007 |
VIN DE PAYS D'OC
★ **$** From the French vineyards of the talented Lurton brothers
(Jacques and François) comes this very drinkable red, with the youthful aromas and flavors of plum, strawberry and blackberry and a lingering finish.

Hecht & Bannier | 2005 | **FAUGÈRES**
★★ **$ $ $** This nicely rustic blend includes small amounts of
Mourvèdre and Carignan, yet it is the majority of Syrah that shines
through in the form of dusty spice and mineral flavors. Black plum,
licorice, spice and roasted meat nuances round out the middle of this
enjoyable red.

Les Deux Rives | 2007 | **CORBIÈRES**
★ **$** The *deux rives*, or two banks, that give this tasty wine its name
refer to those of the Canal du Midi. The 2007 reveals a subtle nose of
plum and red currant that opens to juicy blackberry flavors and a
spicy, peppery finish.

Les Vignerons d'Estézargues Cuvée des Galets | 2007 |
VIN DE PAYS DU GARD
★★ **$** This perfect summer red—juicy, soft and delicious—would
taste great with a slight chill. Made from a blend of Grenache, Syrah,
Carignan and Cinsault grapes grown by a six-farm cooperative, it
bears aromas and flavors of ripe cherry and raspberry beefed up by
notes of leafy green tobacco.

Mas Belles Eaux Les Coteaux | 2005 | **LANGUEDOC**
★★★ **$** Dried, crushed lavender aromas come on strong at first in
this Syrah-Grenache-Mourvèdre blend, then slowly make room for
notes of spice, thyme, pepper and sage. The palate is filled out with
fresh raspberry and red cherry flavors, with lovely minerals taking
over at the end.

Plume Bleue Grenache/Syrah | 2007 | **VIN DE PAYS D'OC**
★★ **$** This affordable red from winemaker Laurence Féraud shows
layers of cherry, blueberry and plum flavors and concludes with a
refreshing, mineral-laden finish.

Puydeval | 2007 | **VIN DE PAYS D'OC**
★ **$** This unique blend, led by Cabernet Franc, proves that the grape
does have its place in the Languedoc region. Pronounced blueberry
aromas mingle with a healthy dose of sage and fennel and are followed by cassis and blackberry flavors held together by grainy tannins on the soft finish.

SOUTHERN FRANCE

provence

Provence is home to one of the world's oldest winemaking traditions, but over the years the region became associated with simple, bulk production. Today, however, thanks to technological innovations and winemaking expertise from other parts of France and abroad, Provence wines have never been better.

Provence Grapes & Styles

Provence's best-known wines are its delicious, dry rosés. Typically made from a blend of Cinsault, Grenache and Mourvèdre grapes, they are meant to be consumed young and with food. Those from Bandol are considered the finest, but many rosés from Côtes de Provence and Coteaux d'Aix-en-Provence are also beautifully crafted. Provence's bright, refreshing, citrusy whites are usually blends of local grapes Bourboulenc, Rolle, Clairette, Grenache Blanc and/or Ugni Blanc; the best come from the seaside village of Cassis. Bandol's mineral-laden whites are full-bodied, as are its more famous, robust reds made primarily from Mourvèdre. Grenache, Carignan, Cabernet, Cinsault and Syrah are also planted throughout Provence, though the best examples of Provence reds are from Les Baux de Provence and Coteaux d'Aix-en-Provence.

provence recommendations

WHITES

Domaine de Granajolo | 2007 | CORSE PORTO-VECCHIO
★ ★ $ Though not technically part of Provence, the nearby island of Corsica shares a similar climate and wine tradition. This 100 percent Vermentino is wonderfully fresh and floral, with zesty lemon flavors and a nutty quality on the finish.

Domaine de la Tour du Bon | 2007 | BANDOL
★ $ This simple yet charming light-bodied blend of three local white grapes, Clairette, Ugni Blanc and Rolle, is made in very small quantities and shows apple, lemon and subtle peach flavors with notes of toasted almonds.

Mas de la Dame Coin Caché | 2005 |
COTEAUX D'AIX-EN-PROVENCE
★ ★ ★ $ $ $ The 16th-century estate Mas de la Dame ("farm of the woman") is owned by two sisters, who work with Rhône superstar Jean-Luc Colombo to craft their excellent range of wines, including this Sémillon-Clairette blend. It spends 12 months in new oak, which imparts richness and body to stone fruit and citrus flavors.

Routas Coquelicot Viognier | 2007 | VIN DE PAYS DU VAR
★ ★ $ Unlike the many viscous, concentrated Viogniers, this version is light and quite crisp, offering refreshing flavors of honeysuckle, peach and flowers.

ROSÉS

Bieler Père et Fils Sabine | 2008 |
COTEAUX D'AIX-EN-PROVENCE
★ ★ ★ $ One of the best rosé deals available (only around $10), this refreshing wine walks the line between New World and Old, with a delicious mix of strawberry, herb and crushed watermelon flavors held up by brisk acidity.

Château Miraval Pink Floyd | 2007 | CÔTES DE PROVENCE
★ ★ $ Made on a pre-Roman estate, this certified organic wine shows intensely fruity aromas of ripe strawberries and cotton candy that give the impression of sweetness, yet the palate tastes entirely dry. Flecks of wild thyme and other herbs add interesting highlights.

Corail de Roquefort | 2008 | CÔTES DE PROVENCE
★ ★ $ This high-altitude vineyard, located near the edge of the Bandol appellation, practices biodynamic viticulture. Made from primarily Grenache, Syrah and Cinsault, this silky-textured rosé has a brilliant pink hue and boasts flavors of wild berries and juicy apples.

Jules | 2008 | CÔTES DE PROVENCE
★ ★ $ Julian Faulkner works with different boutique growers each year, which allows him the flexibility to source grapes "wherever the best value and quality can be found on a particular vintage." His aromatic rosé—a blend of Grenache, Cinsault and the lesser-known Tibouren—is elegant, fruit-forward and herbal.

Mas de la Dame Rosé du Mas | 2008 |
LES BAUX DE PROVENCE
★ ★ $ Grenache dominates in this organically produced rosé, yielding flavors of peach, strawberry and herbs. Served with a good chill, it is an ideal choice for fish, salads or anything off the grill.

REDS

Château Miraval | 2005 | **CÔTES DE PROVENCE**
★ ★ $ This Syrah–Cabernet Sauvignon blend is bolstered by ample oak, which adds weight and spice to rustic flavors of black olives, meat, minerals, earth and dark berries.

Domaine de l'Hermitage L'Oratoire | 2005 | **BANDOL**
★ ★ $ $ $ Having made wine here since the 1970s, the Duffort family has mastered the art of coaxing the best from the mineral-rich clay soils of the Bandol region. The 2005 red, made primarily with the Mourvèdre grape, shows refined graphite and black fruit flavors offset by a charming earthy, rustic quality.

Mas de Gourgonnier | 2006 | **LES BAUX DE PROVENCE**
★ ★ $ An early adopter of organic viticultural practices, Mas de Gourgonnier crafts red blends that taste distinctly Mediterranean. The hearty 2006 offers chewy tannins wrapped around dried herb, black olive and wild blackberry flavors—a perfect match for grilled sausages or cassoulet.

Routas Infernet Grenache/Syrah | 2005 |
COTEAUX VAROIS EN PROVENCE
★ ★ $ This tasty blend of Grenache and Syrah—whose name comes from the Trou de l'Infernet ("Hellhole"), a deep geological formation located near the vineyard where the devil is reputed to live—is a wonderful value for its minty chocolate and spiced red currant flavors and nice structure.

SOUTHERN FRANCE

the southwest

The French region known as the Southwest, or *le Sud-Ouest*, borders the rugged Pyrenees mountains, which separate France from Spain, and is outshone by its formidable neighbor to the northwest, Bordeaux. As a result, the wines of the Southwest remain little known in the U.S., although that situation is starting to change. Three appellations in particular are worth exploring: Bergerac, for its wines of distinctly Bordeaux-like finesse; Cahors, for its prestigious reds of massive ruggedness and power; and Monbazillac, for its excellent Sauternes-like sweet wines that cost a fraction as much as the famed sweet wines of Bordeaux.

The Southwest Grapes & Styles

The red wines of Bergerac are made with the same grapes as those in Bordeaux—Cabernet Sauvignon, Merlot, Malbec and Cabernet Franc. The full-bodied reds of Cahors are based on the grape known elsewhere as Malbec or Côt but here called Auxerrois. In Madiran, vintners use the Tannat grape to craft wines that are even darker, fuller-bodied and more tannic. The hearty wines from the Basque Country are made from a blend of difficult-to-pronounce local grapes. Jurançon is a full-bodied, spicy white wine produced from Petit and Gros Manseng grapes in two styles: dry (labeled "Jurançon Sec") and sweet. Monbazillac and Gaillac are similar wines, with both dry and sweet versions. Vins de Pays des Côtes de Gascogne are light- to medium-bodied wines from local and international grapes.

southwest recommendations

WHITES

Château K Cuvée K | 2007 | BERGERAC
★★ $ The K here stands for owner Katharina Mowinckel, a Norwegian who emigrated to the south of France. Her delicious blend of Sémillon and Sauvignon Blanc boasts a lovely mix of honeysuckle, melon and white peach flavors.

Domaine Bellegarde La Pierre Blanche | 2006 |
JURANÇON SEC
★★★ $ $ This seductive blend of Petit Manseng and Gros Manseng delivers fragrant pear and honey notes amid creamy, nut-infused flavors of sweet apricot, spice and star fruit.

Domaine de Ballade Sauvignon Blanc/Colombard | 2008 |
VIN DE PAYS DES CÔTES DE GASCOGNE
★ $ Gascony's *douceur de vivre,* or sweetness of life, is fully evident here. Zippy citrus and acacia aromas meet creamy lemon curd flavors on the palate, where they are uplifted by bright, mineral-laden acidity.

Premius Sauvignon Blanc | 2007 |
VIN DE PAYS DU COMTÉ TOLOSAN
★ $ A "country wine" from the Midi-Pyrenees region, this Sauvignon Blanc combines aromas of citrus zest, dried pineapple and fresh-cut grass with pure, refreshing citrus flavors and soft minerals.

REDS

Baron d'Ardeuil Vieilles Vignes | 2005 | **BUZET**
★★★ $ Buzet wines are similar to those from neighboring Bordeaux, yet tend to be darker and fruitier. In this concentrated example, aromas of prune, cherry and sweet raisin dominate the nose, while well-integrated tannins support waves of dense black fruit flavors.

Château Lagrézette Cuvée Dame Honneur | 2003 | **CAHORS**
★★★ $ $ $ $ The Cahors region is the home of Malbec, and the grape leads in this stellar, textured red blend, filled out with a bit of Merlot, which contributes a nice softness. Complex layers of violet, chalk and spice aromas are grounded by spiced blackberry flavors and notes of cured meat, mineral and toast.

Clos Siguier | 2006 | **CAHORS**
★★ $ Another great wine from Cahors, this inky-dark blend of Malbec and Tannat is rich and succulent—and true to the region's tradition of "black" wines. Concentrated black fruit flavors abound, wrapped up in supple, chewy tannins on the mouthwatering finish.

Domaine du Crampilh l'Originel | 2005 | **MADIRAN**
★★ $ With a heady nose of dusty herbs and black currants, this 100 percent Tannat brings together juicy black fruit flavors and impressive structure.

Isabelle Carles & Franck Pascal Les Sens du Fruit | 2006 |
BERGERAC
★★ $ This Bergerac blend of Cabernet Sauvignon and Merlot is equal parts lush and firm, thanks to good acidity and tannins that hold up plush flavors of raspberry, blackberry and lots of spice.

Robert & Bernard Plageoles Le Duras | 2006 | **GAILLAC**
★★★ $ $ The Plageoles are champions of Gaillac's nearly forgotten Duras grape, and their organic vines yield rich, character-filled wines. The 2006 is marked by delightful, mouth-coating blackberry flavors and soft tannins on the long finish.

Zette Malbec | 2003 | **CAHORS**
★ $ The second label from the team behind Lagrézette, this wonderfully low-priced red is medium-bodied, yet possesses the bold, powerful tannins typical of Malbec from Cahors.

italy

While wine has been made in Italy for thousands of years, the focus more recently has been on quality, rather than quantity. Today, Italy is the world's leading exporter, and promising wines are made in nearly every corner of the country.

Principal Wine Region

Italy: An Overview

From the foothills of the Alps in the north to the hills of Sicily in the south, almost every region of Italy produces wine. Italian vintners manage to succeed throughout their country's varied terrains and climate zones by utilizing a wide array of indigenous and French grapes as well as cutting-edge winemaking styles and technical innovations. As a result, Italy contains more than 300 DOC and DOCG zones (see Italian Wine Labels, below). Two regions, however, stand out above the rest: Piedmont in the northwest, where the Nebbiolo grape yields famously rich, long-lived Barolo and slightly lighter Barbaresco; and Tuscany, home of the cherry-scented Sangiovese grape, responsible for two of Italy's most recognized wines—Chianti and Brunello di Montalcino. Still, from the mineral-laden whites of Friuli and Trentino–Alto Adige to Umbria's dark, sultry Sagrantino di Montefalco and the powerful reds of Sicily, Italy produces wines for all tastes, budgets and seasons.

Italian Wine Labels

Italian wines are traditionally labeled by their place of origin, though some labels list the grape if it defines a region, such as Montepulciano d'Abruzzo, made from the Montepulciano grape in Abruzzo. Grape names are used most often in the northeastern regions of Alto Adige and Friuli–Venezia Giulia. Italy's regulatory system is the *Denominazione di Origine Controllata* (DOC), which delineates basic areas and standards; more rigorous standards apply to wines with the DOCG (*Denominazione di Origine Controllata e Garantita*) imprimatur. The term *Classico* on a label indicates a prestigious subregion. For much of the system's history, wines not adhering to DOC or DOCG standards were given the humble title *Vino da Tavola* (table wine). In 1992, the *Indicazione Geografica Tipica* (IGT) classification was created for the growing number of superb wines being made with unapproved grape varieties and techniques.

piedmont

Located in northwestern Italy in the foothills of the Alps, Piedmont is home to the Nebbiolo grape, which produces some of the world's most outstanding wines. Chief among them are Barolo and, to a lesser extent, Barbaresco—though both draw comparisons to Burgundies for their elegance and ability to age. The region is also known for light, fruity everyday wines, such as Barbera and Dolcetto, and the popular sparkling white Asti.

piedmont whites

Piedmont's reputation is based upon its reds, but there are still a handful of interesting whites from the region worth seeking out. Gavi di Gavi, from the Cortese grape, is perhaps Piedmont's most famous still white, though Arneis, particularly from the subregion of Roero, is more substantial and more compelling. Chardonnays here can be wonderfully balanced. Sweeter sparkling wines are also prevalent, with the well-known, though rarely exciting, Asti Spumante leading the way. The superior Moscato d'Asti (see p. 262) is unusually delicate and wonderfully fragrant.

piedmont white recommendations

Beni di Batasiolo Granée | 2007 | **GAVI DI GAVI**
★★ **$** This aromatic white—made from the Cortese grape—has notes of acacia flower, minerals and sweet apple. There's a bright kiss of lemon on the palate, rounded out by soft melon undertones.

Ceretto Blangé Arneis | 2007 | **LANGHE**
★★★ **$ $** Riccardo Ceretto founded this winery in the 1930s, when the Langhe region was largely undiscovered. Citrus, apple and wet stone flavors are balanced by crisp acidity on the mouthwatering finish in this excellent Arneis.

Fontanafredda | 2007 | **GAVI DI GAVI**
★★ **$ $** One of the oldest wineries in the region, Fontanafredda can trace its history back to an 1858 royal land grant. The 2007 Gavi boasts flavors of ripe apple and pear layered with ample minerals.

La Scolca (White Label) | 2008 | GAVI DI GAVI
★ ★ $ $ With its mineral-laden, steely nose—typical of traditional Gavi di Gavi—this wine possesses an added whiff of citrus, followed by flavors of sweet lemon zest.

Pertinace | 2007 | ROERO ARNEIS
★ ★ $ Made from Piedmont's toughest-to-grow grape (*Arneis* means "stubborn"), this wine achieves great balance between juicy peach and melon flavors and a touch of lemon curd and minerals.

Villa Sparina | 2007 | GAVI DI GAVI
★ ★ ★ $ Opening with a gorgeous bouquet of white flowers and white peaches, this medium-bodied Gavi offers delicious flavors of stone fruit and fresh herbs balanced by crisp acidity.

piedmont reds

The Nebbiolo grape is responsible for Piedmont's greatest reds: Barolo and Barbaresco. Also called Spanna, Nebbiolo produces the less familiar wines of Gattinara, Ghemme and Langhe as well. The region's most prolific grape, though, is Barbera, a highly acidic chameleon that can yield powerful, ageworthy wines as well as young, light reds. Dolcetto produces a large amount of the region's simpler reds. Cabernet Sauvignon, Pinot Noir and Syrah are also grown here, but the wines generally aren't worth seeking out.

PIEDMONT REDS
barolo & barbaresco

These two renowned reds are among the greatest wines of Italy and the world. Although both are Nebbiolo-based, Barolo tends to be heartier and more aromatic, while Barbaresco is lighter and more subtle. While both improve with age, regulations require Barolo to be aged three years, two in barrel, before release, whereas Barbaresco must be aged only two years, one in barrel. Traditionally, these wines require at least a decade to soften, but many vintners today apply modern techniques that enable their wines to mature earlier. Many traditionalist vintners frown on this approach, and believe the wine is worth waiting for.

barolo & barbaresco recommendations

Beni di Batasiolo Vigneto Corda della Briccolina | 2003 | **BAROLO**

★ ★ ★ ★ **$ $ $ $** From four acres in Serralunga d'Alba comes the only single-vineyard Barolo aged in French oak. Replete with toast and vanilla aromas and a whiff of cream, this silky red is full-bodied, with blackberry and prune flavors and earthy mushroom nuances.

Ceretto Bricco Asili Bernardot | 2005 | **BARBARESCO**

★ ★ ★ ★ **$ $ $ $** A spectacular bouquet of roses, sage and blackberry compote leaps from the glass, followed by a perfect core of succulent black fruit flavors and silky tannins in the mouth. The finish is long and tight—a good indication this will age beautifully.

star producers
barolo & barbaresco

Beni di Batasiolo
Batasiolo's several hundred acres of estate vines in the heart of Piedmont yield an impressive range of wines, including acclaimed Barolos.

Ceretto
Brothers Bruno and Marcello Ceretto began their "reign of terroir" in the 1960s, buying the finest Barolo and Barbaresco houses to make their legendary single-vineyard wines.

Fontanafredda
This pedigreed Langhe estate founded in the 1800s is particularly celebrated for its single-vineyard Barolos but earns praise for a wide spectrum of wines.

Gaja
For nearly half a century, the single-vineyard Nebbiolos of Angelo Gaja—most notably Sorì Tildìn and Sorì San Lorenzo—have been among Piedmont's best.

Massolino
Franco and Roberto Massolino are revered in Piedmont and around the world. Their Vigna Margheria and Vigna Parafada combine power and finesse.

Pio Cesare
Carrying on the traditions of his great-grandfather, Pio Boffa continues to eschew the status quo, ignoring the region's trend toward single-vineyard wines in favor of multi-vineyard blends.

Fontanafredda La Rosa | 2001 | BAROLO
★ ★ ★ ★ $ $ $ $ Fontanafredda's La Rosa vineyard in northern Serralunga d'Alba is known for producing intensely tannic wines. The 2001 is no exception: it's loaded with blackberry and licorice flavors framed by massive tannins that beg for braised osso buco.

Gaja | 2005 | BARBARESCO
★ ★ ★ ★ $ $ $ $ From the "king of Piedmont," Angelo Gaja, comes this gorgeous Nebbiolo bearing violet and ripe blackberry aromas. Full-bodied and chewy, it offers layer upon layer of black fruit and fine-grained tannins well into the lengthy finish.

Massolino | 2005 | BAROLO
★ ★ ★ ★ $ $ $ $ Massolino's stellar reputation is based on delivering robust, concentrated, well-structured Barolos. The 2005 is marked by leafy tobacco and cedar aromas sweetened by raspberry and blackberry flavors; integrated tannins support the lush finish.

Michele Chiarlo Reyna | 2006 | BARBARESCO
★ ★ ★ $ $ $ This is the second vintage of Chiarlo's entry-level Barbaresco under its new name Reyna. It is a formidable wine, wafting sweet plum and dried heather aromas, blackberry, mushroom and mocha flavors and a soft yet memorably long finish.

Parusso | 2004 | BAROLO
★ ★ ★ $ $ $ $ Marco Parusso describes his Barolos in terms of masculine and feminine. This might be likened to the fairer sex, with sweet, fruity lusciousness, alluring vanilla perfume and silky tannins.

Vietti Castiglione | 2005 | BAROLO
★ ★ ★ $ $ $ While it's impossible to miss the full body of this delicious Barolo, it also has a rare delicacy: rising waves of plum, blackberry and cocoa flavors and fine tannins are all in perfect harmony.

PIEDMONT REDS

barbera & dolcetto

If Barolo and Barbaresco are Piedmont's noble wines, Barbera and Dolcetto are the wines of the people. Often produced in large quantities, these wines range from smooth, crowd-pleasing Dolcettos to more complex, aromatic Barberas. Dolcetto is particularly important to vintners here, as it allows them to create marketable young wines while they give their Nebbiolo-based wines time to age properly.

barbera & dolcetto recommendations

Accornero Bricco Battista | 2006 |
BARBERA DEL MONFERRATO SUPERIORE

★ ★ ★ $ $ $ This intensely fragrant wine—with notes of plum, cocoa powder and bright red cherry—is made by the Accornero family, who have been in the wine business since 1897. Black currant and blackberry flavors compete with dusty spice and vanilla, which round out the impressive finish.

Conterno Fantino Bricco Bastia | 2007 | DOLCETTO D'ALBA

★ ★ $ $ *Dolcetto* is Italian for "little sweet one," and indeed the grape is ripe and fleshy here. The entry-level wine from one of Piedmont's top estates, this has sweet plum and red berry flavors held up by mild tannins and a subtle nuttiness on the finish.

Conterno Fantino Vignota | 2007 | BARBERA D'ALBA

★ ★ $ $ Grown in sandy-soiled vineyards and aged in oak for ten months, this big and full-bodied Barbera bears the aromas and flavors of black currants and blackberries. A whiff of citrus zest in the finish gives hefty tannins a nice lift.

Fontanafredda Briccotondo Barbera | 2007 | PIEDMONT

★ ★ ★ $ Fontanafredda is known primarily for its outstanding Barolos, but the winery's excellent Barbera is also delicious. Full-bodied, rich and plush in texture, the 2007 shows a seductive blend of cocoa, dark coffee and blackberry flavors.

Marcarini Fontanazza | 2007 | DOLCETTO D'ALBA

★ ★ $ The Marcarini winery employs many time-consuming traditional winemaking practices, and the results are well worth the effort. This unoaked Dolcetto brings together sweet prune and black fruit flavors with clean minerals and balanced, elegant tannins.

Massolino | 2007 | BARBERA D'ALBA

★ ★ ★ $ $ Aromas of fresh fennel and ripe berries provide an enticing bouquet in this full-bodied wine from one of Barolo's legendary leaders. Flavors of berry jam follow, with soft tannins balancing the refreshing finish.

Pio Cesare | 2006 | BARBERA D'ALBA

★ ★ ★ $ $ Aged in French and Yugoslavian oak, this luscious Barbera is made by the skilled vintner Pio Boffa. Aromas of blackberries and grated chocolate combine with earthy flavors of cocoa powder on the palate of this full-bodied red, where they are balanced with fine-grained tannins.

Poderi Luigi Einaudi | 2007 | DOLCETTO DI DOGLIANI
★★ $ From the estate founded in 1897 by Luigi Einaudi—professor, journalist, winemaker and, eventually, Italy's first elected president—this wine is complex and well balanced. Violet aromas and fresh plum and raspberry flavors are woven with lovely minerals throughout.

Vietti Tre Vigne | 2006 | BARBERA D'ALBA
★★ $ $ As its name suggests, this wine was made from grapes sourced from three different vineyards. The result is a medium-bodied beauty with a berry and violet bouquet followed by ripe plum and blackberry flavors and brightened by a raspberry-like acidity.

other piedmont reds

Piedmont hosts many international grapes, including Cabernet, Merlot and Syrah, all from neighboring France. These grapes are ideal for blending with local varieties, though many native grapes are just as intriguing on their own. Wines from indigenous grapes range from the sweet and effervescent Freisa to the fruity and floral Ruchè. There are also some interesting Nebbiolo-based wines from Gattinara, Ghemme and Langhe, where the grape is often called Spanna, and Nebbiolo d'Alba can somewhat mimic the characteristics of Barolo at a fraction of the cost.

other piedmont red recommendations

Cascina Bongiovanni Faletto | 2006 | LANGHE
★★★ $ $ $ This is a stunning, potent red with ripe raspberry and red currant flavors woven with a ribbon of vanilla and toasted oak notes on the soft, balanced finish.

Poderi Colla Campo Romano Pinot Noir | 2006 | LANGHE
★★ $ $ A delicate, well-crafted red with the refined aromas of plum, cured meat and cedar, this medium-bodied Pinot was made from grapes grown on Campo Romano's Cascine Drago estate near Alba. Thanks to silky tannins, it has a beautiful, lengthy finish.

Produttori del Barbaresco Nebbiolo delle Langhe | 2007 |
LANGHE
★★ $ $ This producer is known for fine Barbaresco, yet its lighter-bodied Nebbiolo from Langhe represents good value for its dark fruit and licorice aromas filled out with spice and tannins on the palate.

Serradenari Nebbiolo | 2005 | LANGHE
★ ★ ★ $ $ Once a haven from an outbreak of the black death, the Serradenari property is now a terraced vineyard famous for superb Nebbiolo. The 2005 gives flavors of *salumi,* plum and raspberry that are rustic and mouth-filling and lead to a powerful yet elegant finish.

Travaglini | 2003 | GATTINARA
★ ★ ★ $ $ $ Don't let the Port-like aromas of caramel and prune fool you: this rich and delicious wine is all Nebbiolo (known locally as Spanna), with black fruit flavors, chewy tannins and a satisfyingly rich finish. Travaglini is *the* name to know in Gattinara.

other northern italian regions

Northeastern Italy's most productive region is Veneto, where popular but inconsistent wines like red Valpolicella and Bardolino and white Soave and Pinot Grigio are made. Throughout the northeast, vintners focused on quality are creating some excellent and unique wines using an array of indigenous grapes not grown in any of the larger regions.

• **TRENTINO–ALTO ADIGE & FRIULI–VENEZIA GIULIA**
Bordering Austria and mainly German-speaking in the north, Trentino–Alto Adige is actually two separate regions often grouped together due to their proximity. A German accent is also evident in the wines here, produced from grapes including Gewürztraminer (also known as Traminer), Sylvaner and Müller-Thurgau. Friuli–Venezia Giulia boasts many unusual grape varieties such as Refosco, Tazzelenghe, Schioppettino and the recently revived Pignolo. Though Friuli is more famous for whites, its subregion Colli Orientali del Friuli is a producer of reds. Even the seemingly desolate hill region of Carso makes some noteworthy wines.
• **VENETO** In spite of its reputation for bulk production, Veneto is responsible for many high-quality wines. The best bottles come from the Soave and Valpolicella zones, especially the hilly Classico regions. Another important wine of note is the popular sparkling white Prosecco (see p. 262).

• **LOMBARDY** The best-known region here is Franciacorta, where Italy's finest sparkling wines are made (see p. 262). Lombardy also encompasses Valtellina, near the Swiss border, where the well-regarded Sforzato wine is made from the Chiavennasca (Nebbiolo) grape.

other northern italian whites

White-wine lovers will find many inspired choices in Italy's northern regions. From Trentino–Alto Adige come German-influenced wines such as Weissburgunder (Pinot Bianco), Müller-Thurgau, Sylvaner and the weighty, incredibly aromatic Gewürztraminer, as well as wines from more common varieties such as Chardonnay, Pinot Grigio and Sauvignon Blanc. Veneto offers the Garganega-based Soave. Much Soave is poorly crafted, but good wines can be found in the Classico zones spanning the hills outside Verona. Indigenous white grape varieties from the Friuli region include Friulano, Ribolla Gialla and Picolit, yet the region is perhaps more renowned for its stunning Pinot Grigio, Pinot Bianco and Sauvignon. The white Prosecco grape flourishes in Veneto, where it is used to produce a refreshingly light sparkling wine of the same name.

other northern italian white recommendations

Brigl Sielo Blu Pinot Grigio | 2007 | **ALTO ADIGE**
★ **$** This is the type of Pinot Grigio that sold many Americans on the grape—lemon-flavored, fresh and delicious. With Granny Smith apple notes and lemonade-like acidity, it has a touch more body than many mainstream versions.

Ca' del Bosco | 2005 | **TERRE DI FRANCIACORTA**
★★★ **$ $ $ $** Ca' del Bosco is famous for its sparkling wines, and this full-bodied Chardonnay shows plenty of Champagne-like richness in the form of butterscotch, marzipan and tarte tatin notes that infuse the flavors of honeysuckle and apple. Thanks to great acidity, it is elegant and complex.

Eugenio Collavini Broy | 2006 | COLLIO
★ ★ ★ $ $ $ The Friulano and Chardonnay grapes used for this wine were slightly dried before pressing, and then blended with Sauvignon Blanc. The result is a pear- and flower-scented wine with spice and tropical fruit on a plush, viscous palate held up by vibrant acidity.

Fantinel Vigneti Sant' Helena Pinot Grigio | 2006 | COLLIO
★ ★ $ $ A slightly rusty, yellow-orange color hints at the full body and flavor-concentration to come. Unlike leaner Pinot Grigios, this is broad and mouth-filling, packed with almond, walnut and stone fruit flavors woven with a fresh streak of minerals.

J. Hofstätter Kolbenhof Gewürztraminer | 2006 |
ALTO ADIGE
★ ★ ★ ★ $ $ $ The Kolbenhof estate sits above the village of Tramin, namesake of the Gewürztraminer grape that grows here. Rich stone fruit, lychee and zesty citrus flavors permeate the palate of this full-bodied yet finely balanced wine.

Kellerei Cantina Andrian Floreado Sauvignon Blanc | 2008 |
ALTO ADIGE
★ $ $ This refreshing Sauvignon is true to varietal form, with candied fruit and passion fruit aromas laced with flowers and fresh hay.

Kellerei Cantina Terlan Lunare Gewürztraminer | 2006 |
ALTO ADIGE
★ ★ $ $ $ Rose petals are on display in this full-bodied wine, coupled with dense clover honey, spice and baked pear flavors. Notes of nutmeg and apricot make this redolent of a chewy Christmas cookie.

Les Crêtes Cuvée Bois Chardonnay | 2006 | VALLE D'AOSTA
★ ★ ★ $ $ $ $ A northern Italian trophy white, this venerable Chardonnay beautifully balances its toasted oak with apple tarte Tatin and creamy pear flavors. Rich and full-bodied on the palate, it is nicely offset by elegant acidity.

Livon Braide Alte | 2004 | COLLIO
★ ★ $ $ $ A combination of Chardonnay, Sauvignon Blanc, Picolit and Moscato Giallo, this wine is rich and complex, with spicy vanilla aromas that turn to peach pie and butter flavors on the plush palate.

Manni Nössing Kerner | 2007 | VALLE ISARCO, ALTO ADIGE
★ ★ ★ $ The 20th-century Kerner grape, a cross between a red grape and Riesling, is incredibly aromatic and a nice alternative for Sauvignon Blanc fans, thanks to its grapefruit flavors and notes of bell peppers and herbs. Thoroughly refreshing, it boasts a steely acidity.

Marcato Le Barche | 2007 | SOAVE CLASSICO

★ **$** This well-priced blend of primarily Garganega, with small additions of Trebbiano di Soave (which is actually Verdicchio) and Chardonnay, offers a mix of chalky minerals and lean white-peach flavors that are mouth-filling and held aloft by fresh acidity.

Muri-Gries Müller-Thurgau | 2008 | ALTO ADIGE

★ **$** Made in a working Benedictine monastery, this white offers lime zest and zippy grapefruit flavors that follow through on the light, crisp and refreshing palate—a perfect seafood pairing.

St. Michael–Eppan Sanct Valentin Sauvignon | 2007 | ALTO ADIGE

★★★ **$ $ $** This excellent Sauvignon Blanc shows gooseberry aromas and sweet and tart flavors of citrus. Juicy and clean, it is pierced by bracing minerals throughout the long finish.

Zanotelli Müller-Thurgau | 2007 | TRENTINO

★★ **$ $** This boutique producer owns a mere 25 acres. Its Müller-Thurgau offers tropical passion fruit flavors that come together with notes of crisp green apple, lime and *yuzu* (a citrus fruit), for a bright, mouth-filling wine with good structure.

other northern italian reds

Valpolicella's popularity is due to its affordability, yet much of it is low quality. Well made Valpolicellas, crafted mainly from the Corvina grape, can, however, be bright, floral and inspired. The best come from the Classico zone and are labeled *Superiore*. Two other notable types of Valpolicella are Amarone and Ripasso. Amarone is a rich wine made from grapes that traditionally have been air-dried for several months prior to pressing, which intensifies the grapes' flavor; Recioto (see p. 278) is a sweet version of Amarone. Ripasso seeks a middle ground by infusing Valpolicella wine with the leftover pressed grapes of Amarone. Other varieties indigenous to the northern regions include rustic Refosco; sharp, tannic Pignolo and Schioppettino; softer Lagrein; and the highly acidic Tazzelenghe (translated locally as "tongue cutter"). Cabernet Sauvignon is increasingly planted here, and wines from long-established Merlot, Cabernet Franc and Carmenère are peppery and herbal.

other northern italian red recommendations

Abtei Muri Riserva Lagrein | 2005 | ALTO ADIGE

★ ★ $ $ An affordable way to discover an underappreciated grape, this inky Lagrein displays earthy black cherry and spicy plum flavors and a supple texture held up by fine tannins. Plenty of acidity and intriguing notes of brandy and licorice on the finish keep it fresh.

Angelini Pinot Noir | 2007 | VENETO

★ $ This is fruit-driven yet tart in a refreshingly Old World way. Brambly raspberry and cherry flavors have just the right amount of green peppercorn and spicy root beer notes.

J. Hofstätter Steinraffler Lagrein | 2000 | ALTO ADIGE

★ ★ ★ $ $ $ A single-vineyard Lagrein, this wine presents the best attributes of the grape, balancing rich and spicy wild berry flavors with wonderfully plush tannins on a medium-bodied frame.

Kellerei Cantina Andrian St. Magdalener | 2008 | SANTA MADDALENA, ALTO ADIGE

★ $ Made with the local Schiava grape, this is an interesting red with the weight of a Cru Beaujolais and bracing acidity. Light flavors of berries are layered with hints of bubblegum, herbs and smoke, making this a perfect wine for summer.

Laimburg Col de Réy | 2004 | VIGNETI DELLE DOLOMITI

★ ★ ★ $ $ $ In this blend, Petit Verdot and Tannat add tannins, while Lagrein contributes black, supple fruit. With a meaty, smoky, black cherry bouquet, the wine is dense and weighty, slowly unleashing flavors of blackberries, cassis and sweet vanilla.

La Roncaia Refosco | 2003 | COLLI ORIENTALI DEL FRIULI

★ ★ ★ ★ $ $ $ An expressive red, this blend of Merlot, Refosco, Cabernet Franc and Cabernet Sauvignon jumps out of the glass with gorgeous aromas of cherry, raspberry, mulberry and cola. The tannins are fine and firm, providing good support for concentrated chocolate-covered cherry flavors.

Le Ragose Ripasso | 2005 | VALPOLICELLA CLASSICO SUPERIORE

★ ★ $ $ From the highest-altitude winery in Valpolicella, this blend of local grapes shows dense red fruit and hints of earth, mocha and smoky oak on the nose. The ripe berry flavors are accented by tart rhubarb and dried fruit that carry through the finish, woven with fine tannins and bright acidity.

Masi Costasera Riserva | 2003 |
AMARONE DELLA VALPOLICELLA CLASSICO
★★★★ $ $ $ $ Amarone's traditional mix of grapes is augmented by 10 percent Oseleta in this full-bodied, decadent red. Tightly wound flavors of chewy dried date and cherry emerge slowly, followed by blackberry jam, prune and chocolate, all framed by supple tannins.

Nino Negri Quadrio | 2005 | **VALTELLINA SUPERIORE**
★★ $ $ Consider this a budget Barbaresco. A blend of 90 percent Chiavennasca—better known as Nebbiolo—and 10 percent Merlot, it unites pretty floral and violet aromas with notes of currant and plum.

Plozza Inferno Riserva | 2004 | **VALTELLINA SUPERIORE**
★★ $ $ $ This Nebbiolo-based wine is introduced by red fruit and herbs followed by licorice notes on the palate that impart a charming rustic quality. The tannins are firm on the cocoa-tinged finish.

news from a wine insider
italy by David Lynch, San Francisco–based author of *Vino Italiano*

Vintage Note

Following the spectacular 2004 vintage in Piedmont, the 2005 Barolos and 2006 Barbarescos have also been released to great fanfare. Meanwhile, Tuscany's Brunello di Montalcino and Rosso di Montalcino producers are still recovering from the 2008 scandal, in which some producers were discovered to be illegally incorporating grapes other than Sangiovese into their wines. Yet, there are still many great wines to be had from Montalcino. In fact, many believe the region will emerge from the scandal stronger.

Regions to Watch

In Calabria, innovative producers such as Odoardi and Statti are making great wines with local grapes Greco and Gaglioppo. Look for Statti's well-priced Gaglioppo reds.

Sicily's Etna region continues to be worth watching. Standouts Benanti and Terre Nere are crafting wines from the indigenous Nerello Mascalese grape that draw comparisons to red Burgundy. A few miles south, near the city of Ragusa, biodynamic wunderkind Arianna Occhipinti makes gorgeous reds from the light and fragrant Frappato variety.

tuscany

Tuscany lies at the heart of Italy's wine heritage. Home to the versatile Sangiovese grape, Tuscany produces what could be called Italy's most popular wine, Chianti, as well as one of its most esteemed, Brunello di Montalcino. In addition, Tuscany's creative vintners make many outstanding blends, such as the modern-style Super-Tuscans classified under the IGT designation (see p. 79).

tuscan whites

Although Tuscany is famous for its reds, the region does produce a decent amount of white wine, most of it based on the bland Trebbiano grape and somewhat overpriced. Two of Tuscany's whites, however, are definitely worth seeking out: Vernaccia from San Gimignano, which is light and crisp on its own but has more body when blended with Chardonnay; and Vermentino, a wine full of mineral and zesty lime flavors.

tuscan white recommendations

Palagetto Santa Chiara | 2006 |
VERNACCIA DI SAN GIMIGNANO
★★ $ Super-Tuscan superstar winemaker Giacomo Tachis helped launch Palagetto in the 1990s. The Vernaccia, marked by white flowers, chalky minerals and sweet apple flavors, has a refreshing, intensely juicy finish.

Rocca di Montemassi Calasole Vermentino | 2007 |
MAREMMA TOSCANA
★★ $ Ripe, rich and round, this tasty white is perfumed with delicate white flowers and brims with clean pineapple flavors balanced with crisp, dry mineral nuances in the finish.

Tenuta Guado al Tasso Vermentino | 2008 | **BOLGHERI**
★★★ $ $ Although Bolgheri has become renowned for its big, full-bodied reds, this refreshing white is worth seeking out. Made with 100 percent Vermentino, it possesses ripe cantaloupe and bright citrus aromas and flavors laced with notes of tart Granny Smith apple on the satisfying finish.

Teruzzi & Puthod Terre di Tufi | 2007 | TUSCANY
★ ★ $ This medium-bodied blend of Vernaccia and small portions of Chardonnay, Malvasia and Vermentino is perfumed with acacia flowers, pineapple and flinty minerals. In the mouth it is plush and round, with clean fruit flavors throughout.

Villa Antinori | 2008 | TUSCANY
★ ★ $ Local Trebbiano and Malvasia are blended with Pinot Bianco and Pinot Grigio to create a mouthwatering wine oozing tropical aromas of banana and pineapple followed by lemon curd and apple flavors and a spritz of citrusy acidity.

tuscan reds

Tuscany's beloved red wines are almost entirely based on the Sangiovese grape. Though the variety's characteristics include high acidity and bright fruit flavors, the wines it produces range from light and simple to bold and complex. There are also many excellent Tuscan blends crafted with other grapes, including relative newcomers Cabernet, Merlot and Syrah, all grown in the regions of Bolgheri and Maremma. Other grapes native to the region, such as Canaiolo (also called Canaiolo Nero), Mammolo and Colorino, are used mainly in blends, particularly in Chianti.

TUSCAN REDS

chianti

Less than 25 years ago, regulations required Chianti producers to blend Sangiovese with several indigenous red and white grapes and to age their wines in large, old casks. Today, while examples of the old-fashioned style still exist, most wineries are crafting modern wines from 100 percent Sangiovese, or adding up to 20 percent Cabernet, Merlot or native grapes like Canaiolo and Colorino. Generic "Chianti," which lists no subregion on the label, is the simplest. Wines labeled *Riserva* require at least two years of aging, and are more concentrated and powerful as a result. Chianti contains eight subregions, which are noted on labels; Chianti Classico and Chianti Rùfina are the finest.

chianti recommendations

Antinori Pèppoli | 2006 | CHIANTI CLASSICO
★ ★ ★ $ $ Produced by the Antinori family—Italian nobles with over six centuries of winemaking experience—this full-bodied wine displays aromas of dried fruit, blackberry, raspberry and minerals, which are augmented on the palate by more juicy black fruit and spice.

Barone Ricasoli Brolio | 2006 | CHIANTI CLASSICO
★ ★ ★ $ $ Baron Bettino Ricasoli—the so-called father of Chianti—was once the winemaker here, and his high standards are well maintained. Beautiful aromas of cocoa, *salumi* (cured meats) and wild berry meet chocolate and silky tannins in the plush finish.

Borgianni | 2006 | CHIANTI
★ $ This easy-drinking red offers a fresh, fruity nose and berry flavors framed by clean minerals, supple tannins and a touch of spice.

Borgo Salcetino Lucarello Riserva | 2003 | CHIANTI CLASSICO
★ ★ $ $ $ In this classic Chianti, Sangiovese is blended with 5 percent Canaiolo Nero, imbuing it with sweet aromas and full-bodied flavors of vanilla and berries that are upheld by mild, juicy tannins.

Castello di Volpaia Riserva | 2004 | CHIANTI CLASSICO
★ ★ $ $ $ From the team behind the well-known Super-Tuscan Balifico comes this delicious 100 percent Sangiovese. With a medium body and aromas of cherries and flowers, it has a palate dominated by black fruit, with highlights of dusty spice and orange zest.

Cecchi Natio | 2007 | CHIANTI
★ ★ $ *Natio* means "native" in Italian, and here refers to the organically grown indigenous grapes from this Tuscan estate. This is a mouthwatering Chianti, full of cherry, raspberry and chalky mineral flavors underpinned by soft tannins.

Coraggio | 2007 | CHIANTI
★ $ The perfect wine for spaghetti dinners, this offers clean, straightforward juicy berry flavors balanced by mineral and mocha notes.

Fattorie Melini Vigneti La Selvanella Riserva | 2003 |
CHIANTI CLASSICO
★ ★ $ $ $ In 1860 Laborel Melini helped to invent the straw jug that maligned the Chianti category for decades, but this wine serves as atonement. Made from 100 percent single-vineyard Sangiovese, it melds dried cherry, mocha and blackberry flavors with good acidity and fine-grained tannins.

Lionello Marchesi Castello di Monastero | 2005 |
CHIANTI CLASSICO
★ ★ $ From one of the estates of Lionello Marchesi, a master of Sangiovese, this wine displays a bright bouquet of leafy tobacco, bright cherry and berry aromas, which are met by crisp acidity on the palate before a soft finish with sweet tannins.

Mazzei Fonterutoli | 2006 | **CHIANTI CLASSICO**
★ ★ ★ $ $ Cocoa powder and blackberry dominate the nose of this sultry red, while the flavors of black cherry, earthy mushroom and chocolate—testament to the 90 percent Sangiovese in the blend—are framed by silky tannins on the smooth finish.

Palagetto Riserva | 2004 | **CHIANTI COLLI SENESI**
★ ★ $ $ Aged in oak for 18 months, this well-constructed Chianti balances the intense aromas and flavors of fennel, blackberry and black cherry with moderately firm tannins on a long finish.

star producers
chianti

Agricola Querciabella
Under the direction of biodynamic advocate Sebastiano Castiglioni, Querciabella has emerged as one of Chianti's best producers.

Antinori
Without a doubt Italy's most dynamic winemaker and important wine ambassador, Antinori has led the charge in transforming Chianti.

Barone Ricasoli
Since taking over at Castello di Brolio in 1993, Francesco Ricasoli has modernized this iconic winery, crafting excellent Super-Tuscans as well as traditional wines.

Castello di Ama
Lorenza Sebasti and winemaker Marco Pallanti tend to this fine estate, and are champions of improving the quality standards of the Classico region as a whole.

Fattoria di Rodáno
Located in Castellina, in the heart of the Chianti Classico district, Fattoria di Rodáno is a go-to source for complex, classically styled Chianti.

Ruffino
Ruffino's Tuscan kingdom is massive, and their influence is international, as they have introduced the wines of Chianti to much of the planet.

Piccini Chianti | 2005 | CHIANTI CLASSICO
★ ★ $ $ Piccini is one of the most prolific vintners in Chianti, and its experience is on display here. Mineral-laden flavors of plum, blackberry and a hint of tobacco finish soft and clean.

Principe Corsini Don Tommaso | 2005 | CHIANTI CLASSICO
★ ★ ★ $ $ $ Blended with 15 percent Merlot, this presents a charming mix of bright cherry, dried flowers and dusty spice on the nose, complemented by red fruit, earth, leather and spice flavors on a medium-long finish.

Ruffino Riserva Ducale Oro | 2004 | CHIANTI CLASSICO
★ ★ ★ $ $ $ Arguably the best-known name in Chianti, Ruffino prides itself on this flagship wine and its ability to age beautifully. Alluring aromas of sweet red cherries and fresh-cut herbs meet tobacco and cocoa in the mouth and toasted oak on the finish.

Terrabianca Scassino | 2006 | CHIANTI CLASSICO
★ ★ $ $ This classic Chianti boasts cherry, berry and plum aromas and flavors. An enticing spiciness and ample minerals are layered between soft tannins.

Valiano Poggio Teo | 2004 | CHIANTI CLASSICO
★ ★ $ $ Another well-made Chianti from Piccini, this 100 percent Sangiovese combines aromas of plum, fig and cocoa with juicy flavors of fresh fruit and spice rounded out by pronounced oak notes.

TUSCAN REDS

montalcino

Brunello di Montalcino is made with 100 percent Sangiovese (called Brunello in Montalcino) and is Tuscany's crowning achievement in wine. Bold, firm and tannic, Brunello requires at least four years of aging before release (five if Riserva). A lighter, less costly version of Brunello can be found in Rosso di Montalcino (a.k.a. "Baby Brunello"). These wines require only one year of aging before release and are usually offered at a fraction of the cost of Brunello. Due to the recent scandal (see "News from a Wine Insider," p. 91) portions of several recent vintages of both Brunello di Montalcino and Rosso di Montalcino have been impounded, including some wines from 2004, 2005, 2006 and 2007.

montalcino recommendations

Caparzo La Casa | 2003 | **BRUNELLO DI MONTALCINO**

★ ★ ★ ★ $ $ $ $ Caparzo's gorgeous 2003 Brunello is well worth the significant investment. Inviting aromas of blackberry, concentrated prune, spice and cocoa precede dense fruit flavors, which are layered seamlessly with chewy, well-integrated tannins on the plush, memorable finish.

Castello Banfi | 2003 | **BRUNELLO DI MONTALCINO**

★ ★ ★ $ $ $ $ A heady blend of spicy licorice and juicy berry *marmellata* (that's Italian for "jam") flavors are upheld by powerful tannins in this Brunello.

Castello Romitorio | 2004 | **BRUNELLO DI MONTALCINO**

★ ★ ★ $ $ $ Artist Sandro Chia returned to his native Italy 25 years ago to buy and restore Castello Romitorio. He and star oenologist Carlo Ferrini crafted this wine, which bears aromas of dried lavender and blackberry jam and a hint of spice. A plush mouthfeel and mouthwatering fruit flavors lead to a long, well-integrated finish.

ColdiSole | 2006 | **ROSSO DI MONTALCINO**

★ ★ $ $ Consider this Rosso a "Baby Brunello." With just eight months of oak aging, it shows fresh berry, plum and leafy tobacco notes on a soft palate infused with raspberry and cocoa flavors and a touch of cedar.

Col d'Orcia | 2004 | **BRUNELLO DI MONTALCINO**

★ ★ ★ ★ $ $ $ While all of Col d'Orcia's wines are built to last, this outstanding 2004 Brunello is also delicious now, thanks to loads of rich and ripe blackberry and plum flavors that beautifully soften the formidable tannins.

Il Poggione | 2006 | **ROSSO DI MONTALCINO**

★ ★ ★ $ $ Il Poggione uses relatively young vines for its Rosso, yet it hardly means a lesser wine. The 2006 has a spicy nose with violet and raspberry aromas and bright juicy fruit flavors that are balanced by soft, chalky tannins.

Marchesi de' Frescobaldi Castelgiocondo | 2004 |
BRUNELLO DI MONTALCINO

★ ★ ★ $ $ $ $ As a result of the wide temperature variations from day to night in the 2004 growing season, this Brunello shows a rich and diverse bouquet, including every imaginable ripe berry and fresh herb. Bold licorice and black fruit flavors in the mouth lead into a long, luscious finish.

Tenimenti Angelini Val di Suga | 2006 | **ROSSO DI MONTALCINO**
★ ★ ★ **$ $** Prune and fruitcake aromas evolve into full-bodied, bold flavors in this rich, plush Rosso, with plenty of supple tannins to keep things balanced.

Terra Rossa | 2004 | **BRUNELLO DI MONTALCINO**
★ ★ ★ **$ $ $ $** Wonderfully fragrant with cherries and jammy strawberries, this treasure is made by winemaker Rodolfo Cosimi. The fresh berry flavors in the mouth are firmed up by great acidity and soft, approachable tannins.

TUSCAN REDS

montepulciano, carmignano, morellino di scansano

Though the wines of Montepulciano are produced less than 30 miles from Montalcino, the wines of the two regions are markedly different. Vino Nobile wines from Montepulciano are made primarily with Prugnolo Gentile (the local name for the Sangiovese grape) and have a minimum aging requirement of two years (three for Riservas). Rosso di Montepulciano requires much less aging—only six months—and is lighter, ready to drink upon release and much less expensive. Carmignano wines are made of Sangiovese grapes blended with Canaiolo and Cabernet Sauvignon and/or Cabernet Franc; they have lower acidity and firmer tannins than typical Chianti Classico. Morellino di Scansano (the "little cherry of Scansano") is a charming, mainly Sangiovese-based wine that has improved considerably in recent years.

montepulciano recommendations

Cecchi | 2004 | **VINO NOBILE DI MONTEPULCIANO**
★ ★ **$ $** Delicate white flower aromas compete with fresh crushed berries and wet stones in the bouquet of this well-built Montepulciano, while the flavors tend toward blackberries, plums and cherries on a very luscious palate.

Dei | 2005 | VINO NOBILE DI MONTEPULCIANO
★ ★ ★ $ $ At once sweet and savory, this wine has both modern appeal and real traditional character, with its dried sausage and prune flavors. The tannins and dark fruit are well integrated, and there is an attractive mineral quality on the finish.

Poliziano | 2005 | VINO NOBILE DI MONTEPULCIANO
★ ★ $ $ This winery takes its name from the Montepulciano-born 15th-century poet Angelo Ambrogini, "Il Poliziano." With its depth of juicy dark fruit and dusty spice flavors married to a touch of vanilla, this red shows good structure and deft balance.

Proprietà Fanetti Riserva | 2004 |
VINO NOBILE DI MONTEPULCIANO
★ ★ $ $ $ As one of the luminary revivalists of traditional Vino Nobile, this producer captures wonderful aromas of dried berries, tobacco and spice here, followed by blackberries and rustic, tight tannins.

Salcheto | 2007 | ROSSO DI MONTEPULCIANO
★ $ This Rosso is made with fruit sourced from newer vineyards, and its youthful verve shines brightly, with sweet red berry and floral aromas that turn slightly darker and richer in the mouth. It is well rounded on the palate, with sweet spice and an earthy finish.

Tenimenti Angelini Trerose | 2005 |
VINO NOBILE DI MONTEPULCIANO
★ ★ $ $ Spiced plum, cherry and orange zest aromas introduce this wine. Showing impressive complexity for the price, it offers dark cherry flavors framed by elegant tannins and sweet, cedary oak notes.

carmignano & morellino di scansano recommendations

Ambra | 2007 | BARCO REALE DI CARMIGNANO
★ ★ ★ $ A quaffable blend of Sangiovese, Canaiolo, Cabernet Sauvignon, Colorino and Merlot, this red is vinified mainly in old-fashioned concrete tanks. The bright cherry flavors are highlighted by dried herbs and char and electrified with lively acidity.

Elisabetta Geppetti Fattoria Le Pupille Poggio Valente
| 2004 | MORELLINO DI SCANSANO
★ ★ ★ $ $ $ Elegance and style are on display here in the form of sweet red berry, vanilla, baking spice and fresh herb aromas. On the palate, mouthwatering red fruit flavors are layered with fine-grained tannins and whispers of spice.

Poggio Argentiera Bellamarsilia | 2007 |
MORELLINO DI SCANSANO
★★ **$ $** A fresh, lively and finely balanced Sangiovese-led blend
from Maremma, this shows the hallmark bright red and black cherry
flavors characteristic to the region alongside notes of ripe plum and
raspberry. A crisp beam of acidity and soft tannins provide the necessary structure.

Villa di Capezzana | 2005 | **CARMIGNANO**
★★★ **$ $** This blend of 80 percent Sangiovese and 20 percent Cabernet Sauvignon has a ruby color and ripe aromas that are reminiscent of raspberry jam laced with anise. Its rich flavors of cherries and
blackberries are nicely layered with tannins and acidity throughout
the long finish.

TUSCAN REDS

super-tuscans

Before the creation of the IGT (*Indicazione Geografica Tipica*) classification in 1992, any Italian wine not produced
under the strict guidelines of the DOC or DOCG was rele-
gated to the lowly category of *Vino da Tavola,* or table wine.
Meanwhile, inventive vintners were experimenting with
different grapes, blending Sangiovese with Cabernet Sauvignon, Syrah and/or Merlot—varieties that were not traditional to the region—to produce the superb wines that
became known as the Super-Tuscans. Once the IGT designation was in place, these innovative vintners could finally
market their wines as their quality merited, adding regional
and compositional information to their labels, which had
been prohibited in the past. Of course, such freedom and
popularity has led to a proliferation of Super-Tuscan wines,
some made with greater care than others. Still, these typically powerful, concentrated and generally quite expensive
red wines remain some of the most sought after and finely
crafted exports Italy has to offer today. Famous Super-
Tuscans include Masseto, Solaia and Sassicaia, the last of
which was granted its own DOC appellation in the late
1990s, the only Italian wine from a single estate to achieve
such an honor.

super-tuscan recommendations

Arceno PrimaVoce | 2005 | TUSCANY
★★ $ Not all Super-Tuscans have to be super expensive, and this Merlot-dominated blend offers a captivating mix of meat and mocha aromas filled out with dusty blackberry flavors. Gentle tannins provide a solid frame.

Borgo Scopeto Borgonero | 2003 | TUSCANY
★★★ $ $ $ Aged in oak casks for 18 months, this wine takes on a slightly rustic character, mingling black fruit with floral aromas and wisps of smoky sausage and tobacco. For a 2003 vintage it shows plenty of youthful tannins, and the long finish has a savory edge.

Castello Banfi Tavernelle Cabernet Sauvignon | 2005 | SANT'ANTIMO
★★ $ $ $ Hailing from Tavernelle, one of Banfi's largest and most northerly vineyards, this is unmistakably Cabernet, with up-front herb and cassis aromas laced with notes of smoldering balsam incense. Soft tannins support violet candy and black fruit flavors.

Coronato | 2005 | BOLGHERI
★★★ $ $ $ $ Showing great complexity from the onset, this blend of Bordeaux grapes wraps its delicious dark fruit in aromas of damp leaves, cigar, spice, oak and leather. Fresh herbs lighten the palate, which is marked by dense blackberry, licorice and chocolate flavors.

Elisabetta Geppetti Fattoria Le Pupille Saffredi | 2004 | MAREMMA TOSCANA
★★★★ $ $ $ $ A seminal Super-Tuscan first produced in 1987, this Maremma is a blend of Cabernet Sauvignon, Merlot and Alicante. Aromas of crushed berry, rose petal and violet precede the full-throttled palate of polished tannins and ripe fruit and licorice flavors.

Fuligni S.J. | 2006 | TUSCANY
★★★ $ $ $ Sangiovese and Merlot come together to powerful, brooding effect in this massive wine. Coffee, leather and earth notes infuse a base of chocolate and concentrated black currant flavors, while well-integrated tannins hold up the juicy fruit and full body.

Gaja Ca' Marcanda Magari | 2006 | TUSCANY
★★★ $ $ $ $ Piedmontese impresario Angelo Gaja crafts this dark, complex Bordeaux blend. The black fruit aromas—mulberry, currant and plum—are accompanied by flowers, chocolate and spice, which follow through on the palate, bolstered by elegant tannins and a firm backbone of acidity.

Marsiliana | 2004 | TUSCANY
★★★ $ $ $ This blend of primarily Cabernet Sauvignon and Merlot is decidedly Bordeaux-like in its rustic, wild earthiness. Sweet berry flavors compete with barnyard, vanilla and cocoa notes on the finish.

Masi Serego Alighieri Bello Ovile | 2005 | TUSCANY
★★ $ Made with traditional grapes (Sangiovese, Canaiolo and Cilie-giolo) and true to the Masi profile, with dried fig, berry and fruitcake flavors, this pretty wine shows a chewy palate and full body. Spice notes woven throughout keep it lively and bright.

Palagetto Uno di Quattro Syrah | 2004 | SAN GIMIGNANO
★★★ $ $ $ $ The Palagetto farm produces olive oil, honey, saffron and exceptional wine. This standout Syrah features an unusual mix of menthol, licorice, graphite and pepper notes, which beautifully com-plement the dark fruit– and plum-laden palate.

Perbruno | 2006 | TUSCANY
★★★ $ $ $ This spectacular 100 percent Syrah from I Giusti & Zanza, a tiny estate, illustrates the grape's potential here. Classic aro-mas of blueberry and pepper show hints of sandalwood spice and lead to a palate marked by juicy fruit and exotic spice.

Sasso al Poggio | 2004 | TUSCANY
★★★ $ With black fruit, dark earth, scorched leaves and charred meat, this wine delivers a lot of flavor for a very accessible price. It is dense and rounded, with integrated tannins that carry it through the licorice-accented finish.

Tenuta Guado al Tasso | 2006 | BOLGHERI SUPERIORE
★★★ $ $ $ Antinori makes this wine on a property named for a badger (*tasso*) crossing area (*guado*) on nearby streams. A striking nose of slate, mineral and blackberry is followed up on the palate, along with chocolate and licorice notes, and supported by ample acidity and balanced tannins.

Terrabianca Campaccio Riserva | 2004 | TUSCANY
★★★ $ $ $ Terrabianca's Riserva is a blend of equal parts Caber-net Sauvignon and Sangiovese. Supple currant and berry flavors aug-ment generous aromas of earth, coffee and violets, and silky tannins are woven beautifully throughout.

Villa Antinori | 2004 | TUSCANY
★★ $ $ Antinori's flagship Sangiovese-based red nicely balances classic Tuscan flavors—earth, barnyard and prunes—with approach-ably modern accents of vanilla and bright berries.

other central italian regions

Beyond Tuscany and its many treasures lie other central Italian regions whose wines are worth exploring. The most notable of these regions is Abruzzo. Responsible for the lion's share of Montepulciano production in Italy, Abruzzo is known for its robust, affordable reds. Other central Italian offerings range from the earthy, smoky Rosso Conero of Le Marche to the popular (if admittedly unremarkable) and slightly sparkling red Lambrusco of Emilia-Romagna.

• **EMILIA-ROMAGNA** Much better known for its culinary contributions, Emilia-Romagna still produces some interesting wines. The most popular is fizzy red Lambrusco, but whites from Chardonnay and the Albana grape are also produced here, as are Sangiovese, Barbera and Cabernet.

• **LE MARCHE** The underestimated region of Le Marche produces both reds and whites, but its signature wine is the distinctively rich white made from the Verdicchio grape. Two interesting reds particular to the region are the bold, full-bodied Rosso Conero and Rosso Piceno.

• **ABRUZZO** Unlike the dull white Trebbiano produced elsewhere, the Trebbiano d'Abruzzo is crisp and lovely. The Montepulciano grape makes dark, spicy wines (no relation to Tuscany's Sangiovese-based Montepulciano, named for a town). Wines from Abruzzo tend to offer excellent value.

• **UMBRIA** Red wines of note from Umbria include the Sagrantino-based wines of Montefalco and the Sangiovese-based wines hailing from Torgiano. Orvieto is the region's most important white wine: simple, less interesting examples are made from the Trebbiano grape alone; those blended with the lively Grechetto grape are far better.

• **LAZIO** The region surrounding Rome provides the capital with one of its simpler pleasures—the lightly sparkling white Frascati. Made from a Trebbiano and Malvasia blend, most versions offer delicate, citrusy refreshment.

other central italian whites

Like many Italian wines, Le Marche's Verdicchio was once a simple, mass-produced commodity with little character. Today, as the region's winemakers focus their attention and resources on the variety, more and more interesting expressions are being crafted. Trebbiano d'Abruzzo is another central Italian white wine making a name for itself internationally. The low-acid Albana grape shines particularly brightly in the Emilia-Romagna region, where it yields a variety of compelling styles, both dry and sweet.

other central italian white recommendations

Cantina Villafranca | 2007 | FRASCATI SUPERIORE
★ $ Frascati is Italy's answer to Portugal's Vinho Verde, and this wine is a perfect example of how refreshing it can be. It is light-bodied and wonderfully crisp, with a tinge of carbonation and a simple mix of cantaloupe and citrus flavors.

Cataldi Madonna | 2007 | TREBBIANO D'ABRUZZO
★ ★ $ $ This is a serious Trebbiano marked by a generous nose of pear and melon, refreshing flavors of concentrated apricot and citrus and a note of bitter almond on the finish.

Lungarotti Torre di Giano Trebbiano/Grechetto | 2007 | TORGIANO BIANCO
★ ★ $ A nose of perfume, flower and citrus is not what you'd expect from a blend of these two grapes, but Lungarotti coaxes the aromas out, followed by subtle flavors of melon and apple.

Palazzone Terre Vineate | 2007 | ORVIETO CLASSICO SUPERIORE
★ ★ $ This 2007 Orvieto is a distinctive blend of five different grape varieties—Procanico, Grechetto, Verdello, Drupeggio and Malvasia. It offers a toasted hazelnut and citrus bouquet and flavors of ripe pear and lemon zest.

Sant'Andrea Dune | 2006 | CIRCEO BIANCO
★ ★ ★ $ $ This blend of Malvasia and Trebbiano spends six months in oak barrels, which explains its intricate nose of honey, vanilla and a hint of sweet banana. The melon-dominated palate is quite dry, with a medium-long finish.

Umani Ronchi Casal di Serra | 2007 |
VERDICCHIO DEI CASTELLI DI JESI CLASSICO SUPERIORE
★ ★ ★ $ Crisp, light and perfect for summer meals, this white is an excellent bargain for its complex mix of almond, citrus and overripe stone fruit flavors balanced by vibrant acidity.

Velenosi Villa Angela Pecorino | 2007 | **OFFIDA**
★ ★ $ This dry, tangy white is profuse with aromas of dried herb, wildflower, toasted nut and zesty citrus fruit. Rich flavors of white peach and honey impart a concentration seldom seen in central Italian white wines.

other central italian reds

The Marche region produces two noteworthy Sangiovese-Montepulciano blends: Rossos Conero and Piceno. Emilia-Romagna, sometimes called the birthplace of Sangiovese, makes a fine, if underappreciated, version of the grape. Umbria's Sagrantino di Montefalco is dark, full-bodied and complex, though small production can lead to high prices. Probably the most popular wine from Italy's other central regions is Montepulciano d'Abruzzo: although typically a simple wine with nice berry flavors, it can also be remarkably robust and tannic.

other central italian red recommendations

Angelini Estate Sangiovese | 2006 | **COLLI PESARESI**
★ ★ $ This medium-bodied Sangiovese hails from northeastern Le Marche. It has dusty, fine-grained tannins, aromas of strawberry, leather and oak and flavors of ripe red berry and earth.

Ca' Montini Cabernet Sauvignon | 2004 | **UMBRIA**
★ ★ ★ $ This well-balanced Cabernet is decidedly French-like: its delightful mix of raspberry, black currant, sweet tobacco and mocha aromas is accompanied by spicy cassis and cedar flavors and nicely integrated tannins.

Corte alla Luna | 2007 | **CESANESE DI OLEVANO ROMANO**
★ ★ $ $ Cesanese is a spicy, aromatic grape variety native to the region of Lazio. This juicy example provides blueberry and flower aromas, while chewy tannins firm the fruit-forward palate.

Farnese | 2007 | MONTEPULCIANO D'ABRUZZO

★ $ Perfect for everyday drinking, this well-priced Montepulciano d'Abruzzo shows a classic profile of oak, earth and dark berry flavors wound up with tight tannins on the rustic finish.

Fattoria Colsanto | 2006 | MONTEFALCO ROSSO

★ ★ $ $ This ripe, jammy blend of Sangiovese and Umbria's Sagrantino grape is a classic representation of the Montefalco Rosso appellation. Firm tannins encase rich flavors of spice, earth and berries.

Fausti Fausto | 2006 | ROSSO PICENO

★ $ A blend of Montepulciano and Sangiovese, this straightforward wine conjures flavors of black fruit, spice and cherry. Although simple, it has a good acidity that makes it ideal for classic Italian fare.

Luciano Landi | 2007 | LACRIMA DI MORRO D'ALBA

★ ★ $ This soft, easy-drinking wine is bright with floral aromas of violet and rose petal. The plush palate of red cherry, mocha and spice flavors melds gracefully with its smooth tannins.

Nicodemi | 2006 | MONTEPULCIANO D'ABRUZZO

★ ★ $ There's more depth and complexity in this delicious Montepulciano d'Abruzzo than one might expect from the appellation. Chewy tannins support flavors of earth, spice and red berry all the way through the lengthy finish.

Quattro Mani | 2007 | MONTEPULCIANO D'ABRUZZO

★ $ This tasty quaffer is medium-bodied and characterized by currant and raspberry flavors set against dusty, fine-grained tannins.

Sant'Andrea Sogno | 2004 | CIRCEO ROSSO

★ ★ $ $ A bit of Cesanese tops off this Merlot-dominated blend, which then spends 12 months aging in new French oak barrels. The result is a modern, full-bodied wine that tastes of sweet vanilla, spice and dense blackberry.

Tenuta Cocci Grifoni Tellus | 2007 | LE MARCHE ROSSO

★ $ Montepulciano, Merlot and Cabernet Sauvignon come together to form this tasty, inexpensive wine. Aromas of raspberry and rose lead to flavors of cherry and earth and chewy tannins on the finish.

Velenosi Ludi | 2005 | OFFIDA ROSSO

★ ★ ★ $ $ $ This full-throttle red presents a nose of vanilla, red fruit and earth that is followed by a jammy palate full of cherry, spice and raspberry compote flavors. Ripe tannins are built to carry the weight of this massive wine.

southern italy

A word often used to describe southern Italy's current wine scene is "exciting." In truth, certain regions, such as Campania and Sicily, are producing excellent wines, among them Sicily's well-priced Nero d'Avola and Campania's red Aglianico and white Falanghina. However, the sunny, hot region as a whole is still in the process of transforming itself from a bulk producer to a land of quality vintners.

• **APULIA** Still known mainly for its mass production of wines that will never reach an international market, Apulia (or Puglia in Italian) is home to an increasing number of high-quality red wines. Look for the spicy reds from Salice Salentino and Copertino, both made from the dark-skinned Negroamaro grape, as well as the fruity Primitivo, which tastes similar to a California Zinfandel.

• **BASILICATA** With the menacingly named Monte Vulture volcano looming in the background, the vineyards of the Basilicata region produce Aglianico-based reds that echo the inherent volcanic soils. Aromatic and spicy, the more tannic versions of these wines require years of aging.

• **CALABRIA** This region, which is located in the "toe" of Italy's boot, is responsible for much low-quality wine. One exception is the Gaglioppo-based red wine of Cirò, which is lightly tannic and flush with berry.

• **CAMPANIA** Campania is the highlight of southern Italian winemaking. The Aglianico-based red Taurasi, which requires a minimum of three years of aging, has earned much well-deserved acclaim since achieving DOCG status in 1993. Both the quality and quantity of Falanghina, the main white in the region, are on the rise, while the two other whites particular to Campania, Fiano di Avellino and floral Greco di Tufo, also deserve recognition.

• **SICILY & SARDINIA** Easily two of southern Italy's most up-and-coming regions, the islands of Sicily and Sardinia have benefited greatly from winemakers' commitment to cultivating grapes indigenous to the regions. While an

107

increasing number of international varieties such as Cabernet Sauvignon, Syrah and Merlot are grown here as well, vintners continue to celebrate their native grapes. Sicily's whites, usually made from Catarratto and often blended with Inzolia, can be bright, citrusy and quite good. The white Vermentino of Sardinia is a standout, as are the spicy reds made from Cannonau (Grenache) and Carignano (Carignane). Meanwhile, the increasingly popular Nero d'Avola is making great strides in solidifying Sicily's reputation as a producer of world-class reds.

southern italian whites

In defiance of their warm climate, southern Italian vintners produce wonderfully light and crisp white wines, such as Falanghina, Fiano di Avellino and Greco di Tufo from Campania and Vermentino from Sardinia.

southern italian white recommendations

Cantina Santa Maria la Palma Aragosta | 2007 |
VERMENTINO DI SARDEGNA
★ $ Light, refreshing and crisp, with an intriguing touch of earthiness, this is an approachable version of Vermentino filled out with juicy ripe apple flavors.

Masseria Altemura Fiano | 2007 | SALENTO
★★ $ From Apulia's peninsula comes this tight-nosed *bianco* with subtle earthy and floral aromas. The ultra-lean palate brings together earth, chalk and minerals with a saline quality that simply begs for fresh seafood.

Planeta La Segreta | 2007 | SICILY
★ $ Golden in color, with delicate melon and pear aromas, this white blend shows a slightly oily texture that nicely carries modest peach and stone fruit flavors and a hint of licorice on a slick finish.

Re Manfredi Bianco | 2007 | BASILICATA
★★ $ This blend of Müller-Thurgau and Traminer is fresh and fruity, with a highly perfumed bouquet of rose petals, fruit and earth. Though the white peach and pear flavors give the impression of sweetness, fresh acidity keeps things balanced and refreshing.

Tormaresca Chardonnay | 2007 | APULIA
★ $ This large-production value-priced Chardonnay offers crisp green apple and citrus aromas followed by a juicy, zesty fruit-forward palate with a kiss of toasted oak on the finish.

Villa Matilde Rocca dei Leoni Falanghina | 2007 | CAMPANIA
★★★ $ Located on the mineral-rich soils of the extinct volcano Roccamonfina, Villa Matilde crafts this wonderfully aromatic white from the local Falanghina grape. It exhibits alpine herbal aromas and stone fruit flavors punctuated by hints of licorice, spice and basil.

Vinosia | 2007 | FIANO DI AVELLINO
★★★ $ This smells like the billowing chalk that emerges from clapping blackboard erasers. Juicy citrus, pear and guava flavors emerge on the palate, alongside a gorgeous minerality woven throughout this superb wine.

Vinosia Doceassaje | 2007 | IRPINIA BIANCO
★★ $ $ A juicy and refreshing blend of Greco Bianco and Fiano, this white kicks off with enticing aromas of ripe fruit and spring blossoms that give way to flavors of tart grapefruit and lime zest with subtle herbal underpinnings.

southern italian reds

There is certainly no shortage of unique red wines to sample from the regions of southern Italy. Running the gamut from soft and simple quaffers to bold and spicy wines suitable for long aging, they are often made from indigenous grapes rarely seen elsewhere.

southern italian red recommendations

Barrua | 2004 | ISOLA DEI NURAGHI
★★★ $ $ $ This blend of 85 percent Carignano, 10 percent Cabernet Sauvignon and 5 percent Merlot aims to be a "Super-Sardinian," with its dense, weighty mix of black cherry, molasses, spiced fig and hefty oak flavors.

Cantina Santadi Grotta Rossa | 2006 |
CARIGNANO DEL SULCIS
★★ $ Hailing from the southwestern coast of Sardinia, this enticing red conjures sweet cassis and ripe cherry aromas, which are met with wild strawberry flavors on the medium-bodied palate, all held aloft by fresh acidity and spice.

Castello Monaci Artas Primitivo | 2006 | SALENTO
★ ★ ★ $ $ $ Primitivo leads in this captivating blend, with the addition of 15 percent Negroamaro. Exotic dried herbs, pumpkin pie spices and sage aromas come on strong, before fresh blueberry and pomegranate flavors take over on the palate.

Conti Zecca Donna Marzia Negramaro | 2006 | SALENTO
★ $ This value-priced wine from Apulia shows the Negroamaro grape's characteristic dark, ripe fruit–filled palate, with chocolate and mocha nuances and a nice dash of fine, dry tannins. For all its fruit and weight, it is quite supple and pleasingly fresh.

Feudi di San Gregorio Rubrato Aglianico | 2006 | IRPINIA AGLIANICO
★ ★ $ Fragrant with dried cherries, cooked plums, violets and touches of earth, smoke and loam, this deep red wine delivers flavors of dense fruit framed by fine, silky tannins and generous acidity, with a lingering finish of black cherry and anise.

Fidatu | 2007 | COLLI DEL LIMBARA
★ $ Simple, sweet and juicy, like an earthy fruit punch, this blend of Cagnulari, Merlot and Sangiovese exhibits some violet candy aromas, sweet fruit flavors, light tannins and refreshing acidity.

Il Matané | 2007 | PRIMITIVO DI MANDURIA
★ ★ $ The tightly wound nose on this well-priced yet serious wine unveils a tapestry of jammy fruit, damp leaf and sultry spice aromas, while the full-bodied palate pours on black fruit mingled with spicy oak, cigar and chunky dark chocolate. The long, very dry finish is bolstered by hearty tannins.

MandraRossa Nero d'Avola | 2006 | SICILY
★ $ For fans of tasty, fruit-forward reds, this affordable wine will satisfy with its concentrated cassis, strawberry and raspberry flavors. It has just enough structure and tannins, and licorice hints on the finish.

Mirabile Nero d'Avola | 2006 | SICILY
★ ★ $ There is an Amarone-like quality to the flavors of raisins and figs in this earthy, rustic wine. Lighter notes of sweet-tart fruit, hints of mocha and nicely integrated tannins balance it out.

Planeta La Segreta | 2007 | SICILY
★ ★ $ Comprised of 50 percent Nero d'Avola, plus some Merlot, Syrah and Cabernet Franc, Planeta's red blend is decidedly New World in style. Its flavors of cherry, vanilla and ripe blackberry show some underlying earthiness and good structure.

Primaterra Syrah | 2007 | SICILY
★ $ This is a nice, simple, fruity Sicilian red worth stocking up on for its juicy blueberry flavors, accents of cocoa and powdery tannins.

Re Manfredi | 2005 | AGLIANICO DEL VULTURE
★★ $ $ This dark, slightly brick-hued red is showing good development, with expressive plum and raspberry aromas coupled with clove and cedary spice. Soft, supple tannins hold together the flavors of cherry, vanilla and pencil shavings.

Saia Nero d'Avola | 2005 | SICILY
★★★ $ $ $ This full-bodied powerhouse of a wine would be perfect for grilled foods. Dark, dense flavors of smoky fruit, kirsch, chocolate and tobacco, as well as a barrage of supple tannins, are uplifted by massive acidity.

Sella & Mosca Riserva | 2005 | CANNONAU DI SARDEGNA
★★ $ Fans of Pinot Noir will appreciate this Cannonau, with its pallid color, delicate berry and earth aromas and barnyard-accented fruit flavors. It is light-bodied, juicy and fresh, with notes of root beer, licorice and earth on the finish.

Tenuta Rapitalà Hugonis | 2006 | SICILY
★★ $ $ $ Cabernet Sauvignon is blended with Nero d'Avola here, bringing concentrated cassis and blackberry flavors, which take a savory turn with herb and green notes on the huge, tannic finish.

Terra dei Re Divinus | 2004 | AGLIANICO DEL VULTURE
★★ $ $ $ Crafted with fruit from 40-year-old vines, this super-inky, modern-style Aglianico is still youthful, bright and lively. Crushed blackberry and black cherry flavors are woven with notes of licorice and tobacco on the medium-bodied, somewhat tannic palate.

Tormaresca Masseria Maìme Negroamaro | 2004 | SALENTO
★★ $ $ $ With its opaque, brick-tinged color, this wine is showing maturity. Flavors of eucalyptus, smoke, meat and leather compete with black fruit in a wine that is ready to drink now.

Vestini Campagnano Casa Vecchia | 2005 |
TERRE DEL VOLTURNO
★★★ $ $ $ A seductive nose rich with barnyard, horse, leather and peppery spice notes leads to a succulent, red fruit–dominated palate in this outstanding red. It walks a fine line between rustic, Old World charm and polished refinement.

spain

Spain has more land planted with vines than any other nation on earth, and its wines are as varied as its topography. But if there is one spirit that unifies all of Spain's winemaking regions, it is innovation. A creative revolution is taking place in practically every region, from the famous ones, such as Rioja, Ribera del Duero and Priorat, to less well known areas like Somontano, La Mancha and Jumilla.

Bay of Biscay

Rías Baixas

Rioja

Bierzo   Cigales   Navarra

Toro   Somontano   Catalonia

Ribera del Duero   Barcelona

Rueda   Calatayud   Priorat   Penedès

Madrid ☆

SPAIN   Utiel-Requena

Ribera del Guadiana   La Mancha   · Valencia

Valdepeñas   Alicante

Jumilla

PORTUGAL

· Seville   *Mediterranean Sea*

Jerez

Málaga

Atlantic Ocean

▇ Principal Wine Region

Spain: An Overview

Spain's mountain ranges divide the country into distinct viticultural areas. Crisp Albariño-based whites hail from the cool Atlantic region of Rías Baixas, while farther east, Rueda produces zippier whites. Catalonia, in the northeast, is home to sparkling Cavas and still wines from Penedès and robust reds from Priorat. Luxurious reds come from along the Duero River in Ribera del Duero, while Bierzo is known for fragrant reds. Toro and Jumilla earn praise for their powerful red wines, and winemakers in Spain's central plain continue their conversion from bulk to fine wine production. Jerez is famous for its fortified Sherries (see p. 267). Whatever the region, Spain's best assets continue to be its indigenous varieties, which are being reclaimed and championed.

Spanish Wine Labels

Spain's *Denominación de Origen* (DO) board determines a region's permitted grapes, harvest limits and vinification techniques, and regulates wine labels. Spanish labels typically list the region; some give the grape used. Terms such as *Joven, Crianza, Reserva* or *Gran Reserva* indicate the length of time spent in oak barrels (see Rioja, below).

rioja

Rioja is often called the Bordeaux of Spain for its celebrated, ageworthy reds. However, many of these traditional wines lacked fruitiness as a result of spending long periods of time aging in oak barrels. Contemporary tastes are driving vintners to make their wines differently, favoring bottle age over barrel (and subtler French oak over American), yielding wines with pronounced fruit flavors augmented by sweet spice and vanilla notes. Rioja whites, too, are now made in a fresher style (though some older-style whites are excellent). Look also for Rioja's dry, flavorful *rosados* (rosés).

Rioja Grapes & Styles

If one grape is synonymous with Rioja, it is Tempranillo. Traditionally, it is blended with Garnacha (Grenache), Graciano and Mazuelo (the Rioja name for Carignane), then aged in American oak. Cabernet Sauvignon is allowed in certain vineyards, and many vintners work with it. Rioja reds are given designations based on aging time in barrel and bottle: Joven wines spend little or no time in oak barrels; Crianza reds must be aged two years, one in barrel. Reservas require three years total, one in oak; Gran Reservas, five years total, two in oak. A growing number of vintners here, however, are now using subtler French oak barrels and aging their wines for shorter lengths of time. Sometimes referred to as *alta expresión* (high expression), these wines have fresh, bold flavors. Rioja's *rosado* wines are dry, with orange and berry flavors. The region's refreshing whites display apple and citrus flavors; they are traditionally made from Viura (the Rioja name for Macabeo) and Malvasia, although since the 2007 vintage, grapes such as Chardonnay, Sauvignon Blanc and Verdejo are also permitted. A few vintners still make traditional, long-aged whites.

rioja recommendations

WHITES

Becquer | 2006 |
★★★ **$** Deliberate oxidation of this Viura-Chardonnay blend makes for a wonderfully funky, traditional white marked by flavors of cinnamon-spiced applesauce, almonds, herbs, citrus and toast, with a hint of white flowers. Refreshing acidity balances the creamy texture.

Marqués de Cáceres | 2007 |
★★ **$** This modern-style Rioja white is made from 100 percent Viura and offers lively citrus, almond and grass aromas, refreshing acidity and a crisp, clean finish.

R. López de Heredia Viña Gravonia | 1999 |
★★★★ **$ $** López de Heredia is devoted to the classic Rioja style and ages its wine for several years before release, allowing oxidation in the process. This shows layered almond and walnut aromas with notes of oak and flowers; its citrusy acidity keeps it vibrant.

ROSÉS

Darien | 2007 |
★★ $ Luis Ilarraza Fernández has built a winemaking facility as modern as his fruit-forward wines. In it, he crafts this bold *rosado*, packed with big, bright flavors of juicy wild strawberries, raspberries, tea and spice.

Muga | 2008 |
★★ $ Muga takes two powerful red wine grapes—Garnacha and Tempranillo—and blends them with white Viura grapes, resulting in this intensely fruity, raspberry- and watermelon-flavored wine that is bright and refreshing.

REDS

Baron de Ley 7 Viñas Reserva | 2001 |
★★★★ $$$$ From the standard-bearer of Rioja's old guard comes this plummy, fruitcake-scented red that, despite its age, exudes youthful berry, spice and cocoa flavors that are impressively complex through the long finish.

Bodegas Bilbaínas Viña Zaco Tempranillo | 2006 |
★★★ $ Bilbaínas has a long history of quality production: their wines were once consumed daily by the Spanish royal court. This 2006 Tempranillo shows fresh black fruit flavors highlighted by spice, cedar and coconut and held up by ripe tannins and medium acidity on the lush finish.

Bodegas Ondarre Ursa Maior Crianza | 2005 |
★★ $ Ondarre's Crianza is old-fashioned and beautiful, with its classic Rioja makeup of strawberry and raspberry jam flavors and notes of tea leaves, vanilla and cinnamon. Bold acidity and ripe tannins complete this well-priced red.

Coto de Imaz Reserva | 2004 |
★★ $$ Coto's Tempranillo is an excellent example of the 2004 vintage, a stellar year for the Rioja region. Ripe red fruit, sweet coconut and floral notes mark the nose, while the palate reveals deeper flavors of cedar and pipe tobacco supported by firm yet approachable tannins and lively acidity.

Cune Imperial Gran Reserva | 1996 |
★★★ $$$$ The aromatics in this impressive Reserva hint at game, dried strawberries, toffee and smoke, while the palate leans toward sweeter flavors of mince pie and licorice wrapped in soft, mellow tannins, with a kick of spice on the finish.

115

Ijalba Graciano Crianza | 2004 |

★ ★ **$** Plush tannins and lively acidity support bright cherry, blackberry and strawberry flavors in this well-priced, organic wine. Notes of black licorice, herbs, cocoa and pepper emerge on the long, complex finish.

Loriñon Crianza | 2005 |

★ ★ ★ **$** Aged 14 months in American oak, this Crianza shows vibrancy and great depth of flavor in the form of herbs, black cherry, red apple, coffee and a hint of ham. Formidable tannins are well integrated, and the finish is beautifully fruity.

Luis Cañas Selección de la Familia Reserva | 2001 |

★ ★ ★ **$ $** Amazingly youthful for its age, this 2001 delivers a lovely mix of blackberry, plum, flower and chocolate notes. With mellow tannins and good acidity, it is delicious now yet could be cellared for another ten years.

star producers
rioja

Baron de Ley

Founded by a small group of prestigious Rioja professionals, Baron de Ley has earned a stellar reputation for classically styled Riojas.

Bodegas Bretón

This vintner is particularly famous for its Loriñon estate, located in the heart of Rioja, which sources excellent fruit from both the Rioja Alta and Rioja Baja regions.

Faustino

Faustino is the largest exporter of Gran Reserva wines from Rioja (representing one-third of the total shipped out), and its prices are very fair.

Muga

Presiding over one of the region's better-known wineries, vintner Jorge Muga takes a modern approach to the art of winemaking.

R. López de Heredia

She may be the most tradition-bound of her contemporaries, but winemaker Mercedes López de Heredia crafts unique, outstanding wines that have an impressive ability to age.

Viña Real

This property is owned by CVNE, among the oldest family-run bodegas in Rioja, but unlike other stalwarts, CVNE embraces innovation.

Marqués de Cáceres Reserva | 2001 |
★ ★ ★ $ $ A great year and a great producer result in this superb wine. Flavors of black cherry, strawberry, spice, leather, dried leaves and mocha are framed by fresh acidity and solid tannins and linger nicely on the palate.

Valsacro Dioro Selección Crianza | 2003 |
★ ★ ★ $ $ $ Great Riojas such as this one can be pleasantly reminiscent of an attic trunk, replete with leather jacket, cigar box and cedar aromas, rounded out with baked pie and cocoa flavors.

Vaza Crianza | 2004 |
★ ★ $ This well-priced Tempranillo is medium-bodied, juicy and luscious, with flavors of chocolate-covered cherries, plums, licorice and herbs held up by soft tannins.

ribera del duero

For decades Ribera del Duero was known for a single producer, Vega Sicilia, whose legendary Unico (a Tempranillo–Cabernet Sauvignon blend) is famous for its longevity—and exorbitant price. Not until Alejandro Fernández's Pesquera—a tremendous bargain by comparison—debuted about a quarter century ago, however, did interest in the region increase significantly. Today Ribera del Duero makes some of Spain's best and most expensive wines.

Ribera del Duero Grapes & Styles

Ribera del Duero reds are mostly made from Tinto Fino (or Tinta Fina), another name for Tempranillo. Bordeaux's Cabernet Sauvignon, Merlot and Malbec are now permitted in the denomination. Garnacha is used in the production of dry *rosados*.

ribera del duero recommendations

Condado de Haza | 2006 |
★ ★ ★ $ $ The much less expensive sibling to Condado de Haza's powerhouse Alenza Gran Reserva, this is a great wine for the price. Mineral, earth and roasted coffee aromas combine with blackberries and espresso on the palate, where they are balanced by ample acidity and plush tannins.

Finca Torremilanos Montecastrillo | 2007 |

★ ★ **$** With just a touch of Cabernet Sauvignon in the mix, this intriguing red delivers a pleasing array of plum, blackberry and black cherry flavors, a cleansing dose of minerals and notes of cocoa and toasted oak.

Legaris Crianza | 2005 |

★ ★ ★ **$ $** Oak-aged for a year, this Tinta Fina (Tempranillo) shows great depth and power. Heady aromas of ripe plum and spice lead into juicy blueberry and blackberry flavors followed by a toast-accented finish with nicely integrated tannins.

Portia | 2006 |

★ ★ **$ $ $** Despite the fact that the winery was named, in part, for a moon of the planet Uranus, this wine is decidedly grounded. Aromas and flavors of cured meats, tobacco and black cherry conclude in a rich, juicy finish.

Valdubón Crianza | 2003 |

★ **$** A robust Tempranillo with flavors of earth, toast, slate and black cherries, this has powerful tannins that make it a perfect choice for hearty meats and flavorful sauces.

catalonia

Although Codorníu's José Raventós put the sparkling Cavas of Penedès (see p. 263) on the map in the early 1870s, only recently have the Catalonia region's still wines merited attention. Thanks to the efforts of vintners like Miguel Torres and René Barbier, Catalonia (Catalunya in the Catalan language) now produces an eclectic range of wines.

Catalonia Grapes & Styles

Catalonia is largely planted with Garnacha, which, along with Cariñena (Carignane), composes the heart of Priorat's full-bodied red wines and is the basis of reds from most subregions. Monastrell (Mourvèdre in French) and Tempranillo are also grown here, as are international grapes Cabernet, Merlot and Syrah. Garnacha Blanca is responsible for the region's nut-flavored whites. Local grapes Macabeo, Parellada and Xarel-lo are used in many generic wines and sparkling Cavas.

catalonia recommendations

WHITES

Abadal Picapoll | 2008 | PLA DE BAGES
★★ $ Named in honor of Bacchus, the Roman god of wine, the Pla de Bages region has a long history of winemaking. The tradition continues with Abadal's delicious 100 percent Picapoll (Picpoul), with its creamy mélange of pear, apple and apricot flavors.

Las Colinas del Ebro Garnacha Blanca | 2007 | TERRA ALTA
★ $ Made from carefully sourced grapes from hundred-year-old vines, this white is intensely mineral-laden, with aromas of slate and chalk filled out by flavors of fresh apple and star fruit on the palate.

René Barbier Mediterranean White | NV | CATALONIA
★ $ A Spanish wine rooted in French tradition, thanks to its founder Léon Barbier's Avignon upbringing, this is delicious and well priced. Pungent aromas of citrus and melon show hints of dried apricot.

Segura Viudas Creu de Lavit Xarel-lo | 2005 | PENEDÈS
★ $ Primarily known for its sparkling wines, Segura Viudas has harnessed knowledge of Cava's Xarel-lo grape to create this crisp wine with enticing flavors of apple, pear, star fruit and spice.

The Spanish Quarter Chardonnay/Albariño | 2007 |
COSTERS DEL SEGRE
★ $ Although this blend consists of slightly more Chardonnay, the Albariño grape hardly takes a backseat. Juicy flavors of sweet peaches, apples and apricots shine in this bargain buy.

Torres Viña Esmeralda Moscato/Gewürztraminer | 2008 |
CATALONIA
★★ $ A blend of fragrant Muscat and Gewürztraminer, this wine includes the rich aromas of acacia flower, orange rind and tangerine. In the mouth, citrus flavors meet pear and vanilla in a spicy finish.

ROSÉS

Las Colinas del Ebro Syrah/Garnacha | 2008 | TERRA ALTA
★★ $ From Celler Batea's new line of wines, this blended rosé delivers red currant and cherry flavors accompanied by fresh herbs. Its great acidity makes for delicious, easy drinking.

René Barbier Mediterranean Rosé | NV | CATALONIA
★ $ This blend of Garnacha, Tempranillo and Cariñena has ample raspberry and dried strawberry flavors that are juicy and clean.

REDS

Elix | 2006 | PRIORAT

★ ★ ★ $ $ $ Elix shares a winemaking director with California's acclaimed Sea Smoke label. This juicy, supple red has tart cherry and berry flavors woven with mineral notes on the vivid, long finish.

Finca El Puig | 2004 | PRIORAT

★ ★ $ $ $ Grapes from hundred-year-old vines were harvested for this wine, which was then aged 14 months in French oak. The result is a rich, aromatic red full of black cherry, blackberry and anise flavors laced with clean minerals.

Mas Sinén Negre | 2005 | PRIORAT

★ ★ ★ $ $ $ $ Aged in primarily French oak for one year, this fragrant blend of Garnacha, Cabernet Sauvignon, Cariñena and Syrah presents an enticing bouquet of black fruit followed by flavors of licorice, spice and berries. Earthy, chewy tannins round out the long and delicious finish.

Morlanda Criança | 2003 | PRIORAT

★ ★ ★ $ $ $ Made with Garnacha and Cariñena grapes (and just a touch of Cabernet Sauvignon), this blend has aromas of ripe black fruit, chalky-sweet violet candy and cherries, underscored by minerals on the juicy finish.

Torres Salmos | 2006 | PRIORAT

★ ★ ★ $ $ $ Created as an homage to the Carthusian monks whose priory gave the region its name, Salmos is an elegant, layered wine with aromas of dusty spice, orange zest, blackberry and licorice, bold flavors of dark berries and tea-accented tannins.

other spanish regions

Spanish regions like Rueda and Toro, once touted as up-and-coming, are now widely recognized as sources of excellent quality and value wines. But there is plenty left to discover in innovative appellations such as Almansa, Bullas, Cariñena, Cigales, Ribera del Júcar, Somontano, Utiel-Requena, Valdeorras and Valdepeñas, which are producing a growing number of outstanding wines.

Other Spanish Grapes & Styles

Spain is undeniably a country of red grapes—and most of them produce fairly full-bodied wines. La Mancha, Vinos de Madrid, Valdepeñas and Ribera del Guadiana make many graceful yet big wines with the standard Spanish mix of grapes. Garnacha is the most important grape in Navarra but is sometimes blended with Tempranillo, Cabernet Sauvignon and Merlot. Navarra's dry *rosados* are considered Spain's best. Vintners in Somontano create polished, earthy reds from Moristel; many bear a striking resemblance to those of nearby Priorat. Toro reds are similar to those from Ribera del Duero, though more concentrated and less elegant. Wines from Bierzo, made from the Mencía grape, are fragrant and graceful. Monastrell rules in eastern regions, joined by Garnacha and the distinctive Bobal grape—a blend that results in black, brooding reds.

Though reds dominate, Spain's finest white wines should not be overlooked. Albariño is the basis for the excellent, steely-crisp whites of Rías Baixas located on the country's northwestern coast. Rueda's impressive whites are made mainly from the Verdejo grape, often supported by Sauvignon Blanc. Txakoli, produced from the Hondarribi Zuri grape in Spain's Basque Country, is slightly sparkling and mineral-laden. And Godello, native to Galicia, is quickly earning a reputation as one of the country's most delicious white grapes, especially in wines bearing the Valdeorras DO.

other spanish recommendations

WHITES

Adega Eidos Viticultores Eidos de Padriñán Albariño
| 2007 | RÍAS BAIXAS

★ ★ ★ $ $ The flagship wine from this standout producer is fresh and delicious, with fragrant citrus and herb aromas. Flavors of honey, melon and pineapple coat the palate, and the finish is complex.

Basa | 2007 | RUEDA

★ $ A blend of Sauvignon Blanc and Spain's native Verdejo and Viura grapes, this crisp, mineral-laden white is saturated with pink grapefruit and lemonade flavors and has a kick of fresh-cut herbs.

Brandal Albariño | 2007 | RÍAS BAIXAS

★ ★ $ The Adegas D'Altamira winery hand-sorts the grapes for this delightful wine. Aromas of white flowers and ripe peach lead into citrus, peach and melon flavors and a mineral-rich finish.

Casal Novo Godello | 2007 | VALDEORRAS

★ ★ ★ $ $ Godello—Valdeorras's indigenous white grape—makes a strong showing in this gorgeous wine, with savory fruit and mineral aromas. The palate is round with flavors of peaches and melons.

Castelo de Medina Verdejo | 2007 | RUEDA

★ ★ $ Castelo de Medina's magnesium- and calcium-rich soils yield a Verdejo marked by citrus, pear and tangerine aromas and grounded by a fresh, lime-tinged acidity.

Condesa Eylo Verdejo | 2007 | RUEDA

★ ★ $ Vibrant green in color, with aromas of apples, pears and limes, this delivers tart, juicy green apple flavors that culminate in a thirst-quenching, citrus-infused finish.

Don Olegario Albariño | 2007 | RÍAS BAIXAS

★ ★ ★ $ $ This luscious unoaked white is fragrant with dried apricots, lemon zest and minerals; the broad, honey-flavored palate is balanced nicely with crisp acidity.

Martínsancho Verdejo | 2008 | RUEDA

★ ★ $ $ Winemaker Angel Rodríguez is often credited with saving the Verdejo grape from extinction with his centuries-old Martínsancho vineyard. His 2008 is a big wine with a honeysuckle and chamomile nose, citrus flavors of tangerine, grapefruit and lemon zest and a soft, mineral-laden finish.

Nessa Albariño | 2008 | RÍAS BAIXAS

★ ★ $ Expressing the pronounced acacia flower, lemon zest and wet stone aromas of good Albariño, this has a crisp, bright palate rounded out by flavors of minerals and guava paste.

Quíbia | 2008 | VINO DE LA TIERRA DE MALLORCA

★ ★ $ Prensal Blanc, the dominant white grape on the island of Majorca, makes up 60 percent of this white blend, filled out with Callet. Defined by bright citrus, melon and tangerine flavors, it is nicely layered with minerals on the complex finish.

Robalino Albariño | 2007 | RÍAS BAIXAS

★ ★ $ This classically styled Albariño shows clean, crisp flavors of peach, pear, mango and citrus, all upheld by a grapefruit-like acidity.

Serra da Estrela Albariño | 2007 | RÍAS BAIXAS

★ ★ $ Crafted in the Condado do Tea subregion—facing Portugal's Vinho Verde region—this displays a bouquet of fennel, peach and melon and a peach-laden palate with notes of minerals and spice.

Valmiñor Albariño | 2008 | RÍAS BAIXAS

★ ★ ★ $ Hailing from the O Rosal ("the rosebush") subregion, this wine delivers flavors of white flowers and super-ripe pears. Its crisp mineral notes and citrusy acidity make it a great choice for seafood.

ROSÉS

Borsao | 2008 | CAMPO DE BORJA

★ $ Like its also-affordable red sibling, Borsao's rosé is a bargain. Cherries and berries compete on the palate of this utterly refreshing, well-structured *rosado*.

Tapeña | 2008 | VINO DE LA TIERRA DE CASTILLA

★ $ A combination of the words *tapas* (small plates) and *peña* (slang for a posse of friends), this food-friendly rosé is a crowd-pleaser.

Vega Sindoa | 2008 | NAVARRA

★ $ This rosé is produced in one of Navarra's best areas, where even pale-colored *rosados* can be both full-bodied and crisp at once. This lovely version shows succulent berry flavors and crisp acidity.

REDS

Bodegas Carchelo Altico "A" | 2006 | JUMILLA

★ ★ $ Located in Spain's arid southeastern countryside, Bodegas Carchelo makes this enticing Syrah infused with aromas of blueberries, blackberries and raspberries. The fruit flavors on the palate are accented by spice notes on a moderately tannic finish.

Casar de Burbia Mencía | 2006 | BIERZO

★ ★ ★ $ $ $ The Mencía grape is something of an underdog, but that is changing, thanks to wines like this elegant red: aromas of cedar and tobacco are rounded out by blueberry and raspberry flavors.

Dehesa Gago | 2007 | TORO

★ ★ ★ $ $ The Telmo Rodríguez Wine Company has cleverly incorporated a bull's horn into the label design of their Toro red, which reveals equal parts earth, smoke and blackberries.

El Albar de J. & F. Lurton Barricas | 2005 | TORO

★ ★ $ $ Aged in partly new French barrels for 12 months, this spicy Tempranillo has pronounced oak flavors in the form of coffee, earth and leather that are set against ripe berry notes and strong tannins.

El Molinet | 2007 | VALENCIA

★ ★ $ Tempranillo is blended with 15 percent Cabernet Sauvignon in this rich wine. Aromas of damp earth, leafy tobacco and sweet cedar mingle with ripe black fruit and spicy overtones in the mouth.

Guímaro Mencía | 2007 | RIBEIRA SACRA

★ ★ $ Although Bierzo is most commonly associated with Mencía, the small DO of Ribeira Sacra north of Portugal also makes great use of the grape. This sweet-savory red shows plum, blackberry and currant aromas fused with notes of coffee and licorice.

Malpaso | 2006 | MÉNTRIDA

★ ★ $ $ Made with 100 percent Syrah, this wine opens with aromas of cedar, blueberries and baking spices before big, luscious fruit takes over the palate. Bright acidity and fine-grained tannins provide great structure and balance.

Marco Real Garnacha | 2005 | NAVARRA

★ $ Hotelier Antonio Catalán made his entrée into the wine business in the late 1980s just as Navarra began to earn a reputation for its non-rosé wines. This 2005 is juicy and fresh, with notes of raspberry, cocoa and dusty spice.

Muret Old Vines Garnacha | 2007 |
VINO DE LA TIERRA RIBERA DEL JILOCA

★ ★ ★ $ $ From the reputed birthplace of Garnacha, this red seduces with spice aromas and vibrant cherry and currant flavors. Tannins frame the sweet, fruity finish.

Palacio de Otazu Altar | 2003 | NAVARRA

★ ★ ★ $ $ $ This limited-edition Navarra red is a well-made blend of Cabernet Sauvignon, Tempranillo and Merlot. Dried flower and black cherry aromas make a big first impression, followed by dusty spice and red cherry flavors with blackberry undertones and a moderately long, supple finish.

Quo Old Vines Grenache | 2007 | CAMPO DE BORJA

★ ★ $ Old-vine Grenache was aged in new French oak to complex effect here. A fascinating nose of clove, musk, sandalwood, blackberry and chocolate is augmented by plum and licorice flavors and well-integrated tannins on the minty, cocoa finish.

Señorío de Unx | 2004 | NAVARRA

★ $ This oak-aged Tempranillo-Garnacha blend is an easygoing and humble wine. Agreeable notes of earth and dried fruit blend quite nicely on the palate.

Son Negre | 2005 | VINO DE LA TERRA DE MALLORCA
★ ★ ★ $ $ $ $ Winemakers Miguel Ángel Cerdà and Pere Obrador craft this super-plush, earthy and elegant wine under the Anima Negra label. Produced from the Callet grape and splashes of Manto Negro and Fogoneu, it is rich and compelling, full of dark tobacco and powerful berry flavors.

Tandem Ars Nova | 2004 | NAVARRA
★ ★ $ $ A captivating array of spicy black currant and dried cherry flavors emerge from this Tempranillo–Merlot–Cabernet Sauvignon blend, offset by earthy coffee accents, chalky minerals and tight tannins that linger on the palate.

Tapeña Tempranillo | 2007 | VINO DE LA TIERRA DE CASTILLA
★ $ This cherry-infused quaffer has a jolt of roasted coffee and cocoa on the finish. Its lush body and low price make it a perfect match for casual tapas.

news from a wine insider

spain by Victor de la Serna, deputy editor, *El Mundo*, Madrid

Producer Making News
Heretat de Cesilia winery, in southeastern Spain's up-and-coming Alicante region (the homeland of the Monastrell grape), has been the subject of growing attention. Its 2005 Ad Gaude release outshone all other wines from southeastern Spain in a blind tasting held by the wine website of the newspaper *El Mundo*. Heretat de Cesilia's talented French vintner, Sébastien Boudon, includes 15 percent each of Syrah and Petit Verdot in his Monastrell-based wine. The result is complex, almost French-seeming and very elegant—an often-elusive quality in wines from hot, dry regions like this.

Significant New Trend
While the producer Gramona started making ice wines more than a decade ago, it wasn't until 2008 that DO Penedès in Catalonia began regulating them with the designation *vinos dulce de frío*. Gramona, whose vineyards do not freeze during harvest months, makes its ice wines by freezing grapes after they've been picked. Producers at Bodegas Vidal Soblechero, in Rueda's La Seca, have been experimenting with ice wines from grapes frozen on the vine.

125

portugal

Portugal is still synonymous with Port, the world-renowned fortified wine, but the country's wine industry is now producing many exciting nonfortified wines as well. Made primarily with Portugal's unique collection of native grapes, these wines are impressively fresh, delicious and well priced.

Vinho Verde

Porto

Douro

Atlantic Ocean

Bairrada

Dão

Beiras

Estremadura

Ribatejo

Bucelas

☆ Lisbon

Borba

Evora

Terras do Sado

Alentejo

Algarve

Principal Wine Region

Portugal: An Overview

For decades Portugal's non-Port wine production was dominated by large cooperatives that prioritized quantity over quality. This began to change in 1986 when Portugal entered the European Union, and outside investment enabled vintners to vastly improve their wines. Results have been particularly dramatic in the Douro—home of the country's famed fortified Port wines (see p. 269)—where producers began making quality strides with their dry reds. While traditional Douro Ports and the new generation of dry reds are indeed wildly different, they do share a similar flavor profile, since they are typically crafted with the same grape varieties. Other regions of note in this small yet geographically diverse country include Alentejo, Bairrada and Dão, where structured, spicy reds are produced. Look to Estremadura, Ribatejo and Terras do Sado near Lisbon for value reds.

Portuguese Grapes & Styles

Though relatively small in size, Portugal is home to many diverse regions where dozens of indigenous grapes thrive. Though largely unknown to most wine drinkers, Vinho Verde should be named the official white wine of summer. It is one of the most refreshing whites made anywhere, thanks to its bracing acidity, slight effervescence and low alcohol. Fuller-bodied examples are made from Alvarinho (called Albariño in Spain) and Loureiro grapes, which are often identified on the label. Whites from other regions such as Alentejo, Dão, Douro, Bairrada and Bucelas are worth seeking out, too. Not surprisingly, Cabernet Sauvignon, Merlot and Syrah have been planted in Portugal, but the country's most compelling reds remain wines made from local varieties such as Baga, Touriga Franca, Touriga Nacional and Tinta Roriz (Tempranillo), appearing in blends or on their own. Baga is especially important in Bairrada, where winemakers use it to make dry and tannic red wines with berry flavors.

Portuguese Wine Labels

Most Portuguese wines are labeled by region and adhere to requirements set up by the country's governing body, the *Denominação de Origem Controlada* (DOC). Wines labeled *Reserva* must be at least half a percent higher in alcohol than the DOC-established minimum. Wines labeled by variety must be made from at least 85 percent of that grape.

portuguese whites

Portugal's enviably long Atlantic coastline yields a lovely range of fish-friendly white wines, from the north's simple, tart Vinho Verde to the long-lived, relatively full-bodied whites from Alentejo in the south.

portuguese white recommendations

Casa de Santar | 2007 | DÃO
★ ★ $ Produced from a blend of the fragrant Encruzado, Cerceal Branca and Bical grapes, this apple- and peach-scented quaffer is mineral-laden and chalky, with flavors of creamy pineapple and Red Delicious apple.

Casa de Vila Verde | 2008 | VINHO VERDE
★ $ Made at one of Portugal's oldest estates—owned by the same family since the 17th century—this fruit-forward white wine bears the aromas and flavors of peach, white flowers and minerals and has a crisp, spicy finish.

Encostas do Lima | 2008 | VINHO VERDE
★ $ An immensely drinkable blend of the Loureiro and Trajadura grapes, this succulent white shows peach and citrus flavors upheld by vibrant acidity.

Esporão Reserva | 2007 | ALENTEJO
★ ★ $ "The World Is a Suitcase" is the title of the artwork on the bottle—which is unique for each vintage. The wine inside features apple pie and baking spice aromas, dried apricot flavors, a rich mouthfeel and a spicy finish.

Fâmega | 2008 | VINHO VERDE
★ $ Between the low alcohol content (around 9 percent) and the very low price, this effervescent young white is a perfect summer sipper. Its peach and mineral flavors are crisp, clean and refreshing.

Marquês de Borba | 2008 | ALENTEJO
★ **$** Made by superstar wine producer João Portugal Ramos, this medium-bodied, unoaked white delivers Granny Smith apple flavors, a plush mouthfeel and a nice kick of spice on the finish.

Quinta da Romeira Arinto | 2007 | BUCELAS
★ **$** Fermented in stainless steel, this wine from Portugal's southern Bucelas region shows creamy apple and citrus flavors accented by notes of spice and nuts on the finish.

Quinta do Crasto | 2007 | DOURO
★★ **$ $** Although Quinta do Crasto is known primarily for Ports and reds, this white table wine is a bright, mineral-rich delight. With a nose of citrus and wild asparagus, it is medium-bodied and has loads of fresh acidity in the mouth.

portuguese reds

Although interest in Portugal's red wines is growing, even most of those from the acclaimed Douro region remain underappreciated. There are many wines to consider here: the simpler examples have a charming rustic quality and a unique array of flavors, while others have the complexity and grace of some of the world's best reds.

portuguese red recommendations

Cabriz Reserva | 2005 | DÃO
★★ **$** Aged in French oak for nine months, this wine is packed with aromas of coffee, mocha and sweet plums. Fine tannins and flavors of black cherry, blackberry and spice fill the mouth.

Casa de Santar Reserva | 2005 | DÃO
★★ **$ $** Produced at the heart of the Dão region in a 17th-century manor house, this oak-aged red has a somewhat shy nose that reveals notes of plum and dusty spice followed by flavors of blueberry, currants and baking spices.

Casa Ferreirinha Reserva | 1996 | DOURO
★★★★ **$ $ $ $** The Ferreirinha brand has been recognized for quality since 1751, so the magnificence of this wine is no surprise. Leafy green notes and rich, dark fruit—including plum, raisin and cherry—lead into spicy, dusty black fruit flavors bolstered by powerful tannins on a finish laden with black pepper and chocolate.

Cedro do Noval | 2006 | VINHO REGIONAL DURIENSE

★ ★ **$** Well-respected Port producer Quinta do Noval blends Syrah with Touriga Nacional, Touriga Franca and Tinto Cão grapes for this table wine. Fresh berry aromas and flavors of plum, blueberry, dusty herb and cocoa are highlighted by savory notes of licorice.

Domaines François Lurton Barco Negro | 2007 | DOURO

★ **$** This dark red is named for a mysterious black ship of Portuguese folklore. Raspberry, cocoa and plum aromas meet bright cherry flavors in this supple wine, which comes at a very fair price.

Esporão Reserva | 2005 | ALENTEJO

★ ★ ★ **$** This heady wine is a blend of Aragonez, Trincadeira and Cabernet that is aged in oak barrels for one year. Its big, powerful aromas of tobacco, coffee, earth and berries precede flavors of black fruit and earth, a supple mouthfeel and well-integrated tannins.

news from a wine insider

portugal by Jamie Goode, UK-based wine journalist

Vintage Note

The unfortified red wines from Portugal's 2007 vintage are being heralded as the country's best yet—particularly from the Douro. Vintners there are establishing an impressive track record: Dirk Niepoort has made Redoma since 1991 and Batuta since 1999, Cristiano van Zeller has produced Vale Dona Maria since 1996, Francisco Olazabal and his son (also Francisco Olazabal) have made Vale Meão since 1999, and relative newcomers Poeira and Pintas each have seven vintages under their belts. And all of these wines seem to be aging well.

Regions to Watch

The number of top producers in the Alentejo continues to grow. Look for Malhadinha Nova, Fita Preta, Herdade dos Grous, Dona Maria, Mouro, Mouchão and Francisco Nunes Garcia.

In Dão and Bairrada, quality levels vary, but the best vintners are making some outstanding wines. Álvaro Castro leads the way in the Dão, while Dão Sul, Quinta dos Roques and Quinta da Vegia also excel. In Bairrada, Luis Pato and Bageiras champion the local Baga grape.

Finally, vintners in the Minho are making great whites with Alvarinho and Loureiro.

José Maria da Fonseca Domini | 2005 | DOURO

★★ $ The head winemaker of José Maria da Fonseca, Domingos Soares Franco, teamed up with one of the "Douro Boys," Cristiano van Zeller, to make this lovely wine, which features juicy, rich sweet plum and raspberry flavors that are enveloped by plush, firm tannins.

Lavradores de Feitoria Três Bagos | 2005 | DOURO

★★ $ Created by a well-regarded team of *lavradores* (growers) under the direction of famed winemaker Dirk Niepoort, this red offers a sweet raspberry and earthy bouquet followed by ripe berry flavors and a mouthwatering acidity balanced by pronounced tannins.

Post Scriptum de Chryseia | 2005 | DOURO

★★★ $ $ A collaboration between Bordeaux legend Bruno Prats and the Port-specializing Symington family, this wine presents big black fruit flavors augmented by tobacco, coffee and leather notes.

Quinta da Gricha | 2005 | DOURO

★★★ $ $ $ From British Port producer Churchill Graham comes this red made with grapes sourced from the bank of the Douro River. Aromas of plum, chocolate and coffee turn earthy in the mouth, with smoky overtones and ripe, well-integrated tannins.

Quinta do Crasto Old Vines Reserva | 2006 | DOURO

★★★ $ $ $ Made from as many as 30 different grape varieties grown in a single vineyard, this oak-aged red has a weighty mouthfeel and brisk acidity. Layers of cocoa, raspberry, plum and tobacco up front compete with cherries and chocolate on the finish.

Red Leg Shiraz/Aragonês | 2007 |
VINHO REGIONAL ALENTEJANO

★ $ This low-priced blend of Shiraz and Aragonez (Tempranillo) delivers juicy black fruit and fresh cherry flavors that are soft and clean.

Roquette e Cazes Xisto | 2004 | DOURO

★★★★ $ $ $ $ Pronounced SHEES-toe—Portuguese for schist soil—this outstanding red is brimming with aromas of spice, blueberry and raspberry. Bold black cherry flavors mingle with cocoa and dusty spice on the palate, which is lush, with grainy tannins.

Vértice Grande Reserva | 2005 | DOURO

★★★ $ $ $ The winery responsible for Vértice was created in 1988 by Jack Davies of Napa's legendary Schramsberg Vineyards. This blend of Touriga Nacional, Tinta Roriz and Touriga Franca is supremely elegant, with an earthy, rustic nose marked by notes of meat and plum. Bright acidity and fine tannins balance the plush mouthfeel.

germany

While most of the winemaking world emulates French traditions, German vintners produce their own unique style of wines: fruit-driven, high-acid, unoaked whites that are usually low in alcohol (though that is changing). The result is wines that are truly some of the world's most distinctive.

■ Principal Wine Region

Germany: An Overview

Given Germany's spectacular success with difficult-to-ripen Riesling, it seems hard to believe that the German government nearly destroyed the grape's reputation when it passed the infamous German Wine Law of 1971. The law granted *Qualitätswein* status (see German Wine Labels, p. 134), similar to France's *Appellation d'Origine Contrôlée,* to many mediocre wines. The result: lots of low-quality wine. Today, fortunately, German vintners are making an increasing number of excellent wines despite the many challenges they face, starting with a relatively frigid climate. Many of the best vineyards cling to steep, south-facing slopes along the river valleys of the Rhine and Mosel and the Mosel's tributaries Saar and Ruwer. It is here that the noble Riesling grape thrives. Rieslings from the Mosel tend to be delicate and mineral-laden; those from the Rheingau are usually drier and fuller-bodied. The hilly terrain of the Rheinhessen yields many low-quality sweet wines, the sort that have besmirched Germany's reputation for years and fueled the common perception that all German wines are sweet (though the region does yield some wonderful wines, particularly from the subregion Rheinterrasse). The relatively warmer Pfalz (Palatinate), Nahe and Baden regions produce lusher Rieslings, as well as a range of interesting wines from other varieties such as Gewürztraminer, Grauburgunder and Weissburgunder.

German Grapes & Styles

Unlike most other Old World countries, Germany is famous for its white wines. The Riesling grape arguably performs better here than anywhere else, thriving in spite of the cold and producing wines of rare delicacy and refinement. Thanks to high levels of residual sugar tempered by equally high acidity, Germany's best Rieslings achieve impressive balance and a range that extends from crisp and dry to concentrated sweet nectars, with many styles in between.

Germany's second most widely planted grape is the white Müller-Thurgau, although with the exception of some compelling wines from Franken (Franconia), it is used mostly for uninspired blends. Germany's other noteworthy grapes include Gewürztraminer, Grauburgunder (Pinot Gris) and Weissburgunder (Pinot Blanc), which particularly excel in the regions of Baden and Pfalz. Centuries of tradition have given German vintners an acute understanding—culled, of course, from experimentation—of their country's *terroir,* which has helped them transform often hard-to-ripen red grapes such as Spätburgunder (Pinot Noir) and Dornfelder into respectable wines.

German Wine Labels

Charming but often difficult to decipher, Germany's distinctive Gothic-script labels usually include the winery name, region, village and sometimes the vineyard where the grapes were grown, as well as the lot and cask numbers. Grapes are mentioned, though in regions like the Rheingau, Riesling is assumed.

German wines carry an official designation of "quality." The first quality category is *Qualitätswein bestimmter Anbaugebiete* (QbA), often simply referred to as "Qualitätswein." This guarantees that the grapes came from a particular region and reached a mandated level of ripeness at harvest time. *Qualitätswein mit Prädikat* (QmP) wines are held to higher standards; they are ranked by grape ripeness at harvest, from *Kabinett* to *Spätlese, Auslese, Beerenauslese* (BA) and *Trockenbeerenauslese* (TBA), in ascending order of ripeness. In theory, riper grapes yield sweeter wines. Yet in practice, sweetness depends more on the balance between acidity and sugar or how much natural grape sugar was allowed to ferment into alcohol. Therefore, depending on how a wine is made, a Kabinett wine can taste sweeter than even an Auslese. Some wineries put *trocken* (dry) or *halbtrocken* (off-dry) on labels to indicate that the wine tastes dry. "Spätlese trocken," for example, means the wine is dry in style and made from grapes picked at Spätlese levels of ripeness.

In an effort to simplify German wine labeling, an additional designation system was established in 2000. Two terms, *Classic* and *Selection,* now denote wines that are dry and high in quality. Classic wines are almost always made with a single grape variety and bear the name of the producer but not the vineyard. Selection wines are higher in quality; they must be made from hand-harvested grapes and list both the producer's name and the vineyard.

riesling

Riesling rivals Chardonnay for the title of noblest white grape, and its wines are the fastest-growing whites in the U.S. Full of citrus and peach flavors, vibrant acidity and a distinct minerality, Rieslings achieve a full range of styles from dry to off-dry, and youthfully fresh to aged and concentrated. Some of the best can age for decades, a process that brings out appealing smoky, steely aromas. Dessert wines made from Riesling (see p. 273) are capable of very long aging, which highlights their intense, sweet flavors.

riesling recommendations

Darting Dürkheimer Hochbenn Kabinett | 2007 | **PFALZ**
★ ★ $ This off-dry Riesling displays both concentration and grace, with a bouquet of fragrant peach, flowers and marshmallow that is echoed on the rich, ripe palate. Crisp acidity provides nice balance on the medium-long finish.

Dr. Fischer Steinbock | 2007 | **MOSEL**
★ ★ $ This medium-bodied Saar Valley Riesling is bone-dry yet still possesses an intensity and depth of fruit. Ripe peach perfumes the nose, followed by flavors of citrus and minerals.

Dr. H. Thanisch Classic | 2007 | **MOSEL**
★ $ This wine is typical of Mosel Riesling: light, nimble and sprightly. Designed to drink now, it boasts flavors of peach and white flowers that are crisp and dry.

Egon Müller Scharzhof | 2007 | **MOSEL-SAAR-RUWER**
★ ★ ★ $ $ Produced by the well-regarded Egon Müller, Scharzhof is the estate's entry-level Riesling. It is off-dry and marked by flavors that lean toward mineral and green apple and a stunningly ripe finish.

Fritz Haag Brauneberger Juffer Sonnenuhr Spätlese
| 2007 | MOSEL

★★★★ $ $ $ From one of the most esteemed names in German winemaking comes this gorgeous off-dry Spätlese, which presents a heavenly mix of slate, thick honey and peach flavors that resonate on the impressively long finish.

Fürst Pur Mineral Trocken | 2007 | FRANKEN

★★ $ $ $ Though Franken's signature grape is Silvaner, the intensity of this Riesling would seem to suggest otherwise. A subtle nose of lime and slate leads to a delicious palate of mineral and citrus fruit.

Gunderloch Jean-Baptiste Kabinett | 2007 | RHEINHESSEN

★ $ This dry, straightforward Riesling exhibits a nose of green apple and flint while delivering generous flavors of peach and apricot. The bright acidity renders it refreshing and immensely drinkable.

star producers
german riesling

C.H. Berres
Inspired by a stint in New Zealand, 21st-generation winemaker Markus Berres calls his new estate Riesling "Impulse" to convey the winery's renewed dynamism.

Dr. Loosen
Not only is Ernst Loosen a champion of spectacular old-vine Rieslings, he's also one of Germany's most important ambassadors for the grape.

Fritz Haag
The current generation at the helm of this top-notch winery— Oliver Haag and his wife, Jessica—have improved quality since they took over in 2005.

Joh. Jos. Prüm
Joh. Jos. Prüm founded this winery in 1911, and it has stayed true to its winemaking strengths: beautifully constructed Rieslings that are vibrant, rich and low in alcohol.

Karthäuserhof
Since Christoph Tyrell took over this winery in 1986, the emphasis has shifted from high-quality sweet wines to even better quality dry wines.

Maximin Grünhaus
The Maximin Grünhaus estate dates back to the Roman era and has built its reputation upon the aging potential of its outstanding Rieslings.

Hexamer Meddersheimer Rheingrafenberg Quarzit | 2007 |
NAHE

★★★ $ $ There is a subtle hint of sweetness here that permeates the ripe flavors of peach and nectarine; firmer notes of tart green apple and wet slate are nicely balanced on the medium-long finish.

J. & H.A. Strub Niersteiner Paterberg Spätlese | 2007 |
RHEINHESSEN

★★ $ $ One of the few producers making Grüner Veltliner in Germany, Strub also specializes in Riesling. This off-dry example brings together lemongrass and spice aromas with apple and peach flavors.

Joh. Jos. Christoffel Erben Ürziger Würzgarten Kabinett
| 2007 | MOSEL

★★★ $ $ This off-dry Riesling offers incredible complexity for the price. Pure, clean flavors of honey, pear and mineral achieve a perfect balance between juicy sweetness and crisp acidity.

Karthäuserhof Eitelsbacher Karthäuserhofberg Auslese
| 2007 | MOSEL-SAAR-RUWER

★★★★ $ $ $ This exceptional Riesling is made from a world-class single-estate vineyard. An intense honey character predominates in this complex wine, which has the capacity to age beautifully.

Kerpen Wehlener Sonnenuhr Spätlese | 2007 | MOSEL

★★★ $ $ Though it seems shy at first, releasing subdued peach aromas, this outstanding wine has a rich, full palate bursting with ripe fruit flavors and a thick texture upheld by vibrant acidity.

Reichsrat von Buhl Armand Kabinett | 2007 | PFALZ

★★ $ Von Buhl has a long history—one of its wines was served to toast the opening of the Suez Canal—but this Riesling is decidedly modern, with a medium-sweet palate of pear and melon flavors preceded by a flinty nose.

Reinhold Haart Piesport Goldtröpfchen 1 Spätlese
| 2007 | MOSEL-SAAR-RUWER

★★★★ $ $ $ This *Erste Lage* (first-growth) Riesling will become only more interesting with time. Even without aging, it demonstrates phenomenal complexity, with aromas of petrol, flint and peach and the concentrated flavor of wildflower honey on the palate.

Rudolf Müller Kabinett | 2007 | MOSEL

★ $ The irresistible baked peach aromas that introduce this wine are filled out by flavors of apricot, honey and pear on the slightly sweet, medium-bodied palate, all supported by zesty acidity.

Selbach-Oster Zeltinger Sonnenuhr Kabinett | 2007 |
MOSEL-SAAR-RUWER

★ ★ ★ $ $ Selbach-Oster has been in family hands since 1660, and its rocky, steep vineyards continue to yield exceptional wines. This wine has a clean, bracing acidity that pierces its subtle sweetness. Rich, pure flavors of pear and stone fruit dominate the palate.

Weingüter Wegeler Geisenheimer Rothenberg Auslese
| 2007 | **RHEINGAU**

★ ★ ★ $ $ $ $ An exceptional Auslese, this Riesling presents candied orange and honey flavors. Crisp acidity ensures that its sweetness is anything but cloying.

Weingut Robert Weil Estate Dry | 2007 | RHEINGAU

★ ★ ★ $ $ Aromas of slate, petrol and pear drive this superb wine. The beautiful, waxy-textured palate is full of grapefruit and mineral flavors. It is already showing some signs of development and will continue to improve with additional aging.

other german whites

The Pfalz and Baden regions benefit from their proximity to France's Alsace, with which they share many of the same white grapes in addition to Riesling. Grauburgunder (Pinot Gris) and Weissburgunder (Pinot Blanc) compare well to their French counterparts. Scheurebe, from the Rheinhessen region, is intriguing for it currant flavors and strong acidity. Kerner is similar to Riesling, while Huxelrebe and Bacchus resemble Muscat. Muskateller (Muscat) and Gewürztraminer make intensely fragrant wines. Silvaner and Müller-Thurgau are used mainly in dull blends, though both can yield lovely whites, especially in Franken.

other german white recommendations

Fitz-Ritter Gewürztraminer Spätlese | 2007 | PFALZ

★ ★ ★ $ $ For a very fair price, this Gewürztraminer provides tremendous aromatic complexity. The pungent nose of spice, honey and perfume aromas is offset by sweet flavors of overripe stone fruit.

Hans Wirsching Dry Silvaner | 2007 | FRANKEN

★ $ This Silvaner shows a straightforward bouquet of melon and citrus, completed by crisp acidity, apple flavors and a waxy texture.

Königschaffhausen Flaneur | 2007 | BADEN

★ ★ $ Flaneur is a particularly well-made Müller-Thurgau from the German wine co-op Königschaffhausen. It is intensely fragrant, with peach and flower aromas, and has a clean, mouthwatering acidity that underscores its subtle lime flavors.

Kruger-Rumpf Scheurebe Spätlese | 2007 | NAHE

★ ★ ★ $ $ This stellar example of the lesser-known German variety Scheurebe conjures aromas and flavors of wet stone, citrus, honey and white peach. The long finish strikes a flawless balance between sweetness and acidity.

Weingut Gysler Scheurebe Halbtrocken | 2008 | RHEINHESSEN

★ ★ $ (1 L) This off-dry white, packaged in a one-liter bottle, makes a lovely first impression, with delicate aromas of citrus, pear and flowers. Delectable flavors of steely minerals and peach mingle with fierce acidity in this nicely priced wine.

news from a wine insider

germany by Peter Moser, Vienna-based wine writer and editor-in-chief of *Falstaff Magazine*

Vintage Note

The weather in 2008 posed considerable challenges throughout Germany, where the largely advantageous summer was offset by a relatively cool, rainy fall. Overall, the resulting wines ranged from good to very good, and "quality" wines (the most basic designation) were better than the previous year. From Kabinett to Auslese, the whites are generally leaner than those from 2007, with a refreshing acidity. The reds have intense color and appealing fruit flavors.

Producers to Watch

Schäfer-Fröhlich (Nahe), Becker and Wehrheim (Pfalz), Schloss Johannisberg and Spreitzer (Rheingau) and Wagner-Stempel (Rheinhessen) have been making some excellent wines in recent years in their respective regions. Among the noteworthy newcomers are Daniel Vollenweider and the outstanding organic producer Clemens Busch (Mosel), Van Volxem (Saar), Markus Schneider (Pfalz) and Andreas Laible and Pinot Noir specialist Ziereisen (Baden).

austria & switzerland

These two Alpine neighbors share more than just a mountain range. Both craft good to excellent white wines as well as some interesting reds. Compared to the white wines of neighboring Germany, Austria's are mainly drier, fuller-bodied and somewhat racier in character. Switzerland's softer, lighter-bodied whites are increasingly available in the U.S., as Swiss winemakers have begun to look beyond their borders for new customers.

austria

In many ways the notorious Austrian wine scandal of 1985 (when a portion of the country's wine was tainted with diethylene glycol, an ingredient used to make antifreeze) was the greatest thing that could have happened to the country's wine industry. It led to the creation of many rigid regulations—the strictest in Europe—that govern all wine-making in Austria and resulted in wines of exceptionally high quality. These range from dry, mineral-laden whites—approximately 70 percent of the country's wines are white—to many interesting reds made from indigenous grapes rarely seen elsewhere.

Austrian Grapes & Styles

Like Germany, Austria is a land of superb white wines. Austria's most popular native grape is the spicy, citrusy Grüner Veltliner. Of the many other white wine grapes, the most prevalent is Riesling, though Weissburgunder (Pinot Blanc), Morillon (Chardonnay), Sauvignon Blanc and Welschriesling are scattered throughout the country as well. A few Austrian reds have come to the forefront in recent years, such as peppery Blaufränkisch (also called Lemberger), juicy Zweigelt, elegant Blauburgunder (Pinot Noir) and smoky St. Laurent.

Austrian Wine Labels

Most Austrian wines list grape and region on the bottle and use a quality system similar to Germany's *Qualitätswein* (see p. 133), though Austria's standards are often higher. Austria's premier area for whites, Wachau, uses its own classification: *Steinfeder* are light wines, *Federspiel* are heavier and *Smaragd* are rich and capable of long aging.

austrian whites

High in minerality and acidity and bursting with expressive fruit flavors, Austrian whites are among the world's most exciting wines. Grüner Veltliner and Riesling are responsible for most of the finest, though some other varieties produce wines worthy of consideration.

AUSTRIAN WHITES

grüner veltliner

Grüner Veltliner, only recently embraced by Americans, is a gem of a wine—light-bodied, versatile and perfect for pairing with food. When aged, it develops intense smoky, mineral flavors, whereas young examples are fresh and apple-scented, perfect for everyday drinking.

grüner veltliner recommendations

Domäne Wachau Terrassen Smaragd | 2008 | **WACHAU**

★ ★ **$ $** This cooperative cultivates one-third of the entire vineyard area of Wachau, yet still manages to pay incredible attention to detail. With bright aromas and flavors of Fuji apple, Bosc pear and passion fruit, this refreshing white is perfect for summer sipping.

Felsner Lössterrassen | 2008 | **KREMSTAL**

★ ★ **$** Fragrant honey, melon and pineapple dominate the nose in this expressive Grüner Veltliner, followed by generous citrus flavors and a pleasing hint of green pepper.

Glatzer | 2007 | **CARNUNTUM**

★ ★ ★ **$** White peach, apple blossom and lychee aromas mingle with hints of wet slate to evoke the scent of a light spring rain in this fine white. On the palate, apple and white pepper flavors are laced by floral and limestone notes that extend through the finish.

star producers
austrian whites

Domäne Wachau
Domäne Wachau represents the very best wines produced by the Wachau Valley's largest cooperative—made up of 600 contributing members.

Heidi Schröck
Heidi Schröck took over the family winery in 1983 and carries on the traditions of her aunts, harvesting grapes from the property's 40-year-old vines.

Hirsch
Josef Hirsch and his son, Johannes, work in "harmonious cooperation" with nature to produce distinctive, complex Rieslings and Grüner Veltliners.

Nikolaihof
The oldest wine estate in Austria, Nikolaihof is a strict practitioner of biodynamic viticulture, even planting and harvesting in accordance with the moon's calendar.

Prager
Prager is easily one of the most famous wineries in Austria, thanks to Toni Bodenstein's winemaking prowess.

Soellner
Since marrying in 1995, Daniela Vigne and Toni Söllner have worked together to create some of Austria's most exceptional biodynamic wines.

Gobelsburger | 2007 | KAMPTAL
★ ★ $ This well-made wine comes at a very low price. Inviting aromas of cantaloupe, mineral and nettles portend flavors of honeydew and cantaloupe that are upheld by acidity.

Grooner | 2007 | NIEDERÖSTERREICH
★ $ Granny Smith apple, bright lime and melon flavors make this zippy Lower Austria white a perfect everyday wine.

Hiedler Löss | 2007 | KAMPTAL
★ ★ $ $ For those who prefer a more voluptuous style of Grüner Veltliner, this substantial Kamptal white will satisfy: green peppers and toasted walnut notes infuse rich flavors of ripe melon, fragrant wildflowers and minerals.

Hirsch Heiligenstein | 2007 | KAMPTAL
★ ★ $ $ This white strikes a perfect balance between fruit-forward and savory characteristics, displaying a mélange of peach, apple, pepper, walnut, olive and chalky mineral flavors.

Nikolaihof Hefeabzug | 2007 | WACHAU
★ ★ ★ $ $ This certified biodynamic gem is taut, subtle and harmonious. Intriguing layers of apple, roasted nuts, smoke, green pea and earth carry through the impressively long finish.

Soellner Hengstberg | 2007 | WAGRAM
★ ★ ★ $ Fermented in stoneware rather than stainless steel or oak, this biodynamic wine is earthy, slightly yeasty and bursting with peach, pear and mineral flavors woven with a thread of honey.

Weingut Johann Donabaum Spitzer Point Smaragd | 2007 | WACHAU
★ ★ ★ $ $ $ The nose here is deceptively restrained; time in the glass reveals grapefruit, papaya and spicy pepper aromas. The palate is elegant, concentrated and waxy, marked by apricot, lemon, white pepper and cream.

AUSTRIAN WHITES
riesling
Austrian Rieslings tend to be drier than German versions, though more fruit-driven than those from France's Alsace region. Intensely mineral-laden and high in acidity, many have the potential to age for a decade or more and can develop an intriguing smoky quality with time.

riesling recommendations

Domäne Wachau Achleiten Smaragd | 2007 | WACHAU

★★★ $ $ $ This delicious, dry Riesling is big on aromatics, displaying intense pear, peach and citrus. The palate is exuberant, with pronounced lemon, lime and grapefruit flavors.

Gobelsburger | 2007 | KAMPTAL

★★ $ $ An ideal choice for sipping on a warm afternoon, this fragrant white is defined by flavors of apple, peach, pear and citrus, with a pronounced core of minerals and earth.

Högl Loibner Vision Smaragd | 2007 | WACHAU

★★★ $ $ $ Ample stone fruit, pineapple and mango on the nose introduce a precise yet rounded palate offering concentrated, juicy ripe fruit balanced by Riesling's classic zippy acidity.

Salomon Undhof Undhof Kögl | 2007 | KREMSTAL

★★ $ $ Ripe pear and toasted walnut aromas make a big first impression in this Riesling, giving way to an assertive, acidic palate loaded with peaches and fine minerals.

other austrian whites

Austria produces many other wonderfully expressive white wines, most notably Welschriesling and Gelber Muskateller, as well as a small amount of Weissburgunder, Grauburgunder (Pinot Gris), Morillon and Muskat-Sylvaner (Sauvignon Blanc). This last grape comes predominantly from the Styria (Steiermark) region, where most of the grapes are hand-picked and the wines well crafted.

other austrian white recommendations

Kracher Illmitz Pinot Gris | 2007 | BURGENLAND

★★ $ Mouthwatering pear, raspberry and passion fruit aromas introduce this dense fruit-forward white, which shows flavors of honey-smothered stone.

Spaetrot Gebeshuber Grosse Reserve | 2006 |
THERMENREGION

★★★ $ $ $ This 50-50 blend of Rotgipfler and Zierfandler is wonderfully complex, showing off the best of both obscure grapes in the form of apple, wildflower, pineapple, earth and flint flavors.

Stift Kloster Neuburg Wiener Nussberg Gemischter Satz
| 2008 | WIEN
★★ $ This is a high-quality, value-priced field blend, composed of Grüner Veltliner, Riesling and Welschriesling, from the Vienna (Wien) region. Flavors of melon, apple and grass finish with a kick of spice.

Wenzel Pinot Gris | 2006 | BURGENLAND
★★★ $ $ This brooding white, with intense flinty aromas, gradually reveals an array of peach and cantaloupe flavors woven with layers of smoke. The palate strikes a compelling balance between sweet vanilla, oak and pear flavors.

austrian reds

Austria's most popular red grape is Zweigelt; it yields light wines with juicy cherry flavors. Blaufränkisch is spicier and more tannic, and responsible for some of the most interesting Austrian reds today. Blauburgunder (Pinot Noir) and St. Laurent (which is similar to Pinot Noir) can also yield some impressive results.

austrian red recommendations

Feiler-Artinger Zweigelt | 2007 | BURGENLAND
★★ $ Smokehouse aromas—meat, embers and earth—dominate the nose of this fascinating red. The palate continues with flavors of loam accompanied by ripe blackberry and plum.

Hannes Schuster Zagersdorf St. Laurent | 2006 |
BURGENLAND
★★★ $ $ $ This wine is characterized by elegance and power. The nose displays layered notes of cassis, vanilla and fresh herbs, while the velvety palate delivers fresh red and black berries.

Moric Alte Reben Neckenmarkt Blaufränkisch | 2006 |
BURGENLAND
★★★★ $ $ $ $ This stunner is assertively tannic on the attack but quickly reveals rich baking spice, black pepper and multiple layers of dark fruit flavors. From mid-palate to finish, it offers waves of blackberry, black currant, huckleberry, black cherry and plum.

Prieler Johanneshöhe Blaufränkisch | 2007 | BURGENLAND
★★ $ $ Concentrated aromas of dark plum, blueberry and fresh lavender precede a hearty palate of ample raspberry flavors and firm tannins in this well-built red.

Rosi Schuster Zweigelt | 2007 | BURGENLAND
★ $ Big, gregarious and utterly enjoyable, this is a crowd-pleaser. Plum, dark berry and a hint of earth mark the nose, while ripe and youthful flavors of blackberry and black cherry arrive on the palate.

Sattler Zweigelt | 2007 | BURGENLAND
★ ★ $ In both aroma and flavor, this red is robust and expressive, conjuring notes of ripe plum, fresh blackberry, violet and a wisp of smoke, all framed by gentle tannins.

Stift Kloster Neuburg Barrique St. Laurent | 2006 |
THERMENREGION
★ ★ $ $ Though this St. Laurent is unapologetically oaky, it is executed with surprising finesse. Warm vanilla and wood mingle with dark berries on the nose, while the palate brings in candied plum and just enough tannic structure to maintain balance.

switzerland

The Swiss export only about 2 percent of their wines, but they are worth hunting for. Roughly half of the country's production is red, and that is increasing. Another notable trend is the shift toward drier wines. Most wine production in Switzerland takes place in the French-speaking western regions and the Italian-speaking southern region, Ticino.

Swiss Grapes & Styles

Chasselas is Switzerland's most prevalent white grape. Chasselas wines (called Fendant in the Valais region) are typically unoaked and mineral-laden. Sylvaner produces fuller-bodied wines. Müller-Thurgau, Chardonnay, Sauvignon Blanc, Aligoté, Completer, Kerner and Sémillon are also planted. Pinot Noir is the principal red wine grape, though Gamay is more important in Vaud and Geneva. Merlot yields relatively full-bodied wines in Ticino. Some well-made Syrah is also crafted in the Valais.

Swiss Wine Labels

Wines tend to be labeled by region and grape. The country adheres to a classification system that uses France's AOC (*Appellation d'Origine Contrôlée*, see p. 21) as a model.

swiss recommendations

WHITES

Château d'Auvernier | 2007 | NEUCHÂTEL

★ $ $ A hint of toasted walnut overlays green apple, pear, lime and subtle brine flavors throughout this lovely Chasselas, and a slight sparkle adds refreshment.

Domaine E. de Montmollin Fils | 2008 | NEUCHÂTEL

★ ★ $ The de Montmollins have tended vineyards in Neuchâtel since the 16th century. Their 2008 vintage displays aromas and flavors of citrus, mineral and pear that are shy at first but blossom with a bit of time in the glass.

Jean-René Germanier Amigne de Vétroz | 2006 | VALAIS

★ ★ $ $ $ This off-dry Amigne boasts candied tangerine, honeysuckle and mineral flavors, and strikes the perfect balance between pronounced acidity, intense flavor and a kiss of sweetness. Notes of elderflower, apricot and lychee assert themselves on the finish.

John & Mike Favre Petite Arvine | 2007 | CHAMOSON-VALAIS

★ ★ $ $ $ Vinified from the rather unusual Petite Arvine grape, this distinctive white shows a delicious harmony of flavors. Honeysuckle, orange blossom, pear and sea air on the nose lead to a palate of citrus rind, mineral and rhubarb.

REDS

Cave de La Côte Dubaril Romand Gamay | 2007 | VIN DE PAYS

★ ★ $ A great value, this well-crafted Gamay balances red cherry, strawberry and loam notes with just a touch of ripe banana—a hallmark characteristic of the grape. It could serve as a tasty alternative to entry-level Pinot Noir.

René Favre & Fils Pinot Noir | 2005 | CHAMOSON-VALAIS

★ ★ $ $ This is a remarkably concentrated Pinot Noir loaded with aromas of raspberry, fresh-baked blueberry pie, violet and lilac. The palate is powerfully floral but also displays ripe strawberry, leather and subtle smoke flavors.

Robert Gilliard Dôle des Monts | 2006 | VALAIS

★ ★ ★ $ $ $ An excellent blend of Pinot Noir and Gamay, this wine weaves together rich aromas of black currant, vanilla, cinnamon and wet soil. Undercurrents of smoke and earth lend interest to flavors of blackberry, raspberry and rose petal.

greece

While Greece has been making wine since long before the very first Olympic Games, the 2004 Athens Games introduced modern Greek wines to the world and drew attention to the dramatic revival of Greece's wine industry after centuries of decline. The finest Greek wines that reach U.S. markets today are made with difficult-to-pronounce indigenous grapes, rather than international varieties like Chardonnay or Cabernet Sauvignon.

Greece: An Overview

As Greek winemakers look to their peers abroad for advice, they're focusing on native grape varieties, and on figuring out the best vineyard sites, determining, for example, that north-facing, high-altitude slopes are key to tempering the extreme summer heat.

There are four main viticultural zones in Greece: north, central, the Peloponnese and the islands. The northern zone encompasses the mountainous regions of Macedonia and Thrace; Naoussa is one of the area's most famous appellations. Central Greece features some of the country's highest-elevation vineyards. The warm valleys and cooler slopes of the Peloponnese peninsula, including the important subregions of Mantinia, Nemea and Patras, have the most appellations. Of the islands, Crete is responsible for a large quantity of wine, while the Aegean islands of Santorini and Samos offer some of the country's finest wines.

Greek Grapes & Styles

Greece is home to more than 300 native grapes—only Italy has more indigenous varieties. International stars such as Chardonnay, Merlot and Cabernet Sauvignon grow here, too, but winemakers typically use them only in blends along with indigenous varieties. Savatiano, used to make Greece's well-known pine resin–flavored wine, Retsina, is the most common grape, but not the most important in terms of quality. Assyrtiko, the best of which comes from the island of Santorini, is used to make crisp, bone-dry wines with pronounced mineral and citrus flavors. Rosy-hued, spicy Moschofilero is produced as a dry white as well as a dry rosé, both of which are high in acidity, low in alcohol and wonderfully aromatic. Agiorgitiko—also known as St. George, as it is sometimes listed on wine labels—is one of Greece's most widely planted red grape varieties; it often draws comparisons to spicy, robust Cabernet Francs. Xynomavro from the Macedonia region of northern Greece yields red wines that are reminiscent of Piedmont's Nebbiolo-based wines, for their high acidity, heavy tannins and impressive aging ability. Honorable mentions go to Roditis, which is responsible for the light-bodied, citrus-flavored white wines of Patras; and Mavrodaphne, a red grape that's vinified in both dry and sweet styles, and often used as a blending grape as well.

Greek Wine Labels

As in the European tradition, wine regions take priority over the names of grape varieties on the majority of Greek wine labels. Red wines from Naoussa are required by law to be made from the Xynomavro grape, while those from Nemea are produced with Agiorgitiko. Mantinia wines must be made from at least 85 percent Moschofilero, and wines from Santorini are dominated by Assyrtiko. Grape varieties that are not traditional to particular areas, however, are usually noted on labels.

greek whites

Greek whites are as distinctive and varied as the appella-tions that produce them. The volcanic soils on the island of Santorini yield bold, mineral-laden whites. Peloponnesian Moschofilero possesses the spiciness of Gewürztraminer. Floral Roditis from Patras, Robola from the Ionian island Cephalonia (Kefalonia) and Assyrtiko from Santorini are universally crisp, mineral-laden and dry.

greek white recommendations

Argyros Estate Argyros | 2007 | SANTORINI
★ ★ ★ $ $ $ This uniquely modern rendition of the Greek Assyrtiko grape is pleasingly oaky without being too heavy or buttery. The ripe, weighty palate offers flavors of citrus, herb and bitter almond and features a long, rich finish.

Domaine Spiropoulos | 2008 | MANTINIA
★ ★ ★ $ Spiropoulos was established in 1870 and has been farmed organically since the early 1990s. Made from the Moschofilero grape, which bears similarities to Gewürztraminer, this standout white is a phenomenal value. Dry and crisp, it shows intense flavors of citrus rind, lemon blossom and peach.

Ktima Tselepos Melissopetra Gewürztraminer | 2008 | VIN DE PAYS D'ARCADIE
★ ★ $ $ (500 ml) Located in the heart of the Peloponnese, Ktima Tselepos was one of the first Greek wineries to experiment with Gewürztraminer. Classic aromas of lychee, white flowers and ripe honeydew are followed by zesty flavors of melon and juicy peach in this dry, well-balanced white.

Lyrarakis Cuvee Grande Colline | 2008 | HERAKLION
★ ★ $ This family-owned winery has been in business since 1966. Muscat and Sauvignon Blanc are joined by the obscure Cretan variety Vilana in this refreshing blend, which displays a grapy nose with whiffs of citrus rind and mango and a crisp, medium-long finish.

Mercouri Estate Folói | 2008 | PISATIS
★ ★ $ This vibrant blend of Viognier and the indigenous Greek variety Roditis offers mouthwatering ripe mango and melon flavors. Look also for Kallisto, Mercouri's other delicious white, a blend of Assyrtiko and Robola.

Semeli Mountain Sun Moschofilero | 2008 | PELOPONNESE
★ $ Moschofilero derives its name from the Greek word meaning "aromatic"—a fitting descriptor for this wine, which is scented with peach, rose and grape. Crisp acidity balances fruit-salad flavors.

Sigalas Asirtiko/Athiri | 2008 | SANTORINI
★ ★ $ This zesty offering from one of Santorini's finest producers yields a nose of lemongrass, mineral and brine. The steely palate and medium body make this a perfect summer sipper.

greek reds

Greek reds range from simple to complex. The best wines of Naoussa and nearby Amyndeon, which tend to be oak-aged Xynomavro, can be compared to quality Barbaresco. Some reds from Nemea possess a Bordeaux-like elegance and others a chewy richness and depth of fruit.

greek red recommendations

Argyros Atlantis | 2006 | SANTORINI
★ ★ $ This Santorini red is made with the Mandelaria grape. Robust flavors of cassis liqueur are upheld by fine-grained tannins.

Boutari Grande Reserve | 2003 | NAOUSSA
★ ★ ★ $ $ Boutari ages this wine for at least four years in both oak and bottle before release, and the result is one of the country's finest reds. The complex nose is defined by animal, plum and cedar notes, while the firm tannins give the palate structure.

Domaine Mercouri | 2005 | VIN DE PAYS DES LETRINON
★ ★ $ $ Made from a combination of the northern Italian grape Refosco and native Greek Mavrodaphne, this wine impresses with its concentration and complexity. It is full-bodied and dense, with flavors of sweet spice, vanilla, licorice and dark cherry.

Gaia Notios Agiorgitiko | 2008 | NEMEA
★ $ This is the straightforward, entry-level red from one of Greece's finest producers. An earthy nose gives way to animal, blackberry and dark cherry flavors on the palate.

Ktima Pavlidis Thema | 2005 | DRAMA
★ ★ $ $ This blend of 40 percent Syrah and 60 percent Agiorgitiko delights with its Bordeaux-like aromas of pencil lead, earth and dark fruit. Ripe tannins frame ripe black currant flavors.

other old world wines

Although Western Europe—France, in particular—sets the benchmark for Old World winemaking, with its emphasis on tradition and terroir, viticulture has far more ancient roots in Eastern Europe, North Africa and the Middle East.

eastern europe

Since the collapse of the Soviet Union, Eastern Europe's wine industry has been virtually reborn. This revival is evident in Croatia, Slovenia and Bulgaria, and especially in Hungary, once considered among the greatest winemaking countries in Europe. In recent years there has been a resurgence of interest in Hungary's indigenous grapes, especially Kadarka. The country also produces blends that include international varieties such as Cabernet Sauvignon, Merlot and Pinot Noir. One of Hungary's best traditional wines, Tokaji Aszú (see p. 274), continues to be among the finest dessert wines made anywhere. Tokaji accounts for only a tiny fraction of Hungary's total wine production, but it is easily the most stunning of Hungarian exports.

Eastern European Wine Labels

The wines of Eastern Europe tend to be labeled according to grape and region. Hungary's famous sweet Tokaji wines—which do not list varieties—are a major exception.

eastern european whites

If one Eastern European country stands out for white wines it is Slovenia, whose blends, made primarily with Pinot Bianco, Pinot Grigio, Ribolla and Malvasia, can hold their own alongside those produced in Italy's Friuli region, just across Slovenia's western border. Look to Hungary for beautiful dry whites from Furmint grapes, and to Croatia for exotic, nutty wines from the Posip grape. Rieslings are made in various parts of Eastern Europe, as is Welschriesling (called Laski Rizling in Slovenia and Olasz Rizling in Hungary), which tastes similar but is unrelated. As in most wine regions, Chardonnay and Sauvignon Blanc make cameo appearances.

eastern european white recommendations

Craftsman Harslevelu | 2006 | NESZMELY, HUNGARY
★ $ Honey dominates in this golden-hued Hungarian white, infusing secondary flavors of raisins and apricot nectar. While it is off-dry, its crisp acidity keeps the sweetness from being overly cloying.

Disznoko Tokaji Dry Furmint | 2006 | TOKAJ, HUNGARY
★ ★ $ The Disznoko estate has been around for a very long time—it was classified as a first-growth property in 1772—yet its winemaking is innovative. This new expression for Furmint is quite dry and full-bodied, with aromas of nuts and apples and crisp pear flavors on a richly textured palate.

Marko Polo Posip | 2007 | KORCULA, CROATIA
★ $ The rare Posip grape grows on the island of Korcula off Croatia's southern Dalmatian coast. This weighty yet refreshing example exhibits a vibrant, clean palate and a nose of green apple and pear.

Monarchia Cellars Olivier | 2007 | MATRA, HUNGARY
★ ★ $ This delicious wine, made from the obscure Irsay Oliver grape, delivers a pleasing mix of grape, lychee and flower flavors that are aromatic and mouthwatering.

Movia Veliko | 2004 | **BRDA, SLOVENIA**
★ ★ ★ $ $ $ The Kristancic family has been making wine here since 1820. This exquisite blend of Ribolla, Sauvignon Blanc and Pinot Grigio displays a complexity that may be unexpected in a wine from Slovenia. The layered palate shows nut, citrus and spice flavors.

Pullus Sauvignon | 2007 | **STAJERSKA, SLOVENIA**
★ $ This Sauvignon Blanc conjures the variety's usual array of expressive citrus, grapefruit and grass aromas and lime and mineral flavors, all upheld by refreshing acidity.

Royal Tokaji Furmint | 2007 | **TOKAJ, HUNGARY**
★ ★ $ In the 16 years that winemaker Karoly Ats has worked here, he has established himself as a master of Furmint. This hefty example weighs in at 14.5 percent alcohol but remains balanced and poised, with a round, full body and flavors of apple, vanilla and waxy lemon.

Zlatan Otok | 2006 | **HVAR, CROATIA**
★ ★ $ This blend of Posip and Marastina is floral, nutty and peach scented; its flavors of pear and citrus are framed by bright acidity.

eastern european reds

Eastern Europe's most interesting reds are from native grapes. Hungary's Egri Bikaver ("Bull's Blood from Eger") is a blend of mainly indigenous grapes. Hungarian vintners also craft wines from Kekfrankos (known elsewhere as Blaufränkisch or Lemberger). Slovenia, Croatia and Bulgaria make fine reds as well. Interestingly, Croatia's Crljenak Kastelanski grape is the parent of California's Zinfandel, and the two taste similar. Plavac Mali is a more widely grown relative, and it, too, offers Zinfandel-like flavors.

eastern european red recommendations

Enjingi Zweigelt | 2006 | **KUTJEVO, CROATIA**
★ $ Zweigelt, an Austrian variety, finds a good home in Croatia, as this fruit-forward red illustrates. Best served chilled, this offers aromas of vanilla and blueberry and flavors of soft cherry and pepper.

Kristof Blue Danube | 2003 | **EGER, HUNGARY**
★ $ This vibrant, earthy red is made from the Kekfrankos grape. Its soft tannins are woven with flavors of raspberry and pomegranate.

Movia Pinot Nero | 2004 | BRDA, SLOVENIA
★ ★ ★ $ $ $ Stylistically, this nuanced and complex Pinot Noir leans more toward Oregon than Burgundy. Four years aging in French oak has imparted notes of smoke and subtle vanilla to the fleshy palate of ripe and juicy red cherry flavors.

Pullus Modri Pinot | 2007 | STAJERSKA, SLOVENIA
★ $ This gulpable Pinot Noir is a perfect party wine for its straight-forward and enjoyable combination of fresh, fruity black cherry and strawberry flavors, balanced by notes of smoke and soft tannins.

Takler Noir Gold Reserve Kekfrankos | 2006 |
SZEKSZARD, HUNGARY
★ ★ ★ $ $ Ferenc Takler and his two sons, Andras and Ferenc, Jr., work as a team to make dependable, dynamic wines. In this excellent red, well-integrated tannins support black plums, smoke and earth flavors, which augment the sweet spice and black fruit on the nose.

Tcherga Merlot/Rubin | 2006 | THRACIAN VALLEY, BULGARIA
★ $ This Merlot-dominated blend is comparable in style to a Califor-nia Central Valley red. Aromas of blackberry and vanilla predict the fruit-forward nature of the palate, offset by robust tannins.

Zlatan Otok Plavac | 2005 | HVAR, CROATIA
★ ★ $ $ $ This delicious red from the island of Hvar has a bouquet of dried herbs and baked fruit, a big body and high alcohol content, which makes it easy to see how Plavac Mali is related to Zinfandel.

middle east & north africa

Winemaking in this part of the world dates back to early biblical times, millennia before the French began ferment-ing grapes. Today, exciting wines are again coming out of these regions, especially from Lebanon. Two producers in particular, Château Musar and Château Kefraya, have helped reinvigorate Lebanon's wine industry and inspire a new generation of vintners. Israel, too, is earning a reputa-tion for world-class wines—not all of them kosher. In North Africa, creative vintners in Morocco, Algeria and Tunisia are emphasizing quality over quantity, with some good results.

Middle Eastern & North African Grapes & Styles

While Lebanon is capable of producing good Chardonnay and Sauvignon Blanc, its winemakers excel with indigenous white varieties such as Merweh, thought to be the same as Sémillon, and Obaideh, thought to be identical to Chardonnay. North African white wines are not nearly as compelling, but some fresh, crisp examples are being made there from the Ugni Blanc, Clairette and Muscat grapes. In both Lebanon's Bekaa Valley and Israel's Golan Heights, vintners are crafting impressive wines from Cabernet Sauvignon, Syrah and Merlot. The finest Lebanese red wines possess a Claret-like elegance, with a slightly fuller body and a more robust character, while Israeli Cabernets and Syrahs are amazingly powerful, with concentrated fruit flavors. Most of North Africa's reds tend to display earthy flavors.

Middle Eastern & North African Wine Labels

France's colonial influence over North Africa and the Middle East is still apparent in the labeling of their wines. Regional names are generally emphasized over grape variety, though labels of wines made exclusively from international grapes like Chardonnay and Cabernet Sauvignon are likely to list them.

middle eastern & north african recommendations

WHITES

Château Musar | 2000 | BEKAA VALLEY, LEBANON
★ ★ ★ $ $ $ Launched in 1930 in a 17th-century castle, Musar has earned international acclaim for its outstanding wines. This blend of indigenous Lebanese varieties Obaideh and Merweh is one of the region's best. Golden-hued, it possesses concentration, balance and complex flavors of dried apricots, nuts and citrus rind.

Dalton Fumé Blanc | 2007 | GALILEE, ISRAEL
★ $ The Fumé Blanc style was created in California, but Israel's Dalton executes it well. This Sauvignon Blanc spends three months in oak, which lends a creamy texture and hints of vanilla to crisp flavors of citrus and grass.

Les Trois Domaines Blanc | 2007 | GUERROUANE, MOROCCO
★ $ This unusual Moroccan white is a refreshing blend of Sauvignon Blanc, Ugni Blanc and Clairette. It smells of flowers and green apples, while the palate is crisp and textured with flavors of pear and lemon.

Yarden Gewürztraminer | 2008 | GALILEE, ISRAEL
★ ★ $ This Israeli Gewürztraminer could easily be mistaken for a German wine, thanks to traditional flavors of lychee, perfume and honey on a weighty, balanced palate.

REDS

Château Kefraya | 2002 | BEKAA VALLEY, LEBANON
★ ★ $ Château Kefraya released its first wine in 1979 after years of selling its grapes to other vintners. This Cabernet Sauvignon–dominated blend is sumptuous and juicy, yet has Old World character in the form of baked dark fruit, earth and dried leaf flavors.

Château Musar | 2000 | BEKAA VALLEY, LEBANON
★ ★ ★ $ $ $ Without a doubt Lebanon's finest red, this garnet-colored blend of equal parts Cabernet Sauvignon, Cinsault and Carignane seduces with a bouquet of spice, oak and dark berry. The harmonious palate hosts fine, satiny tannins and a long, earthy finish.

Domaine Riad Jamil | 2005 | BENI M'TIR, MOROCCO
★ $ This wine is made from 100 percent Carignane—generally a workhorse grape used for beefing up blends. However, this estate's old vines yield a velvety wine with flavors of berries, violet and spice.

Galil Mountain Yiron Syrah | 2005 | GALILEE, ISRAEL
★ ★ $ $ Galil Mountain is the sister winery of Golan Heights Winery—producer of Yarden wines. This voluptuous, inky-purple Syrah is rich with plum and spice aromas followed by dark fruit flavors and ripe tannins on the full-bodied palate.

Massaya Gold Reserve | 2004 | BEKAA VALLEY, LEBANON
★ ★ $ $ $ These three French grapes—Cabernet, Mourvèdre and Syrah—aren't typically blended together, yet in Lebanon the marriage works well. Complex smoke, animal and red fruit aromas precede the cherry-flavored palate, which is filled out with round, soft tannins.

Tabor Adama Volcanic Soil Cabernet Sauvignon | 2006 | GALILEE, ISRAEL
★ ★ $ $ Elegance and power are balanced well in this oak-aged Cabernet: aromas of raspberry, sweet tobacco and cedar give way to dusty tannins and a medium-long finish.

NEW WORLD · UNITED STATES

united states

Winemaking has been part of American life for hundreds of years. European vines were imported to the English colony in Virginia as early as 1619. By 1626, the Spanish were making wine with Old World varieties in what are now Texas and New Mexico, while Franciscan missionaries brought viticulture to California in the late 1770s. Today, the U.S. is the fourth-largest wine-producing nation in the world, and is well on its way to becoming the largest wine consumer, surpassing Italy and France.

The United States: An Overview

While wineries have sprouted up in every state in the U.S., California is still the country's viticultural powerhouse, producing about 90 percent of the nation's wine. Washington, New York and Oregon make up the majority of the remaining 10 percent. Most of the finest wines hail from the temperate, often sun-drenched West Coast, where the European *Vitis vinifera* varieties (Chardonnay, Cabernet Sauvignon, Pinot Noir and so on) thrive. In areas with harsher climates and severe weather fluctuations, only native American grapes like *Vitis labrusca* or *Vitis rotundifolia* can survive—unfortunately, they generally don't make great wines. But while the U.S. may rely on European varieties, its wines are distinctively American in style, typically emphasizing bold fruit flavors over nuances of earth and minerals.

california

California sunshine is actually a mixed blessing. Producers must struggle to find areas that are cool enough to keep grapes from ripening too quickly, thus ensuring proper flavor development. Some of the best wines are made in coastal regions tempered by Pacific breezes, as well as in vineyards at higher elevations; luckily, California happens to have a bounty of such areas up and down the coast.

Mendocino

Lake   Sierra
        Foothills

Sonoma Napa

San
Francisco

Contra Costa

Santa Cruz

Monterey

Pacific Ocean

San Luis Obispo

Santa Barbara

• Los Angeles

Temecula

San Diego

Principal Wine
Region

California: An Overview

The North Coast is the northernmost of California's important winegrowing regions and includes Napa, Sonoma, Mendocino and Lake counties. Mendocino's Anderson Valley provides the perfect climate for producing Chardonnay and Pinot Noir, as well as high-quality sparkling wines (see p. 264). In Sonoma, the legendary Alexander, Russian River and Dry Creek valleys are home to elegant Chardonnays, spicy Zinfandels and fruit-forward Sauvignon Blancs. East of Sonoma is the much smaller yet much more renowned Napa Valley, where the country's greatest Cabernets and Bordeaux-style blends are produced. Nearby Carneros makes many excellent Chardonnays, Pinot Noirs and sparkling wines. California's vast Central Coast region extends southward from Santa Cruz to the northern edge of Los Angeles County. Generally speaking, Pinot Noir and Chardonnay grow well throughout this area; Zinfandel and France's Rhône grape varieties—Syrah, Grenache, Mourvèdre and Viognier—also produce some superb wines here. Farther inland, east of San Francisco Bay, Lodi, in California's Central Valley, and the sprawling Sierra Foothills region are famous for old-vine Zinfandels.

California Wine Labels

California labels list the winery name, region (officially known as an AVA, or American Viticultural Area), vintage and grape. U.S. law dictates that a wine labeled with an AVA must contain at least 85 percent grapes from that specific region. Wines that bear the name of a single grape must contain 75 percent of that variety, though regulations in certain counties are stricter. Blending, however, is an important winemaking technique for many producers, particularly in Napa, where a combination of different grapes often results in wines of greater complexity. Some of California's finest wines are blends of various Bordeaux grapes (see p. 171), a style that carries the legally recognized moniker "Meritage" (pronounced like "heritage"). While the term "Reserve" appears on some vintners' finer wines, it has no legally recognized meaning.

california whites

California's enormous and varied geography gives its wine-makers the ability to craft white wines in a range of styles, from light, floral and crisp to full-bodied, concentrated and high in alcohol. Many of the best whites, however, are produced in the state's cooler regions, such as Sonoma County's Russian River Valley.

CALIFORNIA WHITES

chardonnay

Chardonnay is California's most planted variety and arguably America's most popular grape; almost every wine-maker in the state makes a Chardonnay. In fact, California's hallmark style of Chardonnay—laden with butterscotch and tropical fruit flavors bolstered by spicy toasted oak—was synonymous with "white wine" in the U.S. for many years. While that full-bodied, opulent style still exists, especially in many mass-produced industrial brands, the trend today among quality vintners is to make leaner, more elegant and food-friendly Chardonnays balanced with refreshing acidity and minerality.

chardonnay recommendations

Barefoot | NV | **CALIFORNIA**
★ $ This simple non-vintage white is a perfect picnic wine, complete with crisp, delicious peach and apple flavors.

Byron | 2007 | **SANTA MARIA VALLEY**
★★★ $ $ Both old and new vines in Byron's acclaimed Nielson Vineyard contribute to the delicious complexity of this Chardonnay, which offers layers of soft pear, quince and kiwi fruit, subtle oak creaminess and a broad finish.

Cakebread Cellars Reserve | 2006 | **CARNEROS**
★★★ $ $ $ Cakebread's rich, delicious, fruit-forward Chardonnays serve as benchmarks against which others are measured. This 2006 balances power and refinement with equal parts apple, pear and toasted nut flavors.

Cambria Katherine's Vineyard | 2007 | SANTA MARIA VALLEY

★★ $ Cambria's Katherine's Vineyard stands as testament to the excellent growing conditions in California's relatively cool Santa Maria Valley. A fine minerality imparts elegance and balance to this wine's exuberant tropical fruit flavors.

Clos du Bois Calcaire | 2007 | RUSSIAN RIVER VALLEY

★★★ $ $ Clos du Bois's Calcaire Chardonnays are consistently full-bodied and luscious, packed with apple, melon and pear flavors and a mouth-filling richness.

Cuvaison | 2007 | CARNEROS

★★ $ $ Made in a sustainable solar-powered winery, this white delivers succulent fig flavors along with pears and apples.

Fantesca Estate & Winery | 2006 | CARNEROS

★★★ $ $ $ This stunning Los Carneros Chardonnay brims with tropical fruit, ripe pink grapefruit and quince flavors underscored by zesty citrus, vanilla and a crisp minerality.

star producers
california chardonnay

Grgich Hills
Famous for powerful Cabernets and Chardonnays, this family-owned biodynamic winery uses clean energy from solar panels.

Kendall-Jackson
Although K-J makes wines at every price point, it is probably best known for its consistently delicious, best-selling Vintner's Reserve Chardonnay.

Kistler Vineyards
While his wines stand out for their distinctive Burgundian qualities, Steve Kistler eschews trendy Dijon clones for old California vines.

Patz & Hall
For more than 20 years Patz & Hall has been crafting single-vineyard Chardonnays and Pinot Noirs recognized for their evocative character.

Rochioli
Tom Rochioli has a unique ability to craft world-class wines with a stunning depth of flavor year after year.

Talley Vineyards
Talley's sumptuous, full-bodied Chardonnays have been compared to such Grand Cru white Burgundies as Corton-Charlemagne.

Ferrari-Carano Tré Terre | 2007 | RUSSIAN RIVER VALLEY

★★★ $ $ $ Grapes from six different vineyards endow this blend with a complex layering of super-ripe pear, apple and soft melon flavors; a bright citrus acidity keeps it elegant.

Foodies | 2006 | CALIFORNIA

★ $ As its name implies, this charming wine is designed for people who love food. Refreshing star fruit aromas and a bracing acidity make this a great everyday white.

Frei Brothers Reserve | 2006 | RUSSIAN RIVER VALLEY

★★ $ Russian River Valley Chardonnays tend to have a savory quality in addition to loads of fruit, and this is no exception. Ripe pear and citrus flavors are laced with notes of nutmeg, clove and spice.

Gallo Family Vineyards Two Rock Vineyard | 2005 | SONOMA COAST

★★ $ $ Long before Sonoma was a fashionable winegrowing region, the Gallo family knew it was a place worth exploring. This delightful Chardonnay displays elegant, earth-infused flavors of rich pear, apricot and baking spice.

Grgich Hills Estate | 2006 | NAPA VALLEY

★★★ $ $ $ Mike Grgich is the king of opulent, over-the-top California Chardonnays. This vintage is particularly rich, bursting with tropical fruit, honeysuckle and sweet oak, with nuances of minerals.

Hess Collection Estate Grown | 2007 | MOUNT VEEDER

★★ $ $ $ Swiss business tycoon Donald Hess set his sights on Mount Veeder over 30 years ago, and his winery has become known for beautifully layered wines like this one. Fruit-forward and nutty, it shows fig flavors and a pleasant vanilla finish.

Jordan | 2007 | RUSSIAN RIVER VALLEY

★★★ $ $ Although this powerhouse white is overflowing with thick layers of fruit and spice, it manages to stay remarkably balanced, thanks to a crisp, dry acidity.

Kendall-Jackson Vintner's Reserve | 2007 | CALIFORNIA

★ $ K-J's Chardonnay can be credited with bringing countless American sweet-wine drinkers up the ladder to dry whites. This crowd-pleaser exudes apple and clementine flavors.

Kenwood Vineyards Reserve | 2007 | RUSSIAN RIVER VALLEY

★★ $ $ Apples, spice and toasted oak characterize this wine year after year, and this vintage doesn't disappoint. Filled out with notes of soft melon and a mouthwatering acidity, it is balanced and pleasing.

La Crema | 2007 | **MONTEREY**
★★ $ $ From a longtime producer of dependable, affordable wines, this Monterey bottling is a serious effort, marked by fresh star fruit, spice and vanilla flavors on a creamy, round palate.

Mirassou | 2007 | **CALIFORNIA**
★ $ This is an ideal choice for everyday quaffing. Tangy yet sweet pineapple and passion fruit flavors are balanced by a citrusy acidity.

Ovation | 2006 | **SONOMA COAST**
★★★ $ $ $ Despite the fact that this unctuous Sonoma Coast white is aged in primarily new French oak, it still possesses a cleansing minerality and bright acidity that beautifully offset flavors of toasted nuts, ripe pear, melon and fig.

Patz & Hall Dutton Ranch | 2006 | **RUSSIAN RIVER VALLEY**
★★★ $ $ $ All of Patz & Hall's Chardonnays are delicious, yet this one stands out for its enticing white-flower and star fruit aromas, ripe pear, melon and apple flavors and overall elegance.

Simi | 2006 | **RUSSIAN RIVER VALLEY**
★★ $ $ Perhaps better known for its classy Cabernets, Simi also makes delightful Chardonnays, like this fleshy example full of overripe pear and apricot flavors brightened by citrus zest and nut notes.

St. Francis Winery | 2006 | **SONOMA COUNTY**
★★ $ St. Francis has crafted a great wine for the price here, with a big, expressive array of honeyed apricot and pear flavors. Accents of fig and melon are present in the opulent, butterscotch finish.

Talbott Diamond T Estate Cuvée Audrey | 2005 |
MONTEREY COUNTY
★★★★ $ $ $ $ Here's a stunning New World Chardonnay that overflows with a range of flavors from mango, pineapple and guava to honeysuckle and spice. It is rich and substantial, with generous toasted oak on the lengthy finish.

TAZ | 2007 | **SANTA BARBARA COUNTY**
★★ $ $ Santa Barbara Chardonnays can possess a unique spicy, earthy quality. TAZ's version is rounded out by pear and citrus flavors with ample earth notes.

Terlato Family Vineyards | 2007 | **RUSSIAN RIVER VALLEY**
★★★ $ $ This newcomer from legendary importer-turned-wine-maker Tony Terlato is textbook-perfect Sonoma Chardonnay: sweet fresh fig and spice notes infuse a base of tropical fruit flavors balanced with a hint of toasted oak.

Testarossa Sanford & Benedict Vineyard | 2007 |
SANTA RITA HILLS

★ ★ ★ $ $ $ Winemaker Bill Brosseau has been producing here for about a decade, and his wines just keep getting better and better. This single-vineyard offering serves up peach, nectarine and pear flavors, alongside citrusy acidity and a touch of oak.

Valley of the Moon Unoaked | 2007 | RUSSIAN RIVER VALLEY
★ ★ $ Valley of the Moon dependably produces great-value wines. This unoaked Chardonnay is all about clean, pure pear- and peach-flavored refreshment.

Votre Santé | 2007 | SONOMA COAST
★ ★ $ $ A tribute to Francis Ford Coppola's French-speaking grand-mother, this creamy, pear- and apple-saturated wine shows notes of green apple, lemon curd and minerals.

CALIFORNIA WHITES

sauvignon blanc

Sauvignon Blanc, the white grape of France's Bordeaux and Loire Valley regions, has long been second to Chardonnay in California in terms of popularity. Some versions are simple, fruity and sweet, but others are grassy, herbal and citrus-flavored with lots of refreshing acidity. The term "Fumé Blanc" appears on some labels to evoke a connection to the Loire's Pouilly-Fumé, but few of these wines taste anything like their French counterparts.

sauvignon blanc recommendations

Altamura | 2006 | NAPA VALLEY
★ ★ ★ $ $ $ Napa's Wooden Valley is home to vineyards where Pahl-meyer and Stags' Leap Winery buy fruit, but Altamura is the only winery there. Its Sauvignon is spicy, floral and bright, with layers of peach, pear and apricot flavors, a touch of nuttiness and a lush mouthfeel.

Beckmen Vineyards Purisima Mountain Vineyard | 2007 |
SANTA YNEZ VALLEY

★ ★ ★ $ $ Tom and Steve Beckmen's biodynamic vineyards yield intensely flavored wines. This peachy Sauvignon Blanc is dripping with lime and Granny Smith apple notes and has a luscious, thirst-quenching finish that lingers.

Cakebread Cellars | 2007 | NAPA VALLEY

★★ $ $ Cakebread harvests its Sauvignon Blanc grapes at night to protect the delicate fruit from the heat, which explains the vibrantly fresh aromas and flavors in this wine: vanilla, citrus and green apple are highlighted by spice.

Chateau St. Jean Lyon Vineyard Fumé Blanc | 2007 | ALEXANDER VALLEY

★★ $ All of St. Jean's well-crafted whites are dependably delicious and nicely priced. This blend of Sauvignon Blanc and a small amount of Semillon is marked by melon, apple, pear and fig flavors, vibrant acidity and a creamy mouthfeel.

Duckhorn Vineyards | 2007 | NAPA VALLEY

★★★ $ $ This is Duckhorn's 26th vintage making Sauvignon Blanc, and its style is both fresh and tropical, melding pink grapefruit, pineapple and spice flavors with a creamy finish.

Ferrari-Carano Fumé Blanc | 2008 | SONOMA COUNTY

★ $ Combining grapes from the Dry Creek, Alexander and Russian River valleys, Ferrari-Carano crafts this lush wine offering grapefruit, orange blossom and quince-paste flavors on the palate.

Geyser Peak Winery River Ranches | 2008 | RUSSIAN RIVER VALLEY

★★ $ $ With its cool climate, Russian River Valley is ideal for Sauvignon Blanc, and Geyser Peak's example is bright and floral, with honeysuckle aromas leading to flavors of melon and grapefruit on the lively, balanced finish.

Grgich Hills Fumé Blanc | 2007 | NAPA VALLEY

★★★ $ $ Mike Grgich crafts this biodynamic wine with a decidedly lighter hand than he reserves for his powerful Chardonnays, emphasizing fresh grass and citrus aromas, delicious melon and citrus flavors and a refreshingly bright and layered finish.

Handley | 2007 | DRY CREEK VALLEY

★★ $ Based in Anderson Valley, Handley owns a Dry Creek vineyard, where it makes this nicely priced white. It is perfumed with pear and lime, followed by sweet pear flavors and a crisp minerality.

Hanna | 2008 | RUSSIAN RIVER VALLEY

★★ $ The grapes used to produce this Russian River Sauvignon Blanc survived terrible frosts and a heat wave, yet the wine didn't suffer. Notes of lemon curd and papaya infuse a base of citrus, passion fruit and zesty grapefruit flavors.

Hess | 2007 | LAKE COUNTY
★ $ Vibrant acidity is the hallmark of this delicious bargain, which brings to life honey-coated white flower and citrus flavors.

Hilltown Vineyards | 2007 | MONTEREY COUNTY
★ $ This Monterey County Sauvignon is a perfect everyday wine, packed with citrus flavors and notes of green papaya and apple, balanced by a jolt of crisp acidity.

Honig Reserve | 2007 | RUTHERFORD
★ ★ $ $ An alluring mix of pink grapefruit, acacia flower, grass and lemon zest aromas gives way to intense Bosc pear and fig flavors in this well-built Sauvignon.

Joseph Phelps Vineyards | 2007 | ST. HELENA
★ ★ ★ $ $ $ Joseph Phelps goes tropical in this powerful, delectable wine, with an expressive bouquet of sweet mango, syrupy peaches, guava and dried apricot, upheld by lively acidity and clean minerality.

Kendall-Jackson Vintner's Reserve | 2007 | CALIFORNIA
★ $ Far lighter in style than K-J's iconic Chardonnay, this Sauvignon Blanc is nonetheless plush and refreshing, with sweet pear, peach and pineapple flavors. The finish is crisp and mineral-laden, making it pleasant to the last drop.

Line 39 | 2007 | LAKE COUNTY
★ ★ $ Located at the 39th degree of latitude, Line 39 offers this delicious Sauvignon for a remarkably low price. Pineapple and kiwi flavors have a mouthwatering finish.

Markham Vineyards | 2007 | NAPA VALLEY
★ ★ $ Markham's reputation is based on its fruit-forward Sauvignon Blancs. This affordable, tropical fruit–dominated example is filled out with ripe peach and apricot flavors on the palate, underpinned by a refreshing minerality.

Robert Mondavi Winery To Kalon Vineyard Reserve Fumé Blanc | 2007 | NAPA VALLEY
★ ★ ★ $ $ $ Mondavi's legendary To Kalon Vineyard in Napa creates this complex Sauvignon with a gorgeous bouquet of white peaches, guava and quince. Juicy ripe fruit on the palate is combined with a cleansing acidity.

Tin Roof Cellars | 2007 | CALIFORNIA
★ $ From California's north coast comes this satisfying and straightforward white with notes of fig and fennel, a rich palate of pear and citrus flavors and a crisp, clean finish.

other california whites

More than 100 grape varieties are planted in California, but only about 15 are commonly used for the production of white wine. Riesling makes light, floral, dry and off-dry wines, as well as some late-harvest dessert wines, sometimes with the addition of Semillon in the style of Sauternes. Floral Gewürztraminer and citrusy Pinot Gris (Pinot Grigio) yield respectable wines in cooler climes, while the Rhône Valley's Marsanne, Roussanne and Viognier thrive in the state's more Mediterranean-like regions.

other california white recommendations

Angel Juice Pinot Grigio | 2008 | **CALIFORNIA**
★ **$** (3 L) This light-bodied Pinot Grigio–dominated white comes in a three-liter bag-in-box, which means a lot of wine for not a lot of money. A bright, floral nose is followed by juicy, ripe citrus and creamy baked apple flavors.

AutoMoto Riesling | 2007 | **CALIFORNIA**
★ **$** From California's cool Central Coast comes this easy-drinking Riesling; crafted in a rich style, it offers flavors of peach, tangerine and lemonade accented by minerals.

Blackstone Winery Pinot Grigio | 2007 | **CALIFORNIA**
★ **$** This is Blackstone's third vintage of Pinot Grigio, and it is a pleasing, refreshing white with notes of apple, pear and citrus and a hint of spice on the finish.

Bonny Doon Vineyard Beeswax Vineyard Le Cigare Blanc | 2007 | **ARROYO SECO**
★★★ **$ $** Made from Roussanne and Grenache Blanc grapes, this white blend has an aromatic bouquet of succulent peach, honeydew and orange blossoms. Bright acidity electrifies flavors of stone fruit, ripe pear and minerals.

Bridlewood Estate Winery Reserve Viognier | 2007 | **CENTRAL COAST**
★★ **$ $** Also a working horse farm, Bridlewood Estate is known for its Syrah and Viognier. This delicious version has an intense, spicy-peachy nose, ripe white peach and apricot flavors and a vibrant, orange zest–like finish.

Byron Pinot Blanc | 2007 | SANTA MARIA VALLEY

★ ★ $ Santa Barbara County's cool climate and Byron's gravity-feed techniques combine to produce a superior Pinot Blanc. Aromas of honeysuckle and acacia give way to peach, fig and melon flavors.

Ca' del Solo Muscat | 2008 | MONTEREY COUNTY

★ ★ $ Vintner Randall Grahm—a passionate convert to biodynamic winemaking—makes this fragrant, refreshing Muscat with potent honeysuckle, orange zest and ripe peach on the palate.

Calera Viognier | 2007 | MOUNT HARLAN

★ ★ ★ $ $ Tasting Calera's ultraripe Viognier is like biting into a juicy apricot. Beautifully rich, mouth-filling and unctuous, it is layered with melon, apple, sweet fig and citrus flavors that linger.

Clif Family Winery The Climber White Wine | 2008 | CALIFORNIA

★ $ From the people behind the Clif Bar brand, this blend of five varieties—Sauvignon Blanc, Muscat, Riesling, Chardonnay and Chenin Blanc—is made by the talented Sarah Gott. Spiced flavors of mango, peach and apricot make for a rich finish.

Cline Viognier | 2007 | CALIFORNIA

★ $ A product of Fred Cline's Green String farming technique—a growing practice that goes above and beyond standard organic practices—this bright and drinkable Viognier is rich with citrus and melon flavors and balanced by a lively acidity.

Concannon Selected Vineyards Pinot Grigio | 2008 | CENTRAL COAST

★ ★ $ This tasty Pinot Grigio is a great value for its spicy ripe pear, honeysuckle and subtle nut flavors.

Daniel Gehrs Riesling | 2007 | MONTEREY COUNTY

★ ★ $ A smallish yield brought on by an unusually cold, dry winter didn't diminish the quality of this well-made Monterey Riesling. An enticing blend of dense apricot and honey flavors is accented by rich notes of white peach.

Estancia Pinot Grigio | 2008 | CALIFORNIA

★ $ Crisp and mineral-laden, Estancia's Pinot Grigio has grapefruit zest and sweet peach aromatics and a zingy, citrusy finish.

Handley Gewürztraminer | 2007 | ANDERSON VALLEY

★ ★ $ Handley uses certified organic grapes to produce this textured, expressive wine with sweet lychee flavors woven with grapefruit and tangerine.

Kendall-Jackson Vintner's Reserve Riesling | 2007 |
CALIFORNIA
★ $ A well-crafted wine from a familiar name, this Riesling opens with an acacia flower and peach bouquet, rounded out by zippy, juicy flavors of stone fruit and a touch of sweetness.

Mirassou Riesling | 2007 | CALIFORNIA
★ $ Bold, floral tangerine and honey flavors characterize this juicy Riesling; the fruit-forward palate has a spicy finish that lingers.

Terra d'Oro Pinot Grigio | 2007 | SANTA BARBARA COUNTY
★ $ This winery, which originally made wines under the Montevina label, was named in honor of the region's "gold country" heritage. Its crisp, mineral-laden Pinot Grigio displays delicious melon flavors.

Trefethen Family Vineyards Dry Riesling | 2007 |
OAK KNOLL DISTRICT OF NAPA VALLEY
★ ★ $ $ Trefethen's Chardonnay made headlines when it took top honors in the famous 1979 Wine Olympics. Its enjoyable Riesling, dripping with aromatic flavors of ripe peach, citrus and minerals, is beautifully balanced with snappy acidity.

california rosés

Rosé continues to rise in popularity. Long the underdog of the wine world—thanks to insipid, sweet White Zinfandels, which gave all pink wines a bad name—rosé is increasingly appreciated as dry and food-friendly. Rosé imports have increased in recent years, and California vintners are answering demand with berry-scented wines that are perfect for quaffing during warm weather. The best are made with Sangiovese, Grenache, Pinot Noir or Carignane.

california rosé recommendations

Bonny Doon Vineyard Vin Gris de Cigare | 2008 | CALIFORNIA
★ ★ $ Bonny Doon's much-loved Vin Gris is a consistently delicious bargain, beginning with a beautiful floral bouquet, a generous mouthful of raspberries and a kiss of strawberry and vanilla.

Concannon Selected Vineyards Righteously Rosé | 2008 |
LIVERMORE VALLEY
★ $ With its attractive pink hue and inviting raspberry and watermelon aromas, this drinkable rosé is packed with strawberry flavors.

Francis Coppola Sofia Rosé | 2008 | MONTEREY COUNTY

★ ★ $ Monterey experienced an unusually cold 2008 growing season, which no doubt contributed to the delicate flavors in Coppola's rosé. A blend of Syrah and Grenache, this pretty pink wine is layered with delectable raspberry and strawberry flavors.

Navarro Vineyards Rosé | 2008 | MENDOCINO

★ ★ $ Mendocino County's family-owned Navarro winery crafts this spicy, strawberry-scented quaffer boasting cherry blossom and hyacinth aromas and delicious, spicy red fruit flavors.

Rutherford Hill Rosé | 2007 | NAPA VALLEY

★ ★ $ A pioneer of California Merlot, Rutherford Hill blends Merlot with Cabernet Franc and Zinfandel to make this ginger- and violet-scented beauty of a rosé. Soft and sweet, it offers flavors of cherries, berries and a hint of watermelon.

california reds

Cabernet Sauvignon is the wine that put California on the international map back in the 1970s, most famously when a California Cabernet won the top prize at a tasting in Paris. Although Cabernet remains the state's most iconic wine, fetching the highest praise and prices, there are other standout reds, such as jammy, spicy Zinfandels (especially those crafted from old vines) and the powerful Rhône-style wines championed by the so-called Rhone Rangers (see "Other California Reds," p. 192), made from grapes such as Syrah, Petite Sirah, Grenache, Mourvèdre and Carignane.

CALIFORNIA REDS
cabernet sauvignon & bordeaux blends

Cabernet Sauvignon is the undisputed king of *all* grapes in California, thanks to its ability to create wines of extraordinary complexity, power and longevity. As winemakers have figured out how to manage the development of the grape's formidable tannins, the resulting wines just keep getting more concentrated and better. While Cabernet plantings on California's valley floors can develop intense berry flavors, the trend of late for expensive Cabernets is toward hillside vineyards, where some growers are cultivating vines that yield wines full of blackberry flavors and earthy, smoky characteristics. Cabernet blends beautifully, too, particularly when paired with other Bordeaux varieties such as Merlot, Cabernet Franc, Petit Verdot and Malbec. These blends may be labeled "Meritage," while others carry their own proprietary names, like Conn Creek's "Anthology." Many Bordeaux varieties, including Merlot (see p. 178) and Cabernet Franc, are also bottled separately.

cabernet sauvignon recommendations

Altamura | 2005 | NAPA VALLEY
★ ★ ★ ★ $ $ $ $ Napa natives Frank and Karen Altamura founded this acclaimed vineyard, where they grow only Cabernet Sauvignon and Sangiovese, in 1985. This near-perfect red offers fragrant berry and black fruit aromas that lead to a concentrated, plush palate.

Atlas Peak | 2004 | NAPA VALLEY
★ ★ $ $ $ Sage, spice and black cherry aromas make a big first impression, giving way to flavors of red currants and blackberries held up by sweet tannins.

Brandlin | 2005 | MOUNT VEEDER
★ ★ ★ $ $ $ $ This estate and its vineyards, purchased by Cuvaison in 1998, yield impressive wines like this berry- and cherry-scented red with accents of cigar box and leather. Its firm tannins give structure and make it a perfect match for steak.

Carpe Diem | 2006 | NAPA VALLEY
★ ★ $ $ Overseen by Bordeaux superstar Christian Moueix, this red possesses blackberry and fresh-cut herb aromas, spicy black currant flavors, a firm core of minerals and big, impressive tannins.

Chappellet "Signature" | 2006 | NAPA VALLEY
★ ★ ★ $ $ $ This stunningly complex wine is fragrant with currant, fennel, coffee and sage and delivers supple layers of blackberry, tobacco and mocha on the fine-grained palate.

Charles Krug | 2006 | YOUNTVILLE
★ ★ $ $ Peter Mondavi is in charge of Charles Krug, Napa's first winery, where he crafts delicious wines. This wine has aromas of sage, plum and cedar, while the palate yields ripe plum, currants and spice.

Chateau St. Jean Cinq Cépages | 2005 | **SONOMA COUNTY**
★ ★ ★ $ $ $ $ *Cinq cépages* means "five varieties" in French, yet this wine is undeniably Californian, with its ultraripe nose of dark fruit and fennel and dense, spicy palate.

Chimney Rock | 2006 | **STAGS LEAP DISTRICT**
★ ★ ★ $ $ $ Black cherry, dusty sage and tobacco aromas complement the dark berry, prune and cedar flavors in this Cabernet. Supple tannins make it accessible now, although it is capable of aging.

Clos du Bois Briarcrest | 2004 | **ALEXANDER VALLEY**
★ ★ $ $ $ An explosion of black fruit is accompanied by a whiff of fennel in this Cabernet. Layers of fine tannins support flavors of plum, dried currant and raisin into the sweet, cedary finish.

star producers
california cabernet sauvignon

Altamura
Though hardly a "sleeper" winery, Altamura has been quietly receiving praise from critics for the last ten vintages of their impressive Cabernets.

Beaulieu Vineyard
Beaulieu makes excellent wines for every budget but earns its reputation for its amazingly powerful Georges de Latour Private Reserve Cabernet Sauvignon.

Harlan Estate
This estate's 240 acres of premium Napa terroir yield two of the region's most coveted Cabernet-based Bordeaux-style blends.

Hundred Acre
Consulting winemaker Philippe Melka has a hand in crafting Hundred Acre's highly prized wines; owner Jayson Woodbridge is the bigger-than-life force that drives the legend.

Robert Mondavi Winery
Synonymous with quality and dynamism in California, Napa-based Mondavi has been crafting benchmark wines for more than 40 years.

Staglin Family
This Napa Valley heavyweight produces its full-bodied wines from 100 percent organic grapes that possess intense fruit character and soft tannins.

173

Corison Kronos Vineyard | 2004 | NAPA VALLEY
★★★★ $ $ $ $ Cathy Corison honed her winemaking skills at some of California's finest wineries before setting out on her own. Her elegant 2004 Kronos Cabernet is truly world-class. A complex range of flavors—blackberries, earth, minerals and sage—comes together in the well-integrated finish.

Cuvaison | 2006 | MOUNT VEEDER
★★ $ $ $ This wine engages with fragrant, dusty sage, wet stone and wild berry aromatics and follows up with mouth-filling black fruit and mocha flavors, a full body and chewy tannins.

Dancing Bull | 2006 | CALIFORNIA
★ $ Rancho Zabaco specializes in Zinfandel, but its low-priced and delicious Cabernet is well worth seeking out for its juicy blackberry flavors and sweet, supple tannins.

Eponymous | 2005 | NAPA VALLEY
★★★ $ $ $ Proprietor Bob Pepi sources fruit from a terraced, rocky vineyard 300 feet above the Silverado Trail for this wine. The nose on his robust 2005 is dominated by cassis and black cherry aromas, followed by flavors of blackberries and red currants. Bright acidity and bold tannins ensure a structured and elegant finish.

Gallo Family Vineyards Barrelli Creek Vineyard | 2004 | ALEXANDER VALLEY
★★ $ $ $ Soft, earthy tannins supply the backbone for this well-made wine, which is redolent of spice, fennel, blackberry and cedar and has a lush mouthfeel.

Hess | 2006 | MENDOCINO, LAKE AND NAPA COUNTIES
★★ $ Sourcing fruit from three sustainably farmed vineyards in three separate appellations, Hess produces this enticing red marked by flavors of plum and wild raspberry.

Honig | 2006 | NAPA VALLEY
★★★ $ $ $ Few wineries are as green as Honig, where solar power fuels the winery, biodiesel fuels the tractors, and owls are relied upon to take care of the rodent population. The brawny Cabernet boasts black currant and blackberry flavors and a long finish.

Hundred Acre Kayli Morgan Vineyard | 2006 | NAPA VALLEY
★★★★ $ $ $ $ This masterpiece represents the pinnacle of what Napa Valley is capable of: a spectacular nose of mocha, cassis and wild raspberry yields to opulent dark berry flavors, ripe tannins and a touch of cedar on the long finish.

Jordan | 2005 | ALEXANDER VALLEY

★★★ $ $ $ Jordan serves as a benchmark for classically constructed Sonoma Cabernet. Their juicy, succulent 2005 offers a nose of plum, blackberry and fresh-cut herbs and a palate rich with black cherry, earth and ripe tannins.

Joseph Phelps Vineyards | 2006 | NAPA VALLEY

★★★ $ $ $ More affordable than Phelps's famous Insignia, this is arguably the better value, given its high quality. Its spicy dark berry aromas reveal hints of fresh herbs, and its fine-grained tannins give structure to flavors of black cherry and blackberry.

Justin Vineyards & Winery Reserve | 2006 | PASO ROBLES

★★★ $ $ $ Justin sources grapes from its estate vineyard as well as a select group of growers throughout the appellation. This Cabernet is powerful and big-boned but not at all clumsy. Ripe, juicy blackberry, sage and cedar flavors are savory and balanced.

Kenwood Vineyards 30th Anniversary Artist Series | 2004 | SONOMA COUNTY

★★★★ $ $ $ $ Artist Shepard Fairey (of Obama poster fame) designed the label art for this blockbuster Cabernet. Licorice, blackberry and black cherry aromas come on strong, while flavors of coffee, earth and leather saturate the palate.

Kuleto Estate | 2004 | NAPA VALLEY

★★★ $ $ $ Bay Area restaurateur Pat Kuleto puts just as much thought into his wines as he does his restaurants. The lively black fruit flavors here are framed by supple tannins through the long finish.

L de Lyeth | 2006 | SONOMA COUNTY

★ $ Mint and cherry aromas on the forefront of this low-priced Cabernet are rounded out by notes of mocha, blackberry and vanilla.

Louis M. Martini | 2006 | SONOMA COUNTY

★★ $ This Gallo-owned property has long specialized in Cabernet. The 2006 vintage combines fragrant earth, black currant, raisin and fennel flavors with soft, approachable tannins, for a fair price.

Markham Vineyards | 2005 | NAPA VALLEY

★★ $ $ Markham sources Cabernet grapes from some of the finest vineyards in Napa, and the resulting wine is a delightful mix of red berries, spice and soft, sweet tannins.

Mount Veeder Winery | 2005 | NAPA VALLEY

★★ $ $ $ Notes of plum, cherry and mocha embellish this wine's solid core of black fruit and oak flavors, supported by chewy tannins.

Sequoia Grove | 2005 | NAPA VALLEY
★ ★ $ $ Thanks to 18 months of aging in American oak, this Cabernet has aromas of coffee, earth, sweet spice and cassis that complement the bold flavors of black cherry, plum and leather. Firm tannins add structure and refinement.

The Show | 2006 | CALIFORNIA
★ ★ $ This Cabernet is adorned with a range of eye-catching cowboy-themed labels designed by Nashville's famous Hatch Show Print. Its delicious currant, mocha and spice flavors are just as appealing.

Souverain Winemaker's Reserve | 2005 | ALEXANDER VALLEY
★ ★ $ $ $ There is nothing shy about this hearty Cabernet: a nose of mocha, black cherry, espresso and nutmeg precedes generous flavors of ripe black fruit held up by firm tannins.

Staglin Family Vineyard Estate | 2006 | RUTHERFORD
★ ★ ★ ★ $ $ $ $ Staglin's 2006 release is as elegant as it is powerful. Up-front cedar and plum aromas give way to layers of mineral-laden black fruit flavors in the mouth, supported by well-integrated tannins all the way through the massive finish.

Stags' Leap Winery | 2005 | NAPA VALLEY
★ ★ ★ $ $ $ Not to be confused with Stag's Leap Wine Cellars, this winery holds its own with stellar wines like this bold Cabernet. Waves of flavors—mocha, tobacco and black cherry—are cast upon strong yet approachable tannins.

St. Clement Vineyards Oroppas | 2006 | NAPA VALLEY
★ ★ ★ $ $ $ Winemaker Danielle Cyrot is an up-and-coming Napa star, with winemaking roots that go way back (her ancestors owned the Cyrot vineyard in Burgundy). She ages this wine in French oak for 19 months, which adds a kick of vanilla to flavors of spice, red currant, blackberry and wet stone.

Terlato Family Vineyards | 2005 | STAGS LEAP DISTRICT
★ ★ ★ $ $ $ This ripe, robust wine is loaded with all types of black fruit—berry, currant and cherry. Concentrated and intense, the soft finish makes it immensely drinkable.

Trefethen Family Vineyards | 2005 |
OAK KNOLL DISTRICT OF NAPA VALLEY
★ ★ ★ $ $ $ Trefethen is one of the few Napa wineries that grows Riesling, but Cabernet remains its specialty. This boasts a zippy nose of cherry and licorice, while ripe, dark fruit and earthy flavors predominate on the firm but harmonious palate.

bordeaux blend recommendations

Bond Pluribus | 2005 | NAPA VALLEY
★★★★ $ $ $ $ This wine deserves its cult following. A wonderfully complex blend, it is bursting with aromas of violets, acacia flowers, blueberry pie, earth and sweet spice. Layers of sweet tannins and clean minerals keep it beautifully balanced.

Cakebread Cellars Dancing Bear Ranch Cabernet Sauvignon/Cabernet Franc | 2005 | HOWELL MOUNTAIN
★★ $ $ $ $ Named for the black bears that steal fruit from Cake-bread's vineyards, this savory blend of Cabernets Sauvignon and Franc offers delicious currant, black cherry and juicy plum flavors.

Dominus | 2005 | NAPA VALLEY
★★★ $ $ $ $ Another red made by Bordeaux native Christian Moueix, this is primarily Cabernet Sauvignon, with splashes of Cabernet Franc and Petit Verdot. It is evocative and spicy, with black cherry, currant, licorice and cassis flavors that are both bright and lush.

Eponymous MacAllister Vineyard | 2006 | SONOMA VALLEY
★★ $ $ $ A single vineyard in Sonoma was responsible for the fruit in this blend. The result is a spicy wine with currant and big, chunky black cherry flavors and a plush mouthfeel firmed by tannins.

Harlan Estate | 2005 | NAPA VALLEY
★★★★ $ $ $ $ The exorbitant price tag does nothing to dissuade ardent fans from this highly sought Napa Valley red. Its meaty nose shows hints of plum and violet, and the palate explodes with dense fruit flavors that are perfectly integrated with sweet tannins through the incredibly long finish.

Havens Bourriquot | 2005 | NAPA VALLEY
★★★ $ $ $ This massive yet graceful blend exudes multiple layers of red berries and mint, with robust raspberries and blueberries coming through on the supple finish.

Hess Collection 19 Block Cuvée | 2006 | MOUNT VEEDER
★★ $ $ $ This blend of primarily Cabernet, Syrah and Malbec is defined by ultraripe and juicy plum, dark berry and earth flavors.

Joseph Phelps Insignia | 2006 | NAPA VALLEY
★★★★ $ $ $ $ The nose on Phelps's iconic Napa red is full and fragrant, delivering aromas of berries and minerals and a whiff of dried sage. In the mouth it's all dark berry and baking spice flavors and powerful, sweet tannins on the finish.

Lyeth Meritage | 2006 | **SONOMA COUNTY**
★ ★ $ Cabernet Sauvignon, Merlot and Cabernet Franc are joined to soft, supple effect in this blend, offering mocha, spice and black cherry flavors supported by medium tannins.

Pahlmeyer | 2006 | **NAPA VALLEY**
★ ★ ★ ★ $ $ $ $ This Cabernet Sauvignon–dominated blend proves that Pahlmeyer is capable of more than great Merlot. Heavily laden with minerals and berry flavors, this robust red boasts sweet tannins, a rich mouthfeel and a massive finish.

Roy Estate | 2006 | **NAPA VALLEY**
★ ★ ★ ★ $ $ $ $ Philippe Melka, a terroir-obsessed Bordeaux native, has composed a wine that expresses both Old World elegance and New World concentration. Aromas of red and black currants, cocoa and pepper give way to a palate of dark fruit, earth and oak.

Rubicon | 2005 | **NAPA VALLEY**
★ ★ ★ $ $ $ $ This Coppola wine is the Godfather of Napa blends. Its alluring combination of brooding dark berry fruit accented by earthy undertones, spice and tight tannins is utterly irresistible.

Xtant | 2004 | **NAPA VALLEY**
★ ★ ★ $ $ $ $ Jeff Gaffner, who also owns his own label, Saxon Brown, crafted this full-bodied blend of Cabernet Sauvignon, Merlot and Malbec, which delivers chocolate, plum and berry flavors with beautifully integrated tannins and firming acidity.

CALIFORNIA REDS

merlot

Despite Merlot's well-publicized ups and downs, Americans still drink nearly as much of it as Cabernet—and consumption is rising. The "other half" of the grape duo that creates the world's great Bordeaux and California Bordeaux-style blends, Merlot is the softer counterpart to Cabernet's power. In the 1990s, Merlot became popular as a fruity, accessible red. Unfortunately, with popularity came overproduction, and as many lower-quality Merlots flooded the marketplace, the grape earned a reputation for mediocrity. Fortunately, that reputation is increasingly unwarranted. Today, there are countless stellar Merlots worth seeking out for their plush fruit and flavor concentration.

merlot recommendations

Chateau St. Jean | 2006 | **SONOMA COUNTY**
★★ $ $ This wine displays many layers of red fruit nicely woven with hints of sage and mocha and a pinch of fennel on the earthy finish.

Clos Du Val | 2006 | **NAPA VALLEY**
★★ $ $ A gorgeous nose of tart cherries and rhubarb is followed by rich, concentrated black cherry and blackberry jam flavors; small additions of Cabernet Sauvignon and Cabernet Franc contribute tannins and structure.

Concannon Selected Vineyards | 2007 | **CENTRAL COAST**
★ $ Even though it is low-priced and produced in large quantities, this Central Coast Merlot shows impressive depth. Its plum, cherry and cola flavors lead to a spicy, earthy finish.

news from a wine insider

california by Laurie Daniel, wine columnist, *San Jose Mercury News*

Vintage Note

Weather and wildfires made California's 2008 growing season difficult. The crop was smaller than normal and there was some uneven ripening, but thanks to good harvest-time weather, producers are generally happy with the wines' quality.

Notable New Wines

Winemaker Andy Erickson, vineyard manager David Abreu and consultant Michel Rolland are the creative talents behind Ovid, a relatively new, high-end winery on Pritchard Hill in Napa Valley. The 2005 Ovid is dense and spicy, with plump black fruit flavors and firm structure.

Look also for Bacchant Wines' well-priced Luli Chardonnay, a collaboration between Master Sommelier Sara Floyd and the Pisoni family of Pisoni Vineyards & Winery.

Region to Watch

Happy Canyon, in the Santa Ynez Valley in Santa Barbara County, is awaiting approval as an AVA (American Viticultural Area) but has already made a name for itself with Sauvignon Blancs from producers like Margerum Wine Company, Vogelzang Vineyard, Ojai Vineyard and Fiddlehead Cellars. Now the region's red wines are garnering acclaim.

Duckhorn Vineyards | 2006 | **NAPA VALLEY**
★★ $ $ Having spent 16 months in French oak, this wine starts off tightly wound and structured. A bit of time in the glass reveals aromas of chocolate-covered cherries and a plush palate of black cherry, vanilla, earth and spicy oak.

Ehlers Estate | 2006 | **ST. HELENA**
★★★ $ $ $ Ehlers's certified organic vineyards produce mineral- and herb-infused wines. The 2006 vintage showcases a compelling mix of ripe blackberries, currants, mint, sage and pencil lead.

FishEye | 2006 | **CALIFORNIA**
★ $ (3 L) This fabulous bargain wine (which comes in a three-liter box format) delivers ample bright red cherry and blackberry flavors for a very affordable price.

Gallo Family Vineyards Sonoma Reserve | 2006 | **SONOMA COUNTY**
★ $ A crowd-pleasing, easy-drinking Merlot in the classic juicy style, this offers black cherry flavors with hints of mocha and coffee.

Killer Juice | 2006 | **CENTRAL COAST**
★ $ (3 L) For less than $20, Killer Juice supplies three-liters of well-made, medium-bodied Merlot, full of good tannins to balance the juicy berry flavors laced with black pepper.

Markham Vineyards | 2006 | **NAPA VALLEY**
★★ $ $ Here is a California Merlot with the somewhat rare ability to age, thanks to its tight tannins and good structure. Layered flavors of ripe currants and berries make it drinkable now as well.

Montevina Winery | 2007 | **CALIFORNIA**
★ $ Montevina's debut Merlot is exceptionally refreshing, a result of the invigorating acidity of its cool-climate fruit. Soft in flavor and finish, it offers intriguing violet and cherry aromas on the nose.

Pahlmeyer | 2006 | **NAPA VALLEY**
★★★★ $ $ $ $ A master at Bordeaux-style blending, Pahlmeyer uses 89 percent Merlot and 11 percent Cabernet Sauvignon to craft this gorgeous wine. Bold flavors of mocha, coffee, black cherry and prune are held up by plush tannins and fresh acidity through the intense and lasting finish.

Peju Estate Bottled | 2005 | **NAPA VALLEY**
★★ $ $ $ Peju's organically and sustainably farmed vineyards yield this black fruit–saturated wine with spice and mocha notes. Supple tannins, vanilla and spice mark the long finish.

Rutherford Hill Reserve | 2005 | **NAPA VALLEY**
★ ★ ★ $ $ $ This is a stunning example of what Merlot is capable of in California: mouth-filling and satisfying flavors of black cherry and dark chocolate are upheld by fine tannins and juicy acidity.

St. Clement Vineyards | 2006 | **NAPA VALLEY**
★ ★ $ $ Young winemaker Danielle Cyrot shows her blending prowess, melding flavors of black cherry, raspberry and prune with the perfect touch of oak in this firm yet drinkable wine.

Trefethen Family Vineyards | 2005 |
OAK KNOLL DISTRICT OF NAPA VALLEY
★ ★ $ $ Made in the Oak Knoll District, one of the cooler areas of Napa, this wine offers nice cranberry and tomato-accented flavors alongside riper black cherry and smoky plum notes. A hint of peppery spice on the palate adds complexity.

CALIFORNIA REDS

pinot noir

Pinot Noir is one of the most persnickety of grapes, hard to grow even in its homeland of Burgundy. California vintners have wrestled with it for decades, trying to replicate the smoky, earthy qualities that characterize French examples. While there are many light, cherry-flavored California Pinots at affordable prices, the better ones are costly—a consequence of all the work that goes into making them. The finest come from cool regions like the Russian River Valley, Carneros, Mendocino and the Central Coast, including Santa Barbara County (especially Santa Maria Valley).

pinot noir recommendations

Artesa | 2007 | **CARNEROS**
★ ★ $ $ Owned by the Codorníu Group—the giant Spanish winemaker best known for its sparkling Cavas—Artesa is one of Napa's newer wineries. This $25 Pinot Noir is a great buy, offering notes of cedar and a bounty of strawberry, cherry and cinnamon flavors.

B.R. Cohn | 2006 | **RUSSIAN RIVER VALLEY**
★ ★ ★ $ $ $ B.R. Cohn made fewer than 1,000 cases of this much-acclaimed, silky-textured wine; 19 months in oak adds caramel and spice to flavors of black cherry, fig and earth.

Buena Vista Ramal Vineyard | 2005 | CARNEROS
★★ $ $ $ In this concentrated, spicy bottling, winemaker Jeff Stewart balances red cherry flavors—a hallmark of Carneros Pinot Noir—with a subtle earthy mushroom quality.

Byron | 2007 | SANTA MARIA VALLEY
★★ $ $ As one of California's cooler grape-growing regions, Santa Maria Valley imparts good acidity and an intriguing smoky character to this well-priced wine's full-bodied flavors of flowers and cherries.

Calera Reed Vineyard | 2006 | MOUNT HARLAN
★★★ $ $ $ Reed is one of Calera's oldest vineyards and yields wines with a meaty, wild quality. This lively example has black raspberry, cedar, tar and pepper flavors with a savory finish.

Cambria Bench Break Vineyard | 2007 | SANTA MARIA VALLEY
★★ $ $ Bench Break Vineyard is Cambria's most austere vineyard site, from which this dark, brooding wine picks up a core of minerals that run throughout the ripe dark fruit and cola flavors.

Carmel Road | 2007 | MONTEREY
★★ $ Carmel Road makes another, more expensive Pinot Noir, but it's hard to beat this low-priced beauty, characterized by luscious cherry flavors and accents of vanilla, minerals and earth.

Clos Du Val | 2007 | CARNEROS
★ $ $ Many don't even realize that Cabernet-specialist Clos Du Val produces a Pinot Noir. A near-perfect 2007 growing season makes this an especially good vintage—bursting with ripe cherry and clove flavors—for discovering it.

Cuvaison | 2007 | CARNEROS
★★★ $ $ $ Napa stalwart Cuvaison has been growing grapes here since 1969, and with winemaker Steven Rogstad at the helm today, the wines have never been better. Made with estate fruit, this shows fragrant strawberry flavors underscored by smoke and tobacco.

Daniel Gehrs Limited | 2006 | SANTA BARBARA COUNTY
★★★ $ $ $ In a sea of California Pinot Noirs that taste the same, this limited-edition wine stands out for its distinctive array of deep-earth, spice and heady kirsch flavors.

DeLoach | 2007 | RUSSIAN RIVER VALLEY
★★★ $ $ In 2003 Burgundy's Boisset family purchased this long-time Russian River Valley producer, and the wines shine under their direction. This well-priced, medium-bodied Pinot shows bright rhubarb and strawberry flavors, a medium body and great acidity.

Etude Temblor | 2006 | CARNEROS

★★★ $ $ $ $ Etude founder Tony Soter describes Pinot Noir as the most "unforgiving and quixotic" of all grapes, yet he manages to do amazing things with it. In its second year of production—at a mere 500 cases—his Temblor shows a refined mix of red raspberries, violets, spicy vanilla and a whiff of tobacco.

Fogdog | 2006 | SONOMA COAST

★★ $ $ $ A "fogdog" is a light or clear spot that appears in a fog; in this wine, it could refer to the bright acidity that nicely offsets dark, cedar-tinged flavors of black currant and spice.

Gloria Ferrer José S. Ferrer Selection | 2004 | CARNEROS

★★ $ $ $ Gloria Ferrer is known for some of the state's best sparkling wines but produces stellar still wines, too. This reserve bottling, named in honor of the winery's founder, offers caramel-accented dark fruit flavors balanced by good acidity and a silky texture.

star producers
california pinot noir

Aubert

Mark Aubert's resume includes stints with Peter Michael Winery, Colgin Cellars and Bryant Family Vineyard. Naturally, his Pinot Noirs are delicious—and hard to find.

DuMOL

Winemaker Andy Smith crafts superb Pinot Noirs from the cooler growing regions of the Russian River Valley and Sonoma Coast.

Goldeneye

This terrific Anderson Valley winery is owned by Napa's Duckhorn family. The Migration Pinot Noir made here is outstanding and affordable.

Pahlmeyer

Though generally known for exquisite Cabernets and Merlots, Jayson Pahlmeyer now makes Pinot Noirs under his second label, Jayson.

Paul Hobbs

Hobbs's approach to winemaking—involving the use of indigenous yeast, malolactic fermentation to soften acidity, and no filtration—results in spectacular wines.

Testarossa

Rob and Diana Jensen established Testarossa in 1993 to create terroir-driven Chardonnays and Pinot Noirs that express a sense of place.

Goldeneye | 2006 | ANDERSON VALLEY
★ ★ ★ $ $ $ Over a decade ago, Dan and Margaret Duckhorn traveled north from their eponymous winery in Napa to Anderson Valley to start this winery. Their outstanding Pinot Noir combines intriguing notes of anise and spice with flavors of cherry pie that finish clean.

Handley | 2007 | ANDERSON VALLEY
★ ★ ★ $ $ Winemaker Milla Handley arrived in the then-remote Anderson Valley in 1978. This remarkably elegant Pinot Noir, revealing medium-bodied flavors of vanilla, tart cherries and herbs, demonstates that few know how to express the terroir as beautifully as she.

Jayson | 2007 | SONOMA COAST
★ ★ ★ $ $ $ $ Jayson Pahlmeyer created this second label to find a home for leftover lots of his high-quality fruit. At around 15 percent alcohol, his Pinot is massive, rich and concentrated, with rhubarb and black cherries and a lingering finish.

La Crema | 2007 | RUSSIAN RIVER VALLEY
★ ★ $ $ $ La Crema makes wines from five different Sonoma appellations, and this expression is spicy and ripe yet shows a sturdy, concentrated finish, thanks to the Russian River Valley's cool climate.

Lyeth | 2006 | SONOMA COUNTY
★ ★ $ Credited with championing the meritage concept of Bordeaux blending in California, the Lyeth winery has a way with Pinot Noir as well: with vibrant, minty, baked cherry fruit and a chewy texture, at less than $20, this more than delivers.

Lynmar Estate | 2006 | RUSSIAN RIVER VALLEY
★ ★ ★ $ $ $ Lynn Fritz founded Lynmar Estate in 1990, after years of selling his top-notch grapes to some of Sonoma's most elite producers. His wines are decidedly more Burgundian than most California examples, as this outstanding, earthy Pinot shows.

Patz & Hall Jenkins Ranch | 2007 | SONOMA COAST
★ ★ $ $ $ One of the most coveted Pinot Noir labels, Patz & Hall specializes in single-vineyard bottlings. This smooth, medium-bodied expression is saturated with pomegranates and vibrant spice notes.

Paul Hobbs | 2007 | RUSSIAN RIVER VALLEY
★ ★ ★ ★ $ $ $ These days Hobbs is busy making wines in Argentina, yet spends enough time back home in California to craft some of the region's finest wines. Shy at first, this Pinot opens up in the glass to reveal a dizzying array of complex dark fruit, cola, herb and spiced oak flavors, all framed by supple yet formidable tannins.

Prophet Teac Mor Vineyard | 2006 | RUSSIAN RIVER VALLEY
★★★★ $ $ $ There are few Pinots as excellent as this for under $40. Light in color, with a refined texture, this expressive wine is dominated by smoke, earth and meat and rounded out by well-integrated bright rhubarb and currant notes.

Robert Mondavi Winery | 2007 | CARNEROS
★★ $ $ Tobacco, herbs, tea and fruit share center stage in Mondavi's well-built wine. These flavors are bolstered by sweet notes of vanilla and butterscotch, thanks to eight months in French oak barrels.

Saintsbury Brown Ranch | 2007 | CARNEROS
★★★ $ $ $ Saintsbury prides itself on wines that are robust yet show a rare Burgundian finesse. Brown Ranch was planted with Dijon clones in 1992; its volcanic soils and steep hillsides result in low yields of concentrated, powerful wines.

Saintsbury Garnet | 2007 | CARNEROS
★★ $ Don't be fooled by the screw cap and low price: this is delicious Pinot Noir, with generous cherry fruit and appealing hints of animal funk and smoke.

Sanford | 2007 | SANTA RITA HILLS
★★★ $ $ $ Santa Barbara pioneer Sanford has undergone a makeover by its new owner, and the results are on display in this ripe, rich, multilayered wine. Cranberries and cherries jump out of the glass; they are highlighted by dusty thyme and sage notes and supported by supple tannins.

Sea Smoke Southing | 2006 | SANTA RITA HILLS
★★★ $ $ $ Bob Davids founded Sea Smoke in 1999, and has since established the winery as one of the state's most exciting Pinot Noir producers. Santa Rita Hills' cool evenings endow this rich, floral wine with a firm backbone of acidity.

Sojourn Sangiacomo Vineyard | 2007 | SONOMA COAST
★★ $ $ $ Winemaker Erich Bradley believes 2007's growing conditions have yielded some of Sojourn's best wines ever. The Sangiacomo bottling is marked by cherries, earth and plums, which saturate a plush, creamy palate.

Testarossa Garys' Vineyard | 2007 | SANTA LUCIA HIGHLANDS
★★★★ $ $ $ The Italian word for redhead, Testarossa sources grapes from a vineyard shared by renowned grape-growers Gary Pisoni and Gary Franscioni for this 2007 Pinot. It is robust, spicy and beautifully textured, with a smooth, sappy, cherry-infused finish.

CALIFORNIA REDS

syrah

California's love affair with France's Rhône grape varieties began with Syrah. In cooler climates it yields lean and elegant wines, with spicy berry flavors and smoky aromas—occasionally comparable to northern Rhône wines. Syrah from warmer parts of the state tends to more closely resemble Australian Shiraz (the same grape), displaying spicy, dark berry flavors and often high levels of alcohol.

syrah recommendations

Arrowood Saralee's Vineyard | 2005 | RUSSIAN RIVER VALLEY
★★ $ $ $ This is dark, dense and textured, with aromas of currants, plums and meat. A kiss of oak marks the soft, mildly tannic finish.

Austin Hope Hope Family Vineyard | 2005 | PASO ROBLES
★★★ $ $ $ With both mocha and spice on the nose, Austin Hope's flagship wine opens with an explosion of blueberry and huckleberry flavors in the mouth, where plush tannins and a rich mouthfeel lead into a long, satisfying finish.

Beckmen Vineyards Purisima Mountain Vineyard | 2006 |
SANTA YNEZ VALLEY
★★★ $ $ $ Made with grapes grown on Beckmen's hillside property, this delicious red has a spicy nose, with hints of dusty sage and black tea, leading to a solid core of blackberry and black cherry in the mouth and firm tannins on a long finish.

Big House The Slammer | 2006 | CENTRAL COAST
★ $ With its tongue-in-cheek label humor ("criminally rich Syrah"), this Central Coast Syrah is a great value for everyday drinking, loaded with red cherry and plum flavors.

Blackstone Winery | 2007 | CALIFORNIA
★ $ Blackstone's ability to produce wines that are both wallet- and palate-friendly is once again on display. Well made, with plum and juicy cherry flavors, this is a great party wine.

Bonny Doon Vineyard Le Pousseur | 2006 | CENTRAL COAST
★★ $ This very drinkable blend of mostly Syrah and some Grenache opens with a blueberry pie nose, leading into bright plum flavors and a touch of spice on the satisfying finish.

Clif Gary's Improv | 2006 | NAPA VALLEY

★★ $ $ $ The word "improv" here refers to the different grape varieties that are used to make this Syrah-dominated blend from year to year. The 2006 exudes aromas of rose petals and blueberries, with sweet berries on the palate.

Concannon Selected Vineyards | 2006 | CENTRAL COAST

★★ $ Concannon is known for its Syrah, and rightly so. The 2006 is saturated with juicy, ripe blackberry flavors upheld with moderate tannins and a nice dash of spice on the finish.

Earthquake | 2005 | LODI

★★ $ $ Amazingly, this wine manages to carry its whopping 15.5 percent alcohol content, nicely integrating it with flavors of blackberries and cherries and a soft note of vanilla at the end.

star producers
california syrah

Beckmen Vineyards

Tom Beckmen's impressive line of wines includes such standout Syrahs as his Purisima Mountain Vineyard Block Six and Clone #1.

Bonny Doon Vineyard

The grand guru of Monterey, Bonny Doon's Randall Grahm has become something of a celebrity for his innovative style and fantastic Rhône-inspired range of wines.

Burgess

Tom Burgess's vines are among the few in California that have been phylloxera-free since the 1970s; today they are some of the oldest in Napa.

Elyse

With grit and determination, winemaker Ray Coursen started out picking grapes for other wineries before launching his Elyse label in 1987.

Kuleto Estate

Since it was established in 1993, Kuleto has emerged as one of the best Syrah producers in the state, creating powerful, complex wines.

Sine Qua Non

Winemaker Manfred Krankl earns his reputation as one of California's hardest-working viticulturalists by ceaselessly crafting Syrahs of impeccable purity and richness.

Elyse | 2005 | NAPA VALLEY
★★★ $ $ $ Winemaker and owner Ray Coursen makes this superb wine full of spicy cured meat flavors, chewy tannins and a polished, blackberry-rich ending.

Estancia | 2005 | CENTRAL COAST
★ $ Stony minerals meet dried currants in the nose of this solid, dependable, well-priced Syrah. The medium-bodied palate is filled out with dried berry and subtle earth flavors and toasted oak highlights on the finish.

Fleming Jenkins Madden Ranch | 2006 | LIVERMORE VALLEY
★★ $ $ $ Madden Ranch is purportedly planted with 20 acres of Concannon Syrah clones, among the oldest of their kind in California. The result is an intensely spicy wine with notes of earth and cigar infusing a base of blackberries and soft tannins.

Kuleto Estate | 2006 | NAPA VALLEY
★★★ $ $ $ Loaded with spice and white pepper on the nose, this satisfyingly complex blend of black currant, blackberry, plum and date flavors is framed by firm tannins.

Limerick Lane Collins Vineyard | 2007 |
RUSSIAN RIVER VALLEY
★★ $ $ This wine has all the masculine hallmarks of a good Syrah: cured meat aromas accented by spice and berries, a supple mouthfeel, a rich and dense palate and a balanced finish.

Lost Canyon Trenton Station Vineyard | 2007 |
RUSSIAN RIVER VALLEY
★★ $ $ $ Made with grapes from a relatively new Lost Canyon vineyard, this nicely balanced red shows spicy oak, a wild berry nose and a solid core of blackberry and cedar flavors.

St. Francis Winery & Vineyards Wild Oak | 2005 |
SONOMA COUNTY
★★ $ $ $ St. Francis just celebrated its 30th anniversary, yet has been releasing its Wild Oak line for only a few years. This vintage is herb- and black cherry–scented, with flavors of earth, roasted meat, blackberries and coffee and deftly integrated tannins.

Terlato Family Vineyards | 2006 | DRY CREEK VALLEY
★★★ $ $ $ The Terlato family, headed by longtime wine importer turned vintner Tony Terlato, again succeeds with this exquisite wine. Spicy prune aromas are followed by flavors of berries and nuts and a spicy, sage-accented finish.

CALIFORNIA REDS

zinfandel

In the early 1990s, DNA testing shattered the myth that Zinfandel was a native American grape variety, as many had long believed. Alas, Zinfandel turns out to be identical to an obscure Croatian grape called Crljenak Kastelanski, though how exactly it became Zinfandel, an important variety in California capable of producing world-class wines, remains a mystery. Regardless, Zinfandel's long-established relationship with California (dating as far back as the 1850s) gives it a uniquely American identity. The most prized versions come from vineyards planted with gnarled old vines—some a century old—whose low yield results in grapes of extraordinary richness and concentration.

zinfandel recommendations

Artezin | 2007 | MENDOCINO COUNTY
★ ★ $ This pleasant fruit-forward Zinfandel from Hess Collection winemaker Randle Johnson is nicely oaked and seduces with jammy, juicy strawberry-raspberry flavors.

Bella Lily Hill Estate | 2006 | DRY CREEK VALLEY
★ ★ $ $ $ A small family-owned winery uses fruit from the Dry Creek Valley to craft this wine: a healthy dose of vanilla, sweet oak and violet complements the jammy, blackberry-infused palate.

Cline Ancient Vines | 2007 | CALIFORNIA
★ $ Some of Cline's vines are 80 to 100 years old and yield wines with raspberry and cherry flavors highlighted by coffee and spice.

Dashe | 2007 | DRY CREEK VALLEY
★ ★ ★ $ $ With its plush texture and long-lasting black cherry and red raspberry flavors underscored by leathery earth, this superb wine offers plenty of dimension. An uplifting acidity adds vibrancy to the chewy fruit and peppery finish.

Earthquake | 2006 | LODI
★ ★ $ $ A hefty Zinfandel made in a huge, extracted and hedonistic style, with small amounts of Syrah and Petite Sirah in the mix, it is bursting with smoky oak and berry compote flavors, along with notes of sage, clove and dill.

Edizione Pennino | 2006 | **RUTHERFORD**

★ ★ ★ $ $ $ In a world of plush, soft and round Zinfandels, this stands out for its finely balanced acidity and tannins, which frame red and black berry flavors punctuated by sweet spice and mocha. With a long, peppery finish, this is a food-friendly red.

Edmeades | 2007 | **MENDOCINO COUNTY**

★ ★ $ Made with small additions of Petite Sirah, Syrah, Grenache, Merlot and Barbera, this complex and well-balanced Zinfandel-based wine makes a big impression, with aromas of smoky black plums drizzled with dark chocolate and hints of spice and smoked meat.

Francis Ford Coppola Director's Cut | 2007 |
DRY CREEK VALLEY

★ ★ $ $ Coppola's team crafts Director's Cut at the former Chateau Souverain. Notes of sweet raisin and cedary spice add intrigue to ripe dark plum flavors.

star producers
california zinfandel

Alexander Valley Vineyards
In 1962 the Wetzel family purchased a homestead built by Cyrus Alexander and converted the former plum orchard into an award-winning old-vine Zinfandel vineyard.

Carlisle Winery & Vineyards
Carlisle's Mike Officer makes exuberant Zins from old-vine vineyards in Russian River, Dry Creek and Sonoma valleys.

Dashe
Michael and Anne Dashe, a husband-and-wife winemaking team, craft superlative single-vineyard wines, most famously their standout Zinfandels.

Lolonis
Winemaker Lori Knapp is dedicated to organic grape-growing. Her Mendocino wines offer comparable quality to those from Napa Valley at a fraction of the cost.

Ravenswood
Ravenswood's early focus on Zinfandel has paid off handsomely. Its ripe, concentrated wines serve as the model that many emulate.

Ridge
With around 20 vineyards to choose from, Ridge consistently produces outstanding wines in every vintage.

Haywood Estate Los Chamizal Vineyard | 2006 |
SONOMA VALLEY
★★★ $ $ After being bought and sold by several international wine companies over the course of more than 15 years, this brand is back in the hands of founder Peter Haywood. This concentrated, juicy 2006 Zinfandel has red raspberry flavors accented by cracked pepper notes and balanced by refreshing acidity.

Jacuzzi Family Vineyards Morine Ranch Primitivo | 2006 |
LAKE COUNTY
★★ $ Zinfandel may go by the name Primitivo here, but it delivers the same jammy mix of wild berry, pepper and sage flavors. Hints of black coffee and cedar and chunky tannins add a rustic quality.

Kendall-Jackson Vintner's Reserve | 2006 | CALIFORNIA
★★★ $ Kendall-Jackson uses estate-grown fruit for its Vintner's Reserve line. With its black fruit core and a touch of pepper and tobacco, this juicy wine is one of California's great values.

Kenwood Jack London Vineyard | 2006 | SONOMA VALLEY
★★ $ $ Kenwood proves that Zinfandel can age with this nicely structured wine. Ripe cassis and cherry soda aromas are followed by dense, smoky, spicy dark fruit, vanilla and a good tannic grip.

Murphy-Goode Liar's Dice | 2006 | SONOMA COUNTY
★ $ $ A sweet, blackberry-infused wine with a chewy, mouth-filling texture, this has a brandylike quality on the finish, partly as a result of the 14.9 percent alcohol content.

Paso Creek | 2007 | PASO ROBLES
★★ $ Paso Creek's 350-acre vineyard is arid, rocky and very hot. For such a warm-climate wine, this Zinfandel remains fresh and nimble on the palate, offering a mix of blueberry and raspberry fruit with a touch of mocha and white pepper.

Rancho Zabaco Monte Rosso Vineyard Toreador | 2006 |
SONOMA VALLEY
★★★ $ $ $ Still somewhat tight and closed, this reveals abundant spice and tarry dark fruit flavors with hints of clove and cinnamon. Supple and juicy on the palate, with a bold spicy finish and great length, it's worth decanting.

Rancho Zabaco Reserve | 2007 | DRY CREEK VALLEY
★★ $ $ From a longtime Zinfandel specialist comes this smoky, dill-scented wine with dark blueberry jam and cassis flavors. Fine tannins and dusty spice support the expansive, rich palate.

Ravenswood Teldeschi | 2006 | **DRY CREEK VALLEY**

★★★ $ $ Earth-infused berries are laced with tobacco and spice, giving this wine a savory edge. Generous tannins, good structure and apparent alcohol make this a formidable Zinfandel.

Ridge East Bench | 2007 | **DRY CREEK VALLEY**

★★★ $ $ Ridge is a reliable producer of rich, powerful wines that are also elegant, and this is no exception. Brimming with sweet black raspberry and cherry aromas, it displays a broad mouthfeel and a spicy, peppery finish.

Terra d'Oro Home Vineyard | 2006 | **AMADOR COUNTY**

★★★ $ $ This fresh, fruit-forward wine was crafted with fruit from the four-acre Home Vineyard on Terra d'Oro's estate. Wild raspberry and rose petal aromas are followed by a palate dominated by cracked black pepper and summer strawberries.

Windmill Old Vine | 2006 | **LODI**

★★ $ Brawny and bold, this shows smoky bacon and vanilla aromas woven with ample black fruit. There is 24 percent Petite Sirah in the blend, which explains the slightly rustic flavor and good tannins.

Z-52 Agnes' Vineyard Old Vine | 2006 | **LODI**

★★ $ Few Zinfandels are as well balanced as this example. Sweet berry flavors are tempered with tart Bing cherry and cranberry notes, great acidity and a touch of cocoa on the long, succulent finish.

other california reds

European immigrants brought many different Mediterranean grape cuttings with them long before U.S. Customs prohibited such souvenirs, though most were used to produce simple jug wines. In the 1980s, a group of winemakers calling themselves the "Rhone Rangers" looked beyond the popular Cabernet Sauvignon and began experimenting with varieties such as Grenache, Mourvèdre, Carignane, Syrah and Petite Sirah, which they claimed were ideally suited to California's Mediterranean climate. The gamble paid off, as these grapes are producing some of the state's most interesting and delicious wines. A similar movement to establish Italian grapes such as Sangiovese, Dolcetto and Barbera as "Cal-Ital" varieties has had mixed results, though some of the wines produced are quite good.

other california red recommendations

Altamura Sangiovese | 2005 | **NAPA VALLEY**
★★★ $ $ $ One of California's best Sangioveses, this shows the grape's classic black cherry and violet aromas, accentuated by cocoa and spice. It's full-bodied, with sweet tannins and good acidity.

Austin Hope Hope Family Vineyard Grenache | 2006 |
PASO ROBLES
★★★ $ $ $ A Rhône-variety specialist, Austin Hope crafts this robust Grenache from his high-density vineyard. With dark earth, violet and black fruit aromas highlighted by minerals, it is a worthy companion to his excellent Syrah.

Beckmen Vineyards Purisima Mountain Vineyard Grenache
| 2006 | **SANTA YNEZ VALLEY**
★★★ $ $ $ This dark Grenache was made during the first year Beckmen converted to biodynamic farming. After a bit of time in the glass, fresh raspberry, dusty sage and violet aromas emerge, followed by a soft mouthfeel, supple tannins and a plummy finish.

Big House The Prodigal Son Petite Sirah | 2006 |
CENTRAL COAST
★ $ This value-priced, irreverently marketed wine serves up bright cherry and currant aromas and sweet fruit flavors.

Blackstone Rubric Reserve | 2006 | **SONOMA COUNTY**
★★ $ This mélange includes Cabernet Sauvignon, Cabernet Franc, Merlot, Petit Verdot, Syrah, Petite Sirah and Tannat. The result: a spicy, chalky, chocolate-filled wine with a formidable grip.

Bonny Doon Vineyard Le Cigare Volant | 2004 | **CALIFORNIA**
★★★ $ $ Grenache takes the lead in this Rhône blend and offers layers of pretty floral and raspberry aromas. On the palate, fresh and supple berry flavors are joined by elegant tannins.

Cline Cashmere | 2007 | **CALIFORNIA**
★★ $ In this Grenache-Syrah-Mourvèdre blend, sappy blackberry and blueberry flavors are layered with dusty herbs, spice and black pepper and draped in supple tannins.

Daniel Gehrs Delirio | 2005 | **SANTA BARBARA COUNTY**
★★ $ $ $ Like a California Super-Tuscan, this wine blends Sangiovese and a handful of Bordeaux grapes with great success. Releasing wild strawberry, blackberry, raspberry and blueberry flavors, this mouthwatering red possesses a touch of Italian flair.

Earthquake Petite Sirah | 2006 | LODI
★ ★ $ $ Strutting some of Petite Sirah's inherent strength, this massive wine has a heady cedar bouquet, black fruit flavors and accents of plum and spice. The powerful tannins provide a strong framework.

Ferrari-Carano Siena | 2007 | SONOMA COUNTY
★ ★ $ $ In this odd blend, Sangiovese benefits from the structure and tannins provided by Malbec, beautifully complementing flavors of spicy red currants, earth and dried fruit. A touch of cedary spice marks the chewy, brightly acidic finish.

Horse Play Rollicking Red | 2005 | CALIFORNIA
★ $ The debut vintage for this Cabernet-Merlot-Syrah blend delivers blackberry and sweet vanilla flavors laced with cherry and meat notes. It's easy drinking, at a nice price.

star producers
other california reds

Edmunds St. John
Rhone Rangers cofounder Steve Edmunds and his wife, Cornelia St. John, have what is considered one of the best labels for rich, ripe Rhône Valley–inspired reds.

Kaena
This California brand's name reflects the background of vintner Mikael Sigouin, who hails from Honolulu and also works at Beckmen Vineyards.

Limerick Lane
Winemaker Ross Battersby is responsible for Limerick Lane's distinctive wines, which are unfiltered and made with estate-grown fruit.

The Ojai Vineyard
Regardless of challenging conditions, winemaker Adam Tolmach proves year after year that he knows how to coax power, plushness and structure out of his grapes.

Rosenblum Cellars
Kent Rosenblum remains a champion of Petite Sirah, from which he makes dependably delicious wines.

Stags' Leap Winery
Before joining Stags' Leap as an oenologist a decade ago, Kevin Morrisey interned at Château Pétrus, which accounts for the French-style elegance of his wines.

Kaena Grenache | 2006 | SANTA YNEZ VALLEY

★ ★ ★ $ $ The small-production Grenaches from Kaena offer great value and quality. Made with grapes from two vineyards, this wine brims with plump berries and a generous jammy character upheld by sweet, nicely integrated tannins.

Limerick Lane 1023 | 2007 | RUSSIAN RIVER VALLEY

★ ★ ★ $ $ $ A blend of Syrah and Zinfandel named for the winery's address, this wine packs an intriguing mix of flavors—cherries, currants and pomegranates—joined by cured meat and dried spice notes. A rich mouthfeel and plush tannins add elegance.

Lot 205 No. 1 Red | 2005 | CALIFORNIA

★ $ This simple blend shows a touch of complexity, thanks to tobacco and cigar notes that punctuate the cherry and berry flavors.

Paraduxx | 2006 | NAPA VALLEY

★ ★ ★ $ $ $ Paraduxx is owned by Duckhorn, one of Napa's finest vintners. This 2006 is a Zinfandel-led blend full of delicate violet and sage aromas that give way to spiced plum and prune flavors. Sweet tannins and a touch of mocha make for a memorable finish.

Peju Cabernet Franc | 2006 | NAPA VALLEY

★ ★ ★ $ $ $ Made with the addition of 16 percent Cabernet Sauvignon, this shows spicy cedar and red currant aromas that turn rich and vibrant in the mouth, joining luscious sweet cassis flavors, zesty acidity and well-integrated tannins.

Ravenswood Vintners Blend Petite Sirah | 2007 | CALIFORNIA

★ $ This charming red comes at a very low price. Petite Sirah—with a bit of Syrah—offers blueberry and spice flavors augmented by plum, mocha and tea leaf notes, all supported by chewy tannins.

Ridge Geyserville | 2007 | SONOMA COUNTY

★ ★ ★ $ $ $ As with Ridge's more familiar bottlings, Zinfandel is the star here, but the addition of Carignane, Petite Sirah and a touch of Mataro (Mourvèdre) gives it a structure and power that are rare in pure Zinfandel. The blend is rich with blueberry pie, cracked pepper and sweet vanilla flavors.

Staglin Family Vineyard Stagliano Sangiovese | 2007 | RUTHERFORD

★ ★ ★ $ $ $ $ While renowned for their Cabernet, the Staglins also deserve attention for their Sangiovese. Bearing the region's signature dusty red fruit, this vintage offers earth, tobacco, herbs and spice held together by bracing acidity and soft tannins.

Stags' Leap Winery Petite Syrah | 2006 | NAPA VALLEY

★ ★ $ $ Made with 75 percent Petite Sirah and a splash of Viognier, among others, this "Petite Syrah" is a solidly black wine showing notes of dark chocolate, cocoa and espresso in addition to ample ripe fruit on the plush palate.

St. Francis Winery Red | 2005 | SONOMA COUNTY

★ ★ $ Red fruit aromas and flavors mark this juicy blend of Merlot, Syrah, Cabernet Franc, Cabernet Sauvignon and Zinfandel; notes of toasted oak and nutmeg and firm tannins round it out.

Terra d'Oro Forte | 2006 | AMADOR AND NAPA COUNTIES

★ ★ $ $ The inviting red cherry and rose petal aromas in this Sangiovese–Cabernet Sauvignon blend take on a savory, earthy quality on the palate, where they are joined by juicy wild strawberry notes and firm tannins.

oregon

Although Oregon is sandwiched between Washington to the north and California to the south, its wines are very different from those of its neighbors. This is a consequence mainly of western Oregon's cool, wet weather—exactly the sort of conditions in which Pinot Noir thrives. Vintners here are crafting some of the best Pinot Noirs in the U.S., and a few stellar whites as well.

Oregon: An Overview

The hub of Oregon wine production is the Willamette Valley. Located in the state's northwestern corner and protected against strong winds from the Pacific by the Coast Ranges, the wine region experiences relatively cool temperatures and abundant moisture. Fortunately for vintners, Pinot Noir has taken to the area particularly well. To the south, in the warmer regions of the Umpqua, Rogue and Applegate valleys, some growers work with Pinot Noir, though Bordeaux and Rhône varieties tend to perform better. Northeast of the Willamette Valley, the Columbia Gorge and Valley regions run along the Washington State border, meeting the Walla Walla Valley, where warm-climate-loving Syrah has made a good home for itself.

Oregon Wine Labels

Oregon's labeling rules are slightly stricter than the federal standard followed in other states. Some wines labeled by variety must contain 75 percent of that grape in accordance with federal mandate, but others, such as Pinot Noir, Pinot Gris, Riesling and Chardonnay, are held to a higher state standard of 90 percent. In addition, wines bearing specific region names must contain 95 percent of grapes from that region, a higher proportion than the 85 percent federal standard.

oregon whites

While most of Oregon's vintners focus on reds, their whites can still be impressive. Two of the most notable types are Pinot Gris and Pinot Blanc, with the former showing a bit more substantial body than the latter. The success of Chardonnay in Oregon has been spotty, though several wine-makers have managed to use the cooler climate to their advantage, crafting elegant, mineral-laden examples. Lighter, drier Rieslings also achieve some success in certain areas, particularly the Willamette Valley.

oregon white recommendations

Anne Amie Pinot Gris | 2007 | WILLAMETTE VALLEY
★★★ $ Anne Amie's Pinot Gris offers a lovely mix of soft pear, lemon, almond and flower flavors and a lively acidity. The appealing hint of creaminess on the palate is the result of partial oak fermentation and aging on lees.

Château Benoit Cuvée A Müller-Thurgau | 2007 | WILLAMETTE VALLEY
★★ $ Now owned by the Pamplin family, the Château Benoit label reliably produces great-value wines like this Müller-Thurgau: juicy and fresh, with good acidity and notes of citrus, white flower and almond.

Cristom Estate Viognier | 2007 | EOLA-AMITY HILLS
★★★ $ $ Viognier is one of the most fragrant varieties, but it is also terribly finicky. Cristom is one of the few producers capable of bringing this grape to life, as in this fragrant, floral, silky wine with a rich palate and long, flavorful finish.

Domaine Serene Côte Sud Vineyard Dijon Clones Chardonnay | 2006 | **WILLAMETTE VALLEY**
★ ★ $ $ $ From the southernmost slopes of the Dundee Hills comes this rich and toasty Chardonnay with a creamy texture, layers of green and tropical fruit flavors and notes of yogurt, vanilla and oak.

Erath Pinot Blanc | 2007 | **WILLAMETTE VALLEY**
★ $ Pinot Blanc thrives in the Willamette Valley's mild climate, and Erath shows the grape's full potential in this bright, fresh wine offering citrus, tart peach, bitter almond and expressive mineral flavors.

The Eyrie Vineyards Original Vines Reserve Chardonnay | 2007 | **DUNDEE HILLS**
★ ★ ★ ★ $ $ $ The Lett family's long-held belief in a minimalist approach to winemaking is responsible for wines like this stunning old-vine Chardonnay. Complex flavors of citrus, apple, pear, oak, cream and ginger are mouth-filling and long-lasting.

Hellfire White | 2007 | **COLUMBIA GORGE**
★ ★ ★ $ Named for the fiery Reverend Billy Sunday, who owned farmland in Oregon's Hood River Valley in the early 1900s, Hellfire's blend of Pinot Gris, Gewürztraminer and Chardonnay delivers captivating aromas upheld by vibrant acidity, for a low price.

Montinore Estate Gewürztraminer | 2007 | **WILLAMETTE VALLEY**
★ ★ $ The winemaking Marchesi family produces this charming, silky-textured Gewürztraminer, with aromas of rose, lychee and lime.

RoxyAnn Pinot Gris | 2007 | **ROGUE VALLEY**
★ ★ ★ $ This vintner practices sustainable viticulture, which may explain the pure flavors in this wine. Green fruit and flowers are laced with a vanilla-like creaminess and supported by zippy acidity.

Vista Hills Pinot Gris | 2006 | **DUNDEE HILLS**
★ ★ $ Vista Hills' sustainably farmed vineyards are perched atop the Dundee Hills. Their Pinot Gris offers bold flavors—citrus, pear, melon and almond—backed by firm acidity and a rounded finish.

Willamette Valley Vineyards Pinot Gris | 2007 | **WILLAMETTE VALLEY**
★ ★ ★ ★ $ Jim Bernau was one of the Willamette Valley's earliest winemakers, and he's still one of the best. He and his team of winemakers blend this Pinot Gris with small amounts of Muscat and Pinot Blanc, which creates a gorgeous balance of bright acidity with layers of citrus, pear, melon and almond flavors and a toast-accented finish.

oregon reds

Oregon has benefited from the surging demand for Pinot Noir, despite the fact that its Pinot Noirs are highly susceptible to vintage variation, especially in the Willamette Valley's challenging climate. A dry, hot 2006 produced a crop of bold, high-alcohol wines, while the cooler years of 2005 and 2007 yielded subtler, more elegant and refined bottles. From early reports, conditions in 2008 produced what could be an exceptionally fine vintage. In the state's warmer southern and eastern regions, both Cabernet and Syrah are finding a niche, but the majority of Oregon's winemakers continue to focus on Pinot Noir.

oregon red recommendations

Anna Maria Syrah | 2004 | ROGUE VALLEY
★ ★ $ $ The eastern part of Oregon's mountainous Rogue Valley is ideal for growing Syrah. This one is bursting with ripe blackberry and plum flavors, accompanied by sweet spice, earth, a hint of olive and bold, ripe tannins that hold it together beautifully.

Anne Amie Winemaker's Selection Pinot Noir | 2006 | WILLAMETTE VALLEY
★ ★ $ $ $ Thanks in part to a great vintage, this Pinot Noir is redolent of raspberry, cherry and earth, with a dash of spice and vanilla, refreshing acidity and a juicy finish.

Archery Summit Red Hills Estate Pinot Noir | 2006 | DUNDEE HILLS
★ ★ ★ $ $ $ $ Red Hills is one of Archery Summit's most prized vineyards, yielding wines that are able to age well. This delicious Pinot Noir is fragrant and delicious, packed with cherry, licorice, earth and smoke, with a firm backbone of acidity and medium-soft tannins.

Cliff Creek Claret | 2004 | SOUTHERN OREGON
★ ★ ★ $ $ Three generations of the Garvin family run this excellent winery. This is a complex, mineral-laden Bordeaux-style blend oozing black fruit and earth flavors, balanced by firm tannins and acidity.

Cooper Mountain Vineyards Five Elements Series Doctor's Reserve Pinot Noir | 2006 | WILLAMETTE VALLEY
★ ★ $ $ $ Pepper and dried leaf notes infuse a base of sour cherry, plum and spice flavors in this medium-bodied, smooth Pinot Noir.

Cristom Louise Vineyard Pinot Noir | 2006 |
EOLA-AMITY HILLS

★★★ $ $ $ From the red soils of the Eola-Amity Hills, Cristom produces wonderfully elegant Pinot Noirs. Fragrant, complex fruit and earth aromas are accented by smoked meat and oak and supported by a firming spine of acidity.

Dobbes Family Estate Grande Assemblage Cuvée Syrah
| 2005 | **ROGUE VALLEY**

★★★ $ $ Sourcing fruit from some of the best vineyards in the Rogue, Joe Dobbes fashions this jammy, blueberry-scented wine laced with licorice, cocoa and spice.

Erath Leland Pinot Noir | 2006 | **WILLAMETTE VALLEY**

★★ $ $ $ Produced from a single vineyard in limited quantities, Leland is one of Erath's best wines, defined by bright red berries, minerals, good acidity and notes of herbs, chocolate and bark.

The Eyrie Vineyards Pinot Noir | 2007 | **DUNDEE HILLS**

★★★ $ $ $ The Eyrie Vineyards' famous Pinots have outshone Burgundies in blind tastings. The 2007 offers a delightful mix of cherry, earth, herbs and smoke, upheld by firm acidity on the long finish.

Maysara Jamsheed Pinot Noir | 2007 | **MCMINNVILLE**

★ $ $ Moe Momtazi is following in the footsteps of his grandparents, who grew wine grapes in northern Iran. His 2007 is a classic Oregon Pinot Noir, full of bright berry and sweet spice notes, a hint of earth and smoke and a juicy finish.

Panther Creek Shea Vineyard Pinot Noir | 2006 |
YAMHILL-CARLTON DISTRICT

★★ $ $ $ Shea Vineyard—a longtime grape source for Panther Creek—produces fruit with generous flavors of red berries and earth. The 2006 vintage is especially ripe, with layers of berry, wet earth and licorice and a smooth texture.

Phelps Creek Vineyards Becky's Cuvée Pinot Noir | 2007 |
COLUMBIA GORGE

★ $ $ A soft, juicy palate and fragrant aromas of cherry, spice, banana and violets make this Pinot reminiscent of Beaujolais.

Ponzi Vineyards Pinot Noir | 2007 | **WILLAMETTE VALLEY**

★★★ $ $ $ Winemaker Luisa Ponzi proves her deft understanding of this fickle grape year after year, as evidenced by the vividly pure expression of this wine's black fruit flavors, earthy notes, solid concentration and great depth.

Red Red Wine | 2007 | OREGON

★ ★ ★ **$** This splendid wine comes at a phenomenally low price. Sensual flavors of earth, dark plum and herbs are accented by cocoa, graphite and licorice.

Rockblock Reserve by Domaine Serene Syrah | 2006 |
WALLA WALLA VALLEY

★ ★ ★ **$ $ $** Named for the rocky, nutrient-poor soils in which Syrah thrives, this northeastern Oregon wine exhibits Rhône-like qualities of rich blackberry compote, sweet spice and cinnamon on a dense, concentrated palate.

Sokol Blosser Pinot Noir | 2006 | DUNDEE HILLS

★ ★ ★ **$ $ $** Russ Rosner is the winemaking genius behind Sokol Blosser. His 2006 has an enticing harmony of flavors—berries, earth, bacon—and a sublime balance of acidity and weight.

star producers
oregon pinot noir

Adelsheim
David and Ginny Adelsheim established a sustainable vineyard on the slopes of the Chehalem Mountains in 1971, where they continue to craft distinctive, multilayered wines.

Andrew Rich
Andrew Rich produces beautiful Pinot Noirs and Rhône-style red wines at the Carlton Winemakers Studio, the first green cooperative winery in the country.

Cristom
Owner Paul Gerrie and winemaker Steve Doerner are also both scientists, a shared background that yields brilliant results in the winery.

Domaine Serene
Ken and Grace Evenstad's love of Pinot Noir led them to the Dundee Hills in 1989, where they've since created some of the state's finest wines.

Sokol Blosser
Bill Blosser and Susan Sokol Blosser started making Pinot Noirs in Oregon back in 1971; today their children Alex and Alison follow in their footsteps.

Stoller Vineyards
On land that was once a turkey farm, Bill and Cathy Stoller planted vines and built a state-of-the-art, solar-powered, gravity-flow winery that gets almost as much attention as their stunning wines.

Soter Mineral Springs Pinot Noir | 2006 |
YAMHILL-CARLTON DISTRICT
★ ★ ★ $ $ $ $ This is the second vintage exclusively from Soter Mineral Springs vineyard, located on a gentle slope of siltstone and sandstone. Spiced blackberry flavors make a big first impression, rounded out by earth and a lush, long finish.

Vista Hills Treehouse Pinot Noir | 2006 | **DUNDEE HILLS**
★ ★ ★ $ A particularly fresh, bright Pinot Noir, this shows perfect balance between soft, slightly oaky red cherry flavors and firm, structured mineral notes.

washington state

Washington has the second-largest number of wineries in the U.S. and was responsible for 8 percent of the nation's total wine yield in 2008. Once known primarily for its Merlots, Washington has significantly broadened its range and now produces stellar Cabernet Sauvignons and increasingly fine Syrahs. Chardonnay and Riesling are the state's two most important white grapes, but Sauvignon Blanc and Gewürztraminer are also grown.

Washington State: An Overview

Most winemaking in Washington takes place inland, where vineyards are sheltered from the coastal weather by the Cascade Range and enjoy sunny, relatively dry summers. The state's largest wine region is the Columbia Valley, which encompasses many prominent subregions, including the Yakima Valley, Red Mountain and the Walla Walla Valley (the last of which straddles the border with Oregon in southeastern Washington).

Washington State Wine Labels

Washington wine labels include basic information such as grape variety, winery, vintage and region where the grapes were grown. Some Washington wines are blends of Bordeaux grape varieties and are labeled "Meritage" (see p. 160), which is rare in the U.S. outside of California; other wineries give proprietary names to their signature blends.

washington state whites

Washington was a white-wine-centric state before its reds gained success. Cool nights allow vintners to make crisp, citrusy Chardonnays that are typically lighter and more refreshing than full-bodied California wines. Riesling has surpassed Chardonnay as the state's most harvested wine grape, thanks to a steady climb in domestic demand for the wine. Washington Rieslings tend to reveal vivid fruit flavors complemented by floral aromas, and range in style from dry to sweet. Most of the state's other white wines are made from Sauvignon Blanc and Gewürztraminer.

washington state white recommendations

Abeja Chardonnay | 2007 | **WASHINGTON STATE**
★★ $ $ $ *Sur lie* aging contributes to the creamy texture in this big yet balanced Chardonnay, while the judicious use of barrel fermentation imparts subtle oak and vanilla notes to citrus and apple flavors.

Buty Conner Lee Vineyard Chardonnay | 2007 |
COLUMBIA VALLEY
★★ $ $ $ Pronounced "beauty," this winery makes only 520 cases of this Burgundy-style Chardonnay. It displays lovely pear, melon and mineral flavors and a mouthwatering finish.

Chateau Ste. Michelle & Dr. Loosen Eroica Riesling | 2007 |
COLUMBIA VALLEY
★★★ $ $ Consistently one of Washington's top Rieslings, this off-dry white is the collaboration of two big names in winemaking. Eroica is aromatic and complex, with a mix of slate and citrus flavors that linger nicely on the palate.

Columbia Crest Grand Estates Chardonnay | 2007 |
COLUMBIA VALLEY
★ $ For those who prefer buttery, biscuit-flavored Chardonnays, this round, rich wine from Washington's largest brand is sure to appeal.

Covey Run Riesling | 2007 | **COLUMBIA VALLEY**
★★★ $ Winemaker Kate Michaud got her start at Bonny Doon, and her training is reflected in the way she tempers a gentle sweetness with crisp acidity in this value wine, filled out with citrus and minerals.

Fidélitas Semillon | 2007 | COLUMBIA VALLEY

★ $ Winemaker Charlie Hoppes shows that this Bordeaux variety—usually blended with Sauvignon Blanc—can go it alone. A powerful, full-bodied Semillon, it has pear and spiced vanilla aromas and a round, creamy texture.

L'Ecole Nº 41 Semillon | 2007 | COLUMBIA VALLEY

★ $ L'Ecole Nº 41 has built its reputation on Semillon, and it's easy to see why: this weighty version—made with 10 percent Sauvignon Blanc—offers flavors of melon, pear and citrus.

Maison Bleue Notre Vie Viognier | 2008 | YAKIMA VALLEY

★ $ $ While Maison Bleue focuses its efforts on Rhône Valley varieties, its wines are decidedly New World in style. This big, bold Viognier unleashes an expressive fruit salad of melon and pineapple flavors.

Seven Hills Riesling | 2008 | COLUMBIA VALLEY

★ ★ $ This off-dry Riesling is a textbook Washington value. It's crisp and clean, with floral and tropical fruit aromas, apple and peach flavors and a remarkably lengthy finish.

Snoqualmie Naked Riesling | 2007 | COLUMBIA VALLEY

★ $ Called "naked" because it's made from organically grown grapes in an organic winery, this off-dry, refreshing wine pleases with its surprising depth of mineral and peach flavors upheld by zippy acidity.

washington state reds

Merlot, once Washington's primary red grape, is now second to Cabernet Sauvignon in terms of the amount of vines planted. Washington's best Cabernet Sauvignons, Cabernet Francs and Bordeaux-style blends exhibit smooth textures and bold fruit flavors, though they tend to be somewhat more restrained than California's riper-style red wines. Syrah is Washington's brightest up-and-comer, and is responsible for many of the state's finest wines, which often possess a subtlety missing in warm-region Syrahs, such as those from South Australia (called Shiraz) or California's Central Coast. While winemakers have experimented with varieties like Sangiovese and Nebbiolo, the only other red grape truly of note is Lemberger (also called Blaufränkisch), which yields a fruity, low-acid wine meant to be enjoyed young.

washington state red recommendations

Andrew Will Champoux Vineyard | 2006 |
HORSE HEAVEN HILLS

★ ★ ★ $ $ $ Like a bigger, more concentrated version of a left-bank Bordeaux, this full-bodied, single-vineyard blend boasts flavors of currants and berries and fills the palate with ripe, juicy tannins.

Arbor Crest Wine Cellars Merlot | 2006 | COLUMBIA VALLEY

★ $ After a stint at Ferrari-Carano, Kristina Mielke–van Löben Sels took over her uncle's winemaking responsibilities at Arbor Crest. Her 2006 Merlot is medium-bodied and full of dark cherry, blackberry and vanilla aromas.

Chateau Ste. Michelle Ethos Merlot | 2005 |
COLUMBIA VALLEY

★ ★ $ $ $ This full-bodied Merlot has a marvelously heady nose of oak, spice and black cherry that gives way to soft, ripe fruit flavors and strong yet supple tannins, which nicely hold it together.

Col Solare | 2005 | COLUMBIA VALLEY

★ ★ ★ $ $ $ $ This polished Bordeaux blend is an international collaboration between Washington's Chateau Ste. Michelle and Italy's Marchese Piero Antinori. A rich, spicy red, it is full-bodied, with ripe, peppery berry flavors.

Cougar Crest Estate Winery Estate Grown Cabernet Franc
| 2006 | WALLA WALLA VALLEY

★ ★ $ $ $ Cougar Crest's co-owner and winemaker Deborah Hansen makes one of Washington's finest Cabernet Francs, marked by a medium body, wild berry flavors and approachable tannins.

Gordon Brothers Family Vineyards Merlot | 2007 |
COLUMBIA VALLEY

★ ★ $ $ The Gordon family has a long history of fruit farming in Washington State, and their organic cherry and apple trees surround their vineyards. This crowd-pleasing Merlot, however, is characterized by flavors of plum and spice.

GraEagle Red Wing | 2006 | WALLA WALLA VALLEY

★ ★ $ $ The well-regarded Nicholas Cole Cellars makes this spicy Bordeaux-style red blend. It includes a dollop of Syrah in the mix, which nicely softens its big tannins and adds spice to flavors of bright red fruit and ripe berries.

L'Ecole № 41 Seven Hills Vineyard Estate Syrah | 2006 |
WALLA WALLA VALLEY

★★★ $ $ $ L'Ecole № 41 is famous for its standout whites but makes stellar reds, too. This Syrah is dense and delicious, a mélange of earth, cedar and dark wild berries framed by tannins.

Nelms Road Merlot | 2007 | **WASHINGTON STATE**
★★ $ $ This is the first-rate second label of the renowned Woodward Canyon. Mocha, blackberry and spice dominate the nose of this Merlot, which has medium tannins and a lengthy finish.

Nicholas Cole Cellars Dauphiné Estate Syrah | 2006 |
WALLA WALLA VALLEY

★★ $ $ $ Nicholas Cole's vineyards are situated at a higher altitude than most in Walla Walla, and their wines clearly benefit. This Syrah is inky and ripe, with bold dark fruit, spice and oak.

Northstar Merlot | 2005 | **COLUMBIA VALLEY**
★★ $ $ $ A little Cabernet Sauvignon and Petit Verdot beef up this full-bodied Merlot, marked by spicy, juicy red berry flavors and oak.

Northwest Totem Cellars Potlatch | 2006 | **COLUMBIA VALLEY**
★★ $ $ From one of Washington's very promising newer wineries, this robust red is an unusual blend of Syrah, Tempranillo and Petit Verdot, offering earthy blackberry flavors and firm tannins.

Otis Kenyon Syrah | 2006 | **WALLA WALLA VALLEY**
★★ $ $ Year after year, this winery makes consistently dark and delicious wines. The 2006 Syrah displays spice, violet, plum and animal notes, complemented by a good amount of oak.

Sequel Syrah | 2006 | **COLUMBIA VALLEY**
★★ $ $ $ Made by John Duval of Penfolds fame, this is Washington Syrah by way of Australia—big, bold and plush. It has a complex range of plum, dried fruit, spice and vanilla flavors and a satiny texture.

Spring Valley Vineyard Uriah | 2006 | **WALLA WALLA VALLEY**
★★ $ $ $ This Merlot-dominated blend manages to stay balanced in spite of an alcohol content of 14.9 percent. Its chewy tannins are offset by plush flavors of plum and spice.

Walter Dacon C'est Syrah Beaux | 2006 | **COLUMBIA VALLEY**
★★★★ $ $ $ Founded in 2003 by Lloyd Anderson, this Washington winery is producing some of the state's best Syrahs. The 2006 shows a complex nose of oak, spice, subtle bacon and ripe black fruit—all echoed on the palate and culminating in a velvety, long finish.

William Church Winery Bishop's Blend | 2006 |
COLUMBIA VALLEY

★ ★ $ Bishop's Blend is an odd yet delicious combination of mostly Bordeaux grape varieties, with the addition of a little Syrah and Sangiovese. Red and black cherry and raspberry flavors are supported by rich, smooth tannins.

Woodward Canyon Artist Series Cabernet Sauvignon
| 2006 | **WASHINGTON STATE**

★ ★ ★ $ $ $ Woodward Canyon's Rick Small was largely responsible for the development of the Walla Walla Valley AVA. Woodward's elegant Cabernet contains 13 percent Syrah and could easily be mistaken for a Bordeaux, with its nose of cassis, smoke and pencil lead framed by firm, chewy tannins.

star producers
washington state reds

Andrew Will
Founded in 1989 by former restaurant wine buyer Chris Camarda, this winery specializes in Bordeaux-style blends made with Washington's finest grapes.

Dunham Cellars
Hand-harvesting grapes from some of Washington's finest vineyards, Dunham crafts elegant, ageworthy wines.

Goose Ridge Vineyards
The Monson family has a four-decade history of farming in the Columbia Valley, and their much-acclaimed winery—established here in 1999—is located on some of the region's best south-facing terroir.

L'Ecole Nº 41
The talented Martin Clubb crafts L'Ecole Nº 41's rich, full-bodied reds in what was once a schoolhouse in historic Frenchtown, just outside of Walla Walla.

The Magnificent Wine Co.
Deceptively simple "home-made" labels and under-$20 price tags belie the quality of this producer's handsome, well-balanced Columbia Valley wines.

Walter Dacon
Although the grapes for these delicious and elegant Syrahs are grown in Washington's Yakima and Columbia valleys, their inspiration comes from the Rhône Valley.

other united states

California is by far the country's largest wine-producing state, but it is hardly the only one: today every state can claim at least one winery. A handful of non–West Coast producers have overcome challenges of harsh climate, poor soil, a highly competitive wine market and distribution difficulties to achieve great success.

Other United States: An Overview

Climate is the most challenging problem facing vintners in most states. Cold winters and/or hot, humid summers spell trouble for traditional European *Vitis vinifera* grape varieties (Chardonnay, Cabernet Sauvignon, Sauvignon Blanc, etc.), and as a result, winemakers in many states throughout the U.S. choose to work with the generally lower-quality native American or hybrid grapes that do perform well in less-than-ideal conditions. Parts of New York State prove an exception to this trend: within the two high-quality wine regions, the eastern end of Long Island and the Finger Lakes region in the western part of the state, temperatures are moderated by nearby bodies of water, producing conditions in which *Vitis vinifera* grapes fare well. As a result, Long Island wineries make some exceptional Merlot, Cabernet Franc, Chardonnay and Sauvignon Blanc, while the Finger Lakes region is a source for noteworthy Riesling, Gewürztraminer and Pinot Noir.

Outside of New York, wine regions are developing in northeastern states such as Pennsylvania, New Jersey, Connecticut and Rhode Island. Farther south, in Virginia, successful wineries are moving away from local hybrid grapes toward *vinifera* grapes such as Chardonnay, Viognier and the red Bordeaux varieties. In the Southwest, Arizona is currently focusing on a handful of Rhône Valley varieties, and Texas, too, is making considerable quantities of quality *vinifera*-based white and red wines. The high-elevation vineyards of New Mexico are the source of some fine sparkling wines (see p. 264), as well as appealing reds crafted from Cabernet, Merlot and Pinot Noir.

Still, many wineries in Virginia, North Carolina, Missouri, Ohio and other states continue to rely on hybrid or native grape varieties, such as Baco Noir, Concord, Seyval Blanc, Vignoles and Vidal Blanc, to make wines that are sold mostly to tourists.

Other United States Grapes & Styles

Parts of the Northeast—especially New York's Finger Lakes region—enjoy ideal conditions for growing certain white grape varieties, particularly Riesling and Gewürztraminer. Chardonnay and Sauvignon Blanc benefit from the slightly longer growing season on Long Island, which produces a few good-quality sparkling wines and dry, crisp rosés. Hybrid grapes such as Vidal Blanc are used to make delicious dessert wines in New York, Virginia and Texas. Despite a relatively warm, humid growing season, Virginia winemakers produce a number of high-quality, dry white wines from Chardonnay, Viognier and other *vinifera* grapes. With a growing season marked by cool nights and warm, dry days—much like that of southeastern Washington State to the west—Idaho is also becoming a source of many good *vinifera*-based whites.

Red wine producers are doing well in many pockets throughout the country. Long Island vintners rely on Cabernet Sauvignon, Merlot and Cabernet Franc, while winemakers in the cool-climate Finger Lakes region farther north focus on Pinot Noir, which yields increasingly interesting wines each vintage. In Virginia, local grapes such as Norton grow alongside increasing amounts of *vinifera* varieties, such as Cabernet, Merlot and (surprisingly) Tannat, a powerful red grape from the Madiran region of southwestern France. In Texas and Arizona, Merlot and Cabernet vines do well, and producers are also creating some interesting wines with Grenache, Mourvèdre, Tempranillo and Sangiovese. Pinot Noir does unexpectedly well in New Mexico's high-elevation vineyards.

other u.s. recommendations

WHITES

Barboursville Vineyards Pinot Grigio | 2008 | VIRGINIA

★★ $ From the same region where Thomas Jefferson once produced wine comes this lively Pinot Grigio, crafted by the area's preeminent vintner. Fresh flavors of citrus and green fruit are offset by minerals and good acidity.

Callaghan Vineyards Lisa's Proprietary White | 2007 | SONOITA, ARIZONA

★★ $ $ This unique blend of Riesling, Malvasia Bianca and Rhône varieties is made in Arizona's southeastern corner. It is fragrant with rose hips, peach, tangerine and citrus, and has a fat, fruity palate upheld by medium acidity.

Chaddsford Miller Estate Vineyard Chardonnay | 2007 | PENNSYLVANIA

★★★ $ $ $ In Pennsylvania's historic Brandywine Valley, Eric Miller is making his own history, successfully producing Burgundy-style wines. Chaddsford Miller's 2007 Chardonnay displays fresh green fruit and refreshing acidity balanced by a creamy texture and hints of yogurt, vanilla and spice.

Hermann J. Wiemer Dry Riesling | 2007 | FINGER LAKES, NEW YORK

★★★ $ Raised in the German Mosel, Wiemer recognized the Finger Lakes' terroir as Riesling country early on, and has been producing amazing wines here since the 1970s. Bold acidity balances the juicy, sweet flavors of stone fruit in this version, which is filled out with notes of honey and minerals.

Horton Viognier | 2007 | ORANGE COUNTY, VIRGINIA

★★ $ Viognier has found a second home in Orange County, Virginia, where warm summers bring out its fresh-cut flower aromas. This apricot- and peach-flavored example has a silky mouthfeel and a long, floral finish.

Millbrook Tocai Friulano | 2008 | HUDSON RIVER REGION, NEW YORK

★★★ $ Successful businessman John Dyson founded Millbrook in his hometown 30 years ago, and it is today considered by many to be the region's finest winery. His Tocai is famous for its fragrant pear, citrus and melon flavors, beautifully wrapped up with medium-plus acidity and a juicy, mouth-filling finish.

REDS

Bedell Musée | 2006 | **NORTH FORK OF LONG ISLAND, NEW YORK**
★★★★ $ $ $ $ This Merlot-dominant Bordeaux blend is as elegant as its Chuck Close–commissioned label. Rich black fruit flavors mingle with a complex array of flower, herb and spice notes, balancing acidity and integrated tannins in this beautifully structured wine.

Cinder Syrah | 2007 | **SNAKE RIVER VALLEY, IDAHO**
★★★ $ $ Idaho native winemaker Melanie Krause earned her stripes at Chateau Ste. Michelle's Canoe Ridge Estate in Washington before returning home to craft delicious wines like this berry- and mocha-flavored Syrah, with a plush, velvety mouthfeel.

Gruet Cuvée Gilbert Gruet Pinot Noir | 2007 | **NEW MEXICO**
★★ $ $ Laurent Gruet's sparkling wines have earned national attention ever since he started making them here more than two decades ago. His still wines are just as delicious: this one reveals intense aromas and flavors of black cherry with vanilla and spice.

Llano Estacado Signature Mélange | 2007 | **TEXAS**
★★★ $ This Texas take on a Rhône-style blend is big and bold, with flavors of spice and fresh cherries, plums and blackberries, vibrant acidity and a juicy, clean finish—a great foil for Texas barbecue.

Macari Cabernet Franc | 2004 |
NORTH FORK OF LONG ISLAND, NEW YORK
★★★ $ $ Macari practices biodynamic viticulture, and its Cabernet Franc expresses pure, layered flavors of cranberry, bell pepper, pomegranate and dried fruit, punctuated by spice and pencil lead.

Stone Hill Winery Norton | 2005 | **HERMANN, MISSOURI**
★★ $ Stone Hill was America's second-largest winery before Prohibition forced it to close down. The current owners have revitalized it and produce this zesty native-variety wine full of bright raspberries, tea leaves and bell pepper backed by dry tannins.

Stone House Vineyard Claros Reserve Norton | 2006 |
TEXAS HILL COUNTRY, TEXAS
★★★ $ $ Overlooking Texas's Lake Travis, Stone House grows and produces great wines with the Norton grape. Surprisingly complex and medium-bodied, this wine offers red currant and cherry flavors, minerals, spice and firm acidity.

australia

Australia is now the sixth-largest wine producer in the world, the second-largest exporter to the U.S. and a source of some of the lushest, fullest-bodied wines made anywhere. While the country has dominated the value-wine category for the last decade, it has increasingly become known for acclaimed, top-flight bottles that are on a par with the world's finest.

Western Australia

• Perth

Frankland River

Margaret River

Indian Ocean

Principal Wine Region

Australia: An Overview

Australia has more than 2,000 wineries spread across 64 designated growing regions in six wine-producing states. This island continent's varied climate and geography allow it to produce practically every major wine style. South Australia is the hub of the industry, and home to the majority of the country's most acclaimed regions. Among them are Barossa and McLaren valleys, responsible for much of Australia's acclaimed Shiraz (Syrah); Coonawarra, ideal for Cabernet Sauvignon; and the Clare and Eden valleys, home to Australia's top Rieslings. Pinot Noir thrives in the Yarra Valley, in Victoria, near Melbourne. In New South Wales, the Hunter Valley region north of Sydney is known for its Shiraz, Semillon, Cabernet and Chardonnay, while Tumbarumba has high-altitude vineyards that yield some of Australia's greatest whites, notably Chardonnay.

Australian Wine Labels

Australian labels usually specify producer, region, vintage and grape variety. Blends tend to be named with the dominant grape listed first; in some cases, only the initials of the blend are given, as in "GSM" (Grenache, Shiraz, Mourvèdre).

australian whites

White wines account for around 40 percent of Australia's production. The most popular white is Chardonnay, which is made in a wide variety of styles. Riesling, Semillon and Sauvignon Blanc are also grown, along with lesser-known varieties such as Verdelho, Muscat and Colombard.

AUSTRALIAN WHITES

chardonnay

Australia was slow to embrace Chardonnay. Little of it was planted here until the early 1980s, yet today it is the country's primary white grape. Lighter versions hail from cooler regions, such as South Australia's Adelaide Hills, Mornington Peninsula in Victoria and Tasmania. Chardonnays from the Margaret River region of Western Australia express exquisite elegance, while voluptuous examples are made in South Australia's Riverland, as well as the Hunter Valley, Mudgee and Riverina regions of New South Wales.

chardonnay recommendations

Bulletin Place | 2008 | **SOUTH EASTERN AUSTRALIA**
★ $ This value-priced South Eastern Australia Chardonnay displays fresh apple and pear flavors and a crisp, bright finish.

Deakin Estate | 2007 | **VICTORIA**
★ $ The stony clay of North West Victoria's Red Cliffs yields this well-balanced white with ample flavors of Red Delicious apples and pears, plus a hint of lime zest, that linger on the palate.

Elderton Unoaked | 2008 | **BAROSSA**
★ $ Although the Barossa Valley is most acclaimed for its Shiraz, Elderton crafts a beautiful steel-fermented Chardonnay full of zesty citrus aromas and creamy pear and lime zest flavors.

Gemtree Vineyards Citrine | 2007 | MCLAREN VALE
★ ★ $ By fermenting only 30 percent of their juice in new French oak barriques, Gemtree achieves a perfect balance between lush tropical citrus aromas and sweet-tart pineapple notes in this medium-bodied Chardonnay.

Marquee Classic | 2006 | SOUTH EASTERN AUSTRALIA
★ ★ $ Hand-crafted in small batches, this very approachable Chardonnay opens with a pear, apple and clementine bouquet, which is followed by lush flavors of sweet pear and a nicely balanced finish.

Peace Family Vineyard | 2008 | SOUTH EASTERN AUSTRALIA
★ $ This light and simple offering from Andrew Peace's family-owned vineyard on Australia's Murray River impresses with its mélange of pineapple, citrus and pear flavors—and a great price, too.

Spring Seed Wine Co. Four O'Clock | 2008 | MCLAREN VALE
★ ★ $ Named for a brightly colored, late-afternoon-blooming flower, Spring Seed's certified organic Chardonnay is equally bright. Notes of apricot, tangerine and lime have a spicy, lingering finish.

The Wishing Tree Unoaked | 2007 | WESTERN AUSTRALIA
★ $ Fermented and aged without the use of oak barrels, this medium-bodied white is vibrant and balanced. Apple pie and tropical fruit flavors are offset by refreshing acidity.

Yalumba Wild Ferment | 2008 | EDEN VALLEY
★ ★ ★ $ Its name an Aboriginal term meaning "all the land around," Yalumba makes wines that beautifully express the essence of Eden Valley terroir. This superb Chardonnay is fermented using only the natural yeasts from the grapes' skins; it displays enticing pineapple aromas, pear and citrus flavors and a creamy, lush palate.

other australian whites

Riesling is Australia's second most important white wine. The Clare Valley produces mainly dry versions with mineral flavors and an ability to age nicely. Good Sauvignon Blanc can also be found in Australia, though the Semillon grape fares better, often yielding dry wines with intriguing honey flavors. Rhône grape varieties Marsanne, Roussanne and Viognier are sometimes bottled on their own but generally used in blends. The Portuguese grape Verdelho is widely grown, but produces only a few noteworthy wines.

other australian white recommendations

A.T. Richardson Chockstone Riesling | 2006 | GRAMPIANS

★ $ Named in honor of winemaker Adam Richardson's other great love, rock climbing, this pleasant, breezy wine exhibits subtle petrol and newly mown grass aromas, coupled with the crisp citrus flavors that are the classic Riesling hallmarks.

Frankland Estate Isolation Ridge Riesling | 2007 | FRANKLAND RIVER

★ ★ $ $ Frankland sources these grapes from a vineyard with gravel, loam and clay soils at an elevation of 1,150 feet. The result is a mineral-laden wine with notes of sulfur, petrol and slate and fresh yet richly concentrated flavors of citrus and dried pear.

Gemtree Vineyards Moonstone Albariño | 2008 | MCLAREN VALE

★ ★ $ Gemtree's first 100 percent biodynamic Albariño—fermented without yeast or acid additives and unfiltered—is a delicate white with a gorgeous apple-pear nose and a clean, mineral-laden finish.

Hope Estate Estate Grown Verdelho | 2006 | HUNTER VALLEY

★ $ This Aussie take on the Portuguese Verdelho grape—full of pine-apple, pear and quince flavors and excellent acidity—makes for a fresh, unoaked alternative to Chardonnay.

Kaesler Old Vine Semillon | 2007 | BAROSSA VALLEY

★ ★ $ $ Plagued by drought in 2007, Kaesler's vineyards still yielded flavorful wines like this distinctive Semillon. Floral, citrus and fresh-cut grass aromas are followed by succulent melon and pear flavors.

Oxford Landing Sauvignon Blanc | 2008 | SOUTH AUSTRALIA

★ $ An excellent choice for an everyday wine, Oxford Landing's low-priced Sauvignon Blanc is as refreshing as a tall glass of lemonade. Zippy grapefruit flavors have a zesty, lime-kissed finish.

Peter Lehmann of the Barossa Riesling | 2008 | EDEN VALLEY

★ ★ $ Mostly old vines from 12 separate vineyards produced the fruit for this well-balanced Riesling. Citrus and flowers mingle with a faint hint of petrol on the nose and lead to a bright and fruity palate.

Peter Lehmann Wines Layers | 2008 | ADELAIDE

★ $ Peter Lehmann winemaker Ian Hongell blends Pinot Gris, Mus-cat, Gewürztraminer, Chardonnay and Semillon to lovely effect in this lemon-, pineapple- and apricot-scented wine.

Pewsey Vale Individual Vineyard Selection Dry Riesling
| 2008 | EDEN VALLEY
★ ★ $ Grown in the cool air of Eden Valley's high-altitude country-side, this wonderfully balanced white reveals aromas of honeysuckle and citrus rind, rounded out by pear and melon flavors.

Redbank The Long Paddock Sauvignon Blanc | 2008 |
VICTORIA
★ $ Zingy citrus aromas, crisp pear-nectar flavors and a mouthwatering finish mark this bright, refreshing white.

Woop Woop Verdelho | 2008 | SOUTH EASTERN AUSTRALIA
★ ★ $ A delicious white, Woop Woop Verdelho has peach, lemon and tangerine aromas, tropical fruit flavors and a zippy acidity.

Yalumba Y Series Riesling | 2008 | SOUTH AUSTRALIA
★ $ Affordable and immensely drinkable, Yalumba's well-built Riesling has bright citrus and flower aromas and a fruit-forward palate propped up by great acidity.

australian reds

Robust, ripe, berry-flavored Shiraz is Australia's claim to wine fame, though Cabernet Sauvignon is widely produced and performs well in many regions. Merlot plantings have increased significantly, though the grape has yet to yield results on a par with the country's Shiraz and Cabernet Sauvignon. There is a niche-following for some high-quality Pinot Noirs from a handful of the country's cooler wine regions, and the more obscure varieties of Grenache and Mourvèdre are gaining ground, especially in South Australia's McLaren Vale and Barossa Valley.

AUSTRALIAN REDS

cabernet sauvignon

Cabernet Sauvignon may be second to Shiraz in popularity among Australians when it comes to red wine, but it still is held in high esteem and is responsible for many of the country's best reds. Australian Cabernets run the gamut from simple, often over-acidified wines to ripe, fruity, full-bodied examples; the finest are capable of extensive aging.

Australia's warmer regions tend to highlight berry and chocolate flavors, while cooler climes enhance the grape's mineral qualities. Western Australian regions, like Margaret River, produce refined Cabernets, but some of the best hail from South Australia's relatively tiny Coonawarra region.

cabernet sauvignon recommendations

Aramis Vineyards (Black Label) | 2005 | MCLAREN VALE
★★★ $ $ $ From the *terra rossa* soils of McLaren Vale comes this beautiful Cabernet, showing berry and spice on the nose and stewed fruit, savory spice and a great depth and complexity on the palate.

Bowen Estate | 2006 | COONAWARRA
★★ $ $ $ Doug Bowen is famous for his full-bodied, intensely flavored wines. This Cabernet offers blackberry, eucalyptus and spice flavors held up by powerful, tight tannins that will soften with time.

Glen Eldon Wines | 2005 | BAROSSA
★★ $ $ Barossa's 2005 vintage produced bright, rich fruit, and Glen Eldon took a minimalist winemaking approach in order to let those qualities shine through. Cherry aromas and flavors of earth, fig, tobacco and savory spice define this standout Cabernet.

Henry's Drive Vignerons The Trial of John Montford | 2006 | PADTHAWAY
★★★ $ $ Named for an incident in 1863 when John Montford robbed Henry's mail coach of 75 pounds, this velvety, blackberry-saturated Cabernet lingers nicely on the palate.

Hill of Content | 2005 | SOUTH AUSTRALIA
★★ $ Pure, ripe cherry flavors are highlighted by sweet spice notes in this smooth, generous wine.

Shirvington | 2006 | MCLAREN VALE
★★★ $ $ $ The Shirvington family has received numerous awards and accolades since their first commercial release, a 2001 Cabernet. The 2006 offers blueberry and spice notes with supple tannins.

Two Hands Coach House Block Single Vineyard | 2006 | BAROSSA VALLEY
★★★★ $ $ $ $ Two Hands is a *négociant* lauded by wine lovers and critics alike for its powerful, complex wines. This 2006 Cabernet is full-bodied and ageworthy, packed with flavors of cocoa, eucalyptus, sweet spice and black fruit and woven with formidable tannins.

AUSTRALIAN REDS

shiraz

Shiraz is Australia's iconic red wine grape, revered for producing the country's greatest wines. It is also Australia's most widely planted red grape. Australian Shiraz is remarkably different from its counterpart, the Syrah of France. With a more explosive array of concentrated berry flavors as well as spice, Shiraz is without a doubt Australia's defining wine. Grown in a variety of regions throughout the country, Shiraz is at its best in the Barossa Valley and McLaren Vale in South Australia, Hunter Valley in New South Wales and several Victoria regions. Most examples are drinkable when young, though some well-made versions have the ability to benefit from long aging, sometimes even more so than comparable Cabernet Sauvignons.

shiraz recommendations

Brothers in Arms | 2002 | LANGHORNE CREEK
★★★ $ $ $ The Adamses have grown grapes since the 1890s but didn't start making their own wine until more than 100 years later. This Shiraz—full of sumptuous layers of blackberry, cassis and leather flavors—shows off their skill in the winery.

Bulletin Place | 2007 | SOUTH EASTERN AUSTRALIA
★ $ Bulletin Place pays homage to a Sydney dining club and wine store where many of Australia's modern winemakers got their start. This well-priced Shiraz buzzes with the youthful vibrancy of fresh blueberries and peppery spice, balanced by mouthwatering acidity.

Cimicky Trumps | 2007 | BAROSSA VALLEY
★★★ $ Charles Cimicky believes in a very meticulous approach to winemaking, and consequently his wines show a rare purity. Licorice, spicy currant and cassis-syrup flavors take a savory turn on the palate in this lovely bottling.

Expatriate | 2006 | MCLAREN VALE
★★★ $ $ $ Made with top-quality fruit by one of the country's finest young winemakers, Corrina Rayment, this Shiraz makes a powerful first impression, with explosive blackberry, cassis and black pepper flavors that linger on the palate.

Fireblock Old Vine | 2005 | CLARE VALLEY
★★ $ As its name suggests, Fireblock warms the palate with an intense spiciness, lush black fruit flavors, licorice highlights and a subtly sweet, lasting finish.

Geoff Merrill Reserve | 2003 | MCLAREN VALE
★★ $ $ $ Geoff Merrill restored an historic but dilapidated gravity-fed winery to realize his dream of producing excellent wine. The effort was well worth it, as this spicy prune- and blackberry-infused McLaren Vale Shiraz demonstrates.

Henry's Drive Vignerons Dead Letter Office | 2006 |
MCLAREN VALE/PADTHAWAY
★★ $ $ Grapes from two appellations come together to create a wine with intriguing aromas of cigar box and black pepper and luscious blueberry flavors supported by smooth tannins.

star producers
australian shiraz

Charles Cimicky
When Charles took over from his father, Karl, he made important quality strides at the winery, gaining a reputation as one of the most meticulous winemakers in South Australia.

Domaine Terlato & Chapoutier
French winemaker Michel Chapoutier and U.S. importer Anthony Terlato teamed up to build this highly lauded winery in the Australian Pyrenees.

Penfolds
Aussie pioneer Penfolds makes delicious wines for every taste and budget, as well as a flagship wine, Grange, that is legendary.

Peter Lehmann
Since 1982 Peter Lehmann has made wine from the best Barossa Valley grapes available from 185 independent growers.

S.C. Pannell
Stephen Pannell sculpts Australian wines with European-style complexity, reflecting his various French apprenticeships and respect for the Syrah grape.

Two Hands
The team of Michael Twelftree and Richard Mintz has been called one of the best *négociant* operations south of the equator, sourcing fruit from prized parcels in Australia.

Hewitson Ned & Henry's | 2006 | BAROSSA VALLEY
★ ★ $ $ Hewitson uses grapes from some of the finest vineyards in the Barossa Valley to craft this elegant Shiraz. Blackberries and pepper emerge from the glass, alongside spicy fruit and sweet currants.

Jim Barry The Lodge Hill | 2006 | CLARE VALLEY
★ ★ $ The children of pioneering winemaker Jim Barry pay honorable tribute to his memory with top-notch wines like this 2006 Shiraz. A cherry-berry nose perfumed with dusty spice is followed by a sweet, ripe palate and a mocha-mint finish.

Layer Cake | 2008 | SOUTH AUSTRALIA
★ ★ ★ $ Juicy and brimming with plum, raspberry and violets, Layer Cake's Shiraz has a lovely hint of spearmint and a wonderfully layered, mouthwatering finish.

Marquee Classic | 2007 | VICTORIA
★ $ A hot vintage in Victoria resulted in especially concentrated wines. Marquee's well-priced bottling gushes with black cherry, blackberry and stewed prune notes.

Peter Lehmann Stonewell | 2004 | BAROSSA
★ ★ ★ ★ $ $ $ $ Peter Lehmann is a household name in the Barossa, and the Stonewell vineyard has been especially good to the winemaker. This vintage unearths blackberry, blueberry, sage, nutmeg, chocolate and coffee flavors that are woven with muscular tannins.

Revolution | 2007 | MCLAREN VALE
★ ★ ★ $ $ Another wine by Corrina Rayment, this Shiraz is a good bargain. Its complex melody of flavors—blueberries, mushrooms and cured meats—makes it a weighty, plush yet balanced mouthful.

S.C. Pannell | 2006 | MCLAREN VALE
★ ★ ★ ★ $ $ $ Stephen Pannell wakes up the senses with a generous bounty of wild blueberry, blackberry and cassis aromas highlighted by violets and mocha. The massive palate shows a perfect integration of flavors and a lengthy, concentrated finish.

Shirvington | 2006 | MCLAREN VALE
★ ★ ★ $ $ $ $ Shirvington uses small-batch fermentation in order to emphasize the natural flavors of the grapes. This vintage displays a gorgeous mix of cassis and coffee upheld by smooth tannins.

Slipstream Fastback | 2006 | MCLAREN VALE
★ ★ $ $ The importer Epicurean created this label to showcase different winemakers each year. This Shiraz-Grenache blend made by Ben Glaetzer offers full-bodied blueberry, violet and pepper flavors.

Two Hands Lily's Garden | 2006 | MCLAREN VALE
★★★ $ $ $ $ This Shiraz is another top-flight wine from Two Hands. Mouth-filling flavors of black fruit, cocoa and cedar ooze on the palate, backed up by substantial tannins.

The Winner's Tank | 2007 | LANGHORNE CREEK
★★ $ Named for a water tank on the vineyard that is painted with the colors of the local winning football team, this Shiraz overdelivers for the price, with fragrant cured meat, spicy black cherry and ripe cassis flavors.

Woop Woop | 2007 | SOUTH EASTERN AUSTRALIA
★★★ $ Here is an outstanding Shiraz at a price that makes it perfect for everyday drinking. With its ample, lush, spiced blackberry flavors, this is an ideal choice for barbecue.

other australian reds

Australia's unheralded red grapes are Grenache and Mourvèdre, both originally from France's Rhône Valley. Grenache displays many of the same fruit-forward characteristics as Shiraz but with a somewhat lighter body, while Mourvèdre shows a smokier, spicier composition. Many vintners combine the two with Shiraz in blends labeled "GSM." Pinot Noir has tried to take hold in several wine regions throughout Australia, though success is mainly restricted to the island of Tasmania and Victoria's Yarra Valley. Merlot has increased in presence in South Australia over the last decade.

other australian red recommendations

The Black Chook Shiraz/Viognier | 2007 | SOUTH AUSTRALIA
★★★ $ Made with grapes sourced from vineyards in McLaren Vale and Langhorne Creek, this fabulous value possesses great complexity and length. The Shiraz provides layers of ripe black fruit, while a touch of Viognier softens the texture.

Brothers in Arms No. 6 Shiraz/Cabernet Sauvignon | 2004 | LANGHORNE CREEK
★★ $ $ This powerful blend of 85 percent Shiraz and 15 percent Cabernet Sauvignon tastes of dark berry, plum and violet, with pleasant oak notes, and has a persistent length.

Domaine Terlato & Chapoutier Shiraz/Viognier | 2006 |
VICTORIA

★★★ $ $ The French winemaker Chapoutier and the U.S. importer Terlato partnered to create this impressive blockbuster. Dark berry and dusty sage notes make a first impression, followed by crème de cassis flavors.

Gemtree Vineyards The Phantom Petit Verdot | 2007 |
MCLAREN VALE

★★ $ The traditional Bordeaux blending grape can excel on its own in the hands of the right winemaker. This stellar version is unusual yet appealing for its blueberry, sage and white pepper flavors and fruity, firm structure.

Henry's Drive Vignerons Parson's Flat Shiraz/Cabernet
| 2005 | PADTHAWAY

★★★ $ $ $ This Shiraz-dominated blend hails from Padthaway, located on Australia's Limestone Coast, and displays a hefty structure, considerable oak and loads of lavender, black currant and blueberry pie flavors that remain remarkably balanced.

Henschke Henry's Seven | 2006 | BAROSSA

★★★ $ $ $ Named after Harry Evans, an Australian wine pioneer who planted a seven-acre vineyard in 1853, this southern Rhône–style blend shows a French-like profile, with black fruit and cigar box aromas, sweet tannins and a rich finish.

Hewitson Miss Harry Dry Grown & Ancient Grenache/
Shiraz/Mourvèdre | 2006 | BAROSSA VALLEY

★★★ $ $ The product of old vines dating back to the late 1800s, this wine unfurls a complex bouquet of eucalyptus, dense blackberry and mineral, which is echoed in its flavor profile. It is rich yet elegant, with supple tannins and a tight finish.

Kaesler Stonehorse Grenache/Shiraz/Mourvèdre | 2006 |
BAROSSA VALLEY

★★ $ Earth, berries and cedar dominate the nose of this Barossa beauty. Made with nearly equal parts Shiraz and Grenache and a small amount of Mourvèdre, it offers the richness of blueberry pie, accented by savory notes.

Massena The Moonlight Run | 2006 | BAROSSA VALLEY

★★★ $ $ $ Low yields, old vines and the judicious use of oak all contribute to the concentration of this silky Rhône-fashioned blend. Layers of flavors range from cedar, eucalyptus and spice to blueberry, blackberry and mocha.

The Old Faithful Sandhill Grenache | 2006 | MCLAREN VALE
★★ $$$ Concentrated violet and blueberry flavors mark this Grenache, named after the ancient and reliable vines on which the partnership behind it has built its reputation.

Pillar Box Red | 2007 | PADTHAWAY
★ $ This easy-drinking Shiraz–Cabernet Sauvignon–Merlot medley is made by the same team behind Henry's Drive. Flavors of meat, black cherry and blackberry are infused with spice notes.

Primo Estate Il Briccone Shiraz/Sangiovese | 2006 |
MCLAREN VALE
★★ $$ The unusual marriage between Shiraz and Sangiovese results in an interesting and enjoyable wine. Complex flavors of cedar, cherry, spice and blueberry are set against a plush-textured palate.

Rocky Gully Shiraz/Viognier | 2007 | FRANKLAND RIVER
★★ $ A first-rate effort from Frankland Estate in Western Australia, Rocky Gully displays violet and blackberry aromas that lead to a peppery, cherry-saturated palate and a bright, balanced finish.

**Rutherglen Estates The Reunion Mourvèdre/Shiraz/
Grenache** | 2006 | VICTORIA
★★ $ This spicy blend is a heavyweight, with 58 percent Mourvèdre and equal parts Shiraz and Grenache. Ripe cherries and plums abound on a plush, medium-bodied palate.

Slipstream Shiraz/Grenache | 2006 | MCLAREN VALE
★★★ $ This is a true value, considering it's crafted by superstar winemakers Stephen Pannell and Ben Glaetzer. Powerful, dark and inky, it shows off spicy berry and ripe black fruit flavors.

Taltarni Cephas | 2003 | PYRENEES
★★ $$$ Winemaker Loïc Le Calvez says his proudest moment was when he finished blending this vintage. A blend of Shiraz and Cabernet, it is a perfect fusion of cocoa, blackberry and bright raspberry.

Tir Na N'Og Old Vines Grenache | 2006 | MCLAREN VALE
★★★ $$$ Easier to drink than to pronounce (*tír na nÓg* is Gaelic for "land of eternal youth"), this plush and mouth-filling wine displays spicy aromas, blackberry and cherry flavors and soft, ripe tannins.

Two Hands Brave Faces Shiraz/Grenache/Mataro | 2007 |
BAROSSA VALLEY
★★ $$$ Mataro is an Aussie synonym for the Mourvèdre grape, and here it contributes spice notes to a meaty, earthy blend that is rounded out by red and black fruit flavors and mighty tannins.

Wallace by Ben Glaetzer Shiraz/Grenache | 2007 |
BAROSSA VALLEY

★ ★ ★ **$ $** Made with more Shiraz than Grenache, this inky, dark blend possesses a soft and supple palate overflowing with layers of ripe berry and pencil shavings augmented by up-front oak flavors. Its concentrated finish stands testament to Glaetzer's skill in crafting world-class, good-value wines.

Yangarra Estate Vineyard Cadenzia Grenache/Shiraz/ Mourvèdre | 2006 | **MCLAREN VALE**

★ ★ **$ $** Cadenzia is a collection of Grenache-dominated wines made by five different McLaren Vale producers. Yangarra's effort is round and well built and displays fragrant spiced vanilla and bright red cherry aromas followed by earthy, black fruit flavors, all held up by well-integrated tannins.

news from a wine insider

australia by Sophie Otton, Australia-based wine buyer, judge and journalist

Vintage Note

Australia's 2008 vintage was marked by weather extremes. In South Australia, a hot spell hit at the end of the ripening season and many producers suffered some damage and crop loss. Excessive rain was a problem in eastern Australia, particularly in the Hunter Valley and Mudgee regions, where rot occurred in some places. Despite uneven conditions, industry experts deemed the overall quality of the 2008 vintage good to excellent, especially in the South Eastern Australia region. Tasmania and most of Western Australia had their best vintages in years.

Significant New Trend

Australia continues to be a red-wine country, with Shiraz the most planted grape. Plantings of white grapes, however, are not far behind. Chardonnay is still Australia's dominant white variety, but the production of Sauvignon Blanc and Pinot Gris has increased significantly.

Producer Making News

After years of making wine in the south of France, Peter Schell is now producing Mediterranean-style wines at Barossa Valley's Spinifex. His complex red blend Papillon integrates Grenache, Cinsault and Carignane.

new zealand

New Zealand has been so successful with Sauvignon Blanc and Pinot Noir that it has come to be identified almost exclusively with these two signature grapes. However, the country's talented winemakers also produce impressive wines from a broad range of other grapes.

■ Principal Wine Region

Kumeu
Auckland • Waiheke Island

Tasman Sea

Gisborne

Hawkes Bay

Wairarapa
Martinborough
Nelson ☆ Wellington
Blenheim Marlborough

Waipara

Canterbury • Christchurch

Central Otago
Queenstown

South Pacific Ocean

New Zealand: An Overview

Despite the challenges of a highly unpredictable maritime climate, both of New Zealand's main islands, the North Island and the South Island, produce great wine. The country's best Sauvignon Blancs come from the Marlborough region, on the northeastern tip of the South Island. Pinot Noir excels in Marlborough, too, as well as in Central Otago (also on the South Island) and Martinborough, near the southern tip of the North Island. The North Island's warmer Hawkes Bay region focuses on elegant Bordeaux-style wines and, from the region's up-and-coming Gimblett Gravels district, top-quality Syrah.

New Zealand Wine Labels

Labels generally list region, grape and vintage, and in some cases, vineyard name. The term "Reserve" may be used to designate higher-quality wines but has no legal meaning.

new zealand whites

Historically, New Zealand has been known as a white wine country. Although many excellent Chardonnays and Rieslings are crafted here, it is Sauvignon Blanc that has emerged as the defining white grape of New Zealand.

NEW ZEALAND WHITES

sauvignon blanc

Sauvignon Blanc is the keystone of New Zealand's wine industry. The grape here yields wines with a freshness that recalls examples from Sancerre in France's Loire Valley. Yet New Zealand Sauvignons are in a category of their own, possessing flavors of grass, limes and exotic tropical fruit. This distinctive flavor profile, in combination with a comparatively low mineral content and high acidity, results in fresh, citrusy wines unburdened by overtly herbal flavors.

sauvignon blanc recommendations

Craggy Range Te Muna Road Vineyard | 2008 |
MARTINBOROUGH

★ ★ ★ **$ $** According to renowned New Zealand viticulturist (and Master of Wine) Steve Smith, Martinborough Sauvignon Blancs can possess more complexity than those from Marlborough, thanks to a harvest that occurs one to three weeks later. His exceptional Sauvignon offers white peach and tropical fruit flavors, supported by a fierce acidity and lime-infused minerals.

The Crossings | 2008 | **MARLBOROUGH**

★ ★ ★ **$** Awatere Valley is a distinct subregion of Marlborough, and this wine beautifully reflects the area's clay and limestone soils. A vibrant, lemony tartness and ripe peach and gooseberry flavors round out the palate.

star producers
new zealand sauvignon blanc

Brancott

Brancott helped establish Marlborough Sauvignon Blanc as New Zealand's signature wine by planting the region's first modern vineyards.

Cloudy Bay

Among the first Sauvignon Blanc producers to draw international acclaim for a grape too often dismissed as inferior to Chardonnay, Cloudy Bay crafts wines that recall white Burgundies in their elegance and complexity.

Craggy Range

In just over a decade, Craggy Range has emerged as one of New Zealand's most dynamic and highly lauded wineries.

Kim Crawford Wines

Crawford began by renting winery space before acquiring his own vineyards and facility. Today, Kim Crawford Wines is one of the country's largest and best producers.

Spy Valley

Bryan and Jan Johnson planted vines in the lower Waihopai Valley and in 2000 launched their own label to showcase their outstanding fruit.

Vavasour

Under both Vavasour and Dashwood labels, this producer is credited with pioneering the Awatere Valley, a Marlborough subregion that has become one of New Zealand's finest.

Cupcake Vineyards | 2008 | MARLBOROUGH
★ ★ $ Cupcake is a California-based vintner that turns to New Zealand for its Sauvignon Blanc; this well-priced result shows a perfect balance of key lime, kiwi and racy acidity.

Drylands | 2008 | MARLBOROUGH
★ ★ $ Made from some of the longest-established vines in Marlborough, this multilayered wine offers round melon and passion fruit flavors punctuated by grass, herbs and pleasing hints of earth.

Giesen | 2008 | MARLBOROUGH
★ ★ ★ $ Giesen has been making Marlborough wines since the early 1980s, and the winery has stayed true to its zippy, light-bodied, wonderfully refreshing style. With expressive aromas of lemongrass and stone, this is the perfect summer wine.

Goldwater | 2008 | WAIRAU VALLEY
★ ★ $ Pineapple and grapefruit come together in this fresh, zingy Sauvignon from Marlborough's Wairau Valley subregion.

Long Boat | 2008 | MARLBOROUGH
★ $ This Sauvignon Blanc from Long Boat's high-altitude vineyards is medium-bodied, with flavors of wet stone and lemonade highlighted by grass and plum.

Omaka Springs Estates | 2008 | MARLBOROUGH
★ ★ ★ $ Omaka Springs Estates owns 178 acres in Omaka Valley in the heart of the Marlborough wine region. Their light-bodied, crisp Sauvignon is augmented by a touch of Semillon, which adds a lovely herblike greenness to delicious flavors of grapefruit and lemon.

Origin Reserve Series | 2008 | MARLBOROUGH
★ $ Not all New Zealand Sauvignons are lean and green: in this fuller-bodied example, apple and lime flavors take on a rounder, richer profile, though ample acidity and minerals maintain good balance.

Piko | 2008 | MARLBOROUGH
★ ★ $ This winery takes its name from an edible fern native to New Zealand that can be used in cooking as a pepper substitute. True to its namesake, this green-hued wine radiates with white pepper and green pepper aromas, which are filled out by herb and lemon notes.

Spy Valley | 2008 | MARLBOROUGH
★ ★ ★ $ Marlborough's near-perfect growing conditions in 2008 endowed the always-excellent Spy Valley Sauvignon with a riper, richer mouthfeel and a tropical palate—though the signature pungent grass, sweet pea, grapefruit and mineral flavors still shine through.

Vavasour | 2008 | **AWATERE VALLEY**
★★★ **$** Vavasour makes big wines regardless of grape variety, and this complex bottling is no exception. Full-bodied and palate-coating, it is slightly smoky and refreshingly offset by a bright minerality, courtesy of the Awatere Valley's stony soil.

Wild Rock Elevation | 2008 | **MARLBOROUGH**
★★ **$** The Craggy Range team is behind this relatively new line of wines. Their 2008 Sauvignon Blanc is pure lime- and peach-scented refreshment, with intriguing notes of cherry.

other new zealand whites

New Zealand's second most planted white grape, Chardonnay is grown in many regions on both islands. Although skilled winemakers have worked hard to produce high-quality Rieslings in New Zealand, the grape still ranks fourth in total acreage behind Pinot Gris.

other new zealand white recommendations

Kim Crawford Unoaked Chardonnay | 2008 | **NEW ZEALAND**
★★ **$** This well-crafted, pleasant Chardonnay from one of New Zealand's most reliably consistent producers is brisk, with aromas of lemon and apple; malolactic fermentation—a process used to soften acidity—imparts notes of toffee and honey and a bit of weight.

Nautilus Pinot Gris | 2008 | **MARLBOROUGH**
★★★ **$** Nautilus makes elegant, serious whites, and this stunning Pinot Gris is just one example. A portion of this wine was aged for three months in old barrels, which lends a rich, smoky quality to succulent flavors of pear and peach.

Omaka Springs Estates Pinot Gris | 2008 | **MARLBOROUGH**
★★★ **$** Expressive floral aromas and pure flavors of ripe apple and juicy peach are polished by a clean, stony minerality in this well-built Marlborough Pinot Gris.

Wairau River Riesling | 2007 | **MARLBOROUGH**
★★★ **$** The owners of Wairau have been cultivating vines on the banks of the Wairau River since 1978. Their Riesling is an explosion of lychee and stone fruit infused by minerals and spice, all supported by a bracing acidity.

new zealand reds

New Zealand's efforts in red wine have been focused mainly on Pinot Noir, a grape that makes exceptional wines here. Many refined Cabernets and Merlots are produced as well, and some Syrahs are worth noting.

NEW ZEALAND REDS

pinot noir

Pinot Noir is New Zealand's most planted red grape. This notoriously finicky variety thrives on both islands, thanks to cool temperatures moderated by the ocean's influence. On the North Island, Pinot Noir performs especially well in Martinborough. On the South Island, it excels in Marlborough and particularly in Central Otago, in the southern part of the island, where the country's finest Pinot Noirs are made from low-yielding vines that produce intensely concentrated yet elegant wines.

pinot noir recommendations

Amisfield | 2007 | **CENTRAL OTAGO**
★★★ **$ $ $** Once used to raise sheep, Amisfield's vineyard land yields concentrated wines. This decidedly New World–style Pinot—made from single-vineyard estate fruit—oozes dark berry flavors.

Kawarau Estate | 2007 | **CENTRAL OTAGO**
★★ **$ $** Made from organic vineyards, Kawarau's elegant estate Pinot Noir is medium-bodied and marked by bright fruits like currants and wild raspberries, with hints of barnyard and earth.

Martin's Rake | 2008 | **MARLBOROUGH**
★★ **$** A leaner Pinot Noir than many other New Zealand examples, this is by no means shy on flavor. The juicy cherry, citrus and fresh-ground white pepper notes finish crisply.

Mt. Difficulty Roaring Meg | 2008 | **CENTRAL OTAGO**
★★★ **$ $** At just over $20, this is the least expensive Pinot from one of the South Island's finest producers. With aromas of granite and sweet raspberry, it is classic Central Otago Pinot Noir, complete with a medium-weight body and clean, balanced flavors.

Opawa | 2007 | **MARLBOROUGH**
★ ★ ★ $ Another fabulous and affordable Pinot, this is an immensely drinkable, silky-textured wine, with loads of red cherry and raspberry flavors that aren't overdone.

Palliser Estate | 2007 | **MARTINBOROUGH**
★ ★ $ $ Credited with making some of the North Island's best Pinots, winemaker Allan Johnson strives for a "ripe, full and rich" style. He achieves it here: powerful and spicy, this Pinot shows intense dark berry flavors and vanilla notes.

Rippon | 2006 | **CENTRAL OTAGO**
★ ★ ★ $ $ $ One of the region's oldest and most stunning vineyards also yields one of its finest wines. This Pinot Noir shows what old (and biodynamically farmed) vines are capable of: dense and richly textured, yet elegant, it is packed with deep flavors of earth, anise and ripe red and black fruit.

news from a wine insider
new zealand by Sue Courtney, New Zealand–based editor of wineoftheweek.com

Vintage Note

The 2008 vintage produced a bumper harvest, up 39 percent over 2007. This is the result of favorable weather as well as increased plantings, particularly of Sauvignon Blanc but also of Pinot Noir and Pinot Gris. Most of New Zealand did well, with the significant exceptions of Gisborne and Hawkes Bay, where yields were down.

Most Significant Trends

The number of New Zealand wineries continues to grow, and around 600 were recorded in 2008. Throughout the industry the current buzzwords are "sustainability" and "varietal diversity." Environmentally friendly practices are on the rise in vineyards and wineries, as well as in the marketing, packaging and transporting of the country's wines.

Meanwhile, growers are focusing on new grapes in their vineyards. While Sauvignon Blanc and Pinot Noir remain the most planted, and Chardonnay, Pinot Gris, Gewürztraminer, Riesling, Viognier, Merlot, Syrah and Bordeaux varieties are also popular, winemakers are now experimenting with Dolcetto, Montepulciano and Tempranillo, often with impressive results.

Saint Clair | 2007 | **MARLBOROUGH**
★★ $ St. Clair's owners named the vineyard for pioneer James Sinclair, who helped develop the town of Blenheim—and are pioneers in their own right, growing grapes here since 1978. This well-priced Pinot offers ample fruit flavors underscored by earth and tobacco.

Spy Valley | 2007 | **MARLBOROUGH**
★★ $ $ In the lower Waihopai Valley, a subregion of Marlborough, Spy Valley does things the old-fashioned way—handpicking grapes and using wild yeasts—and it shows. Richly perfumed with plum, flowers, earth and mushrooms, this is a refined, complex Pinot Noir.

Vavasour | 2007 | **AWATERE VALLEY**
★★ $ $ A heady mix of black cherry, tobacco and spice, this wine is dark, rich and generously oaked—a firm acidity keeps it balanced.

other new zealand reds

The warmer pockets of its two main islands yield New Zealand's finest Cabernet Sauvignon, Merlot and Cabernet Franc, most of which are used in blends. Many of these Bordeaux-style blends achieve a rare elegance and can taste very French-like. A growing number of vintners are working with Syrah, which is showing real promise here.

other new zealand red recommendations

Craggy Range Te Kahu Gimblett Gravels Vineyard | 2006 |
HAWKES BAY
★★★ $ $ This serious, multilayered red evokes the elegance of Bordeaux. Made from mostly Merlot, with bits of Cabernet Sauvignon, Cabernet Franc and Malbec to add weight and spice, it offers plum, leather and cedar, with a lengthy, memorable finish.

Crossroads Winery Merlot | 2006 | **HAWKES BAY**
★★ $ The intense minerality of Gimblett Gravels' soils is on display in this full-bodied Merlot. It is powerful, yet not overblown, with ample ripe fruit, a round texture and softened tannins on the finish.

Villa Maria Private Bin Merlot/Cabernet Sauvignon | 2006 |
HAWKES BAY
★ $ Made by one of New Zealand's larger producers, this Merlot-dominated blend is peppery, fresh, juicy and supple.

argentina

Argentina is the world's fifth-largest
wine producer, but only in the last
decade or two did it begin exporting
high-quality wines. Today, thanks
largely to the growing popularity of
Argentine Malbec, the U.S. imports
one-quarter of Argentina's entire
wine production.

■ Principal Wine
Region

CHILE

*South
Pacific
Ocean*

Salta
· Cafayate

ARGENTINA

La Rioja

Aconcagua —
Casablanca — · Valparaíso
San Antonio — ☆ Santiago   San Juan
Maipo —
Rapel — · Colchagua   Mendoza   Buenos Aires ☆
Curicó — · Maipú
Maule — · Luján
Concepción ● · Tupungato
Mendoza

*South
Atlantic
Ocean*

Río Negro
· Neuquén

Argentina: An Overview

Argentina's wine regions enjoy both an abundance of sunshine and natural irrigation from the Andes mountains. Mendoza—with its important subregions Maipú and Luján de Cuyo—is the largest region and produces most of the country's finest bottles, but winemakers are experimenting in many recently developed regions with promising results. Argentina's high-altitude vineyards—particularly in the Uco Valley in Mendoza and the Cafayate Valley in the Salta region—yield excellent white wines, while cool-climate regions, including Río Negro and Neuquén farther south, show potential as well. In San Juan, the country's second-largest wine-producing region, volume is down and wine quality is up. La Rioja's up-and-coming Famatina Valley is another region to watch.

Argentine Wine Labels

Most Argentine wine labels identify grape variety, the region where the grapes were grown, the producer's name and the vintage. Proprietary names are sometimes listed as well. The terms *Reserva* and *Reserve* are commonly used on higher-quality wines, though these terms have no regulated legal meaning.

argentine whites

Torrontés is Argentina's most distinctive white grape variety. It makes floral, light-bodied, refreshing wines, the best of which come from Cafayate. Chardonnay, however, is a more important grape in terms of quantity and is grown in most of the country's wine regions. Argentine Chardonnays range in style from lightly oaked, light-bodied and refreshing to full-bodied, decadent and creamy. Argentina is home to many other international white grape varieties, including Sauvignon Blanc, Pinot Gris (Pinot Grigio), Riesling, Semillon and Viognier.

argentine white recommendations

Catena Chardonnay | 2007 | MENDOZA

★ ★ $ This great value from one of Argentina's most important wine families is a complex white made with grapes from two different vineyards. Succulent aromas of quince, pear and honeysuckle dominate, while fresh acidity balances the rich, creamy mouthfeel.

Cobos Bramare Marchiori Vineyard Chardonnay | 2007 | MENDOZA

★ ★ ★ ★ $ $ $ Those familiar with California vintner Paul Hobbs know what to expect from his Argentine endeavor: a big, heady, yeasty Chardonnay, redolent of warm apple pie, with a dense, juicy palate of dried figs and pineapple.

Colomé Torrontés | 2008 | CALCHAQUÍ VALLEY

★ ★ $ Hailing from Salta, a region responsible for some of the highest-altitude vines in the world, this white reveals mineral, wet stone and citrus aromas, followed by juicy flavors of quince fruit.

Luigi Bosca Reserva Sauvignon Blanc | 2008 | MAIPÚ

★ ★ $ $ Fermented on lees in stainless steel, this gains a smooth texture while preserving the zesty fruit and zippy lime flavors. The aromas of grapefruit and lemon are unmistakably Sauvignon Blanc.

Michel Torino Estate Cuma Torrontés | 2008 | CAFAYATE VALLEY

★ $ Made from estate-grown, certified organic grapes, this white exemplifies the qualities of Cafayate Torrontés: light, refreshing flavors of kiwi, banana and clementine, with a touch of spice.

Pascual Toso Torrontés | 2008 | MAIPÚ

★ ★ $ Founded in 1890—and now with Paul Hobbs as a consultant—Pascual Toso is a great example of an old winery that has embraced Argentina's quality-wine revolution. Citrus, tropical fruit and lychee dominate the nose of this medium-bodied, crisp Torrontés.

Tamarí Reserva Torrontés | 2008 | LA RIOJA

★ ★ $ Not to be confused with the Spanish region of the same name, La Rioja is an up-and-comer in Argentina. This wine's citrus rind and orange blossom aromas lead to a plush, generous mouthfeel, balanced by good acidity on the finish.

Trapiche Torrontés | 2007 | MENDOZA

★ $ This lovely white is a terrific value. Full of spicy citrus and stone fruit flavors that are crisp and light, it is a perfect aperitif wine.

argentine reds

In the 1980s and 1990s, Argentina, like most New World wine-growing countries, focused on Cabernet Sauvignon (it still does, to an extent). But now Malbec, long considered a second-class grape, has become Argentina's signature red. It yields robust wines full of intense fruit flavors concentrated by oak aging. The cherry-flavored, medium-bodied Bonarda grape also thrives here. Merlot, Pinot Noir and Tempranillo have a minor presence, while Syrah has proved successful recently in the San Juan region.

argentine red recommendations

Barda Pinot Noir | 2007 | RÍO NEGRO
★★ $ $ This wine demonstrates the great potential for Pinot in the south of Argentina with its bright red cherry and berry nose, laced with earth and spice. Medium-bodied, with wild strawberry on the palate, it is a fresh, lively red.

Catena Alta Malbec | 2005 | MENDOZA
★★★ $ $ $ Grapes from four different vineyards meld seamlessly in this powerful, rich and meaty red. Malbec's dark fruit flavors—blackberry, black cherry and ripe plum—are complemented by notes of earth and leather.

Clos de los Siete | 2007 | MENDOZA
★★★ $ Made primarily with Malbec, with the addition of Merlot, Syrah and Cabernet Sauvignon, this red blend shows amazing elegance and complexity, with spicy lavender aromas, pronounced cherry and currant flavors, silky tannins and a long finish.

Cobos Bramare Malbec | 2006 | LUJÁN DE CUYO
★★★★ $ $ $ Another blockbuster effort involving California winemaker Paul Hobbs, this impressive, multilayered Malbec offers expressive aromas that range from leather, cigar box and tobacco to ripe fig and cherry. Partly because the wine is unfined and unfiltered, it has a plush, broad palate balanced by supple tannins.

Colomé Estate Malbec | 2007 | CALCHAQUÍ VALLEY
★★ $ $ This Malbec has the deep color typical of wines from Argentina's Salta province. Small additions of Cabernet Sauvignon, Syrah and Tannat add complexity to the richly textured palate of blueberries, blackberries, smoke and violets in this fruit-forward red.

Domaines Barons de Rothschild (Lafite) and Nicolás Catena Amancaya Malbec/Cabernet Sauvignon | 2007 | MENDOZA

★★★ $ $ This collaboration of two of the wine world's biggest names pays homage to its Bordeaux coproducer with dense flavors of black fruit, earth and cedar. With such immense concentration, depth and structure, it has great potential for the cellar.

Enrique Foster Limited Edition Malbec | 2004 | LUJÁN DE CUYO

★★★★ $ $ $ From the first—and most prestigious—of Argentina's designated wine regions, this Malbec shows dense black currant and cocoa flavors joined by eucalyptus, mint and dusty cedar.

Familia Marguery Malbec | 2004 | MENDOZA

★★★ $ $ With 12 months in French oak, this small-production wine achieves a lush texture and elegant oak integration. Powerful flavors of blueberry pie and chocolate make it a decadent mouthful.

Kaiken Malbec | 2007 | LUJÁN DE CUYO

★★★ $ A textbook Mendoza Malbec made by Chilean winemaker Aurelio Montes, this offers great character and value. Blueberry and violet aromas yield to black fruit flavors on the rich, round palate.

Luigi Bosca Single Vineyard Malbec | 2006 | LUJÁN DE CUYO

★★★ $ $ Aged in French oak, this complex Malbec shows spiced berry compote and pepper on the nose and waves of dark fruit flowing through the mid-palate. The chewy fruit is nicely balanced with tannins, resulting in a big, but balanced, red.

Marchiori & Barraud Malbec | 2007 | PERDRIEL

★★★ $ This delicious effort from the winemaking duo behind Viña Cobos is worth seeking out for its lovely aromas of wildflowers, cigar box, berry and cherry. The dark fruit palate, with hints of spice, coffee and mocha, is exquisitely balanced.

Nicolás Catena Zapata | 2005 | MENDOZA

★★★★ $ $ $ $ Lest you think Argentina is strictly Malbec-centric, this powerhouse blend, dominated by Cabernet Sauvignon (with some Malbec), is truly world-class. Dark flavors of coffee, dried figs, violets and roasted fruit are impressively structured and intense.

Salentein Reserve Malbec | 2006 | UCO VALLEY

★★ $ This wine, typical of the up-and-coming Uco Valley, showcases red cherry and black fruit along with elegant floral aromas. The oak is nicely integrated, lending spicy complexity to its finely tuned and nicely balanced flavors.

Trapiche Broquel Malbec | 2006 | **MENDOZA**
★★ $ Sourced from vineyards across Mendoza, this is a good example of a large-production wine that overdelivers for the price. Marked by layers of spice, smoke and blueberry flavors, a full body and firm tannins, it is a perfect wine for summer grilling.

Viña Cobos Felino Malbec | 2007 | **MENDOZA**
★★★ $ This Cobos bottling impresses from the start with a dark berry, black licorice and mineral-laden nose. It offers pure, clean fruit flavors, highlighted by pepper notes, on the plush palate, and a long, satisfying finish.

Weinert Carrascal | 2005 | **MENDOZA**
★★★ $ An excellent value for the price, this Malbec–Merlot–Cabernet Sauvignon blend is supple and juicy, with a rustic, dried fig and date quality that gives it an Old World flavor. Its herb-infused, meaty palate shows great structure.

news from a wine insider

argentina by Ian Mount, Buenos Aires–based journalist and wine writer

Vintage Note
Mendoza was hit by a lot of rain in early 2008. While the quality of some white wines suffered, it made many reds easier to drink, since acidity levels are higher and alcohol contents are lower.

Most Significant Trends
Malbec is still the king of Argentine red wines, but local winemakers are experimenting with other grapes today. Despite Mendoza's hot climate, Pulenta Estate and O. Fournier are producing surprisingly good, citrusy Sauvignon Blancs, while Ricominciare and Achaval Ferrer are bottling powerful but elegant Cabernet Francs. High-quality Syrah, Viognier and Petit Verdot are also receiving well-deserved acclaim.

Notable Restaurants
In Mendoza, pioneer Lucas Bustos, who launched popular restaurants at the Altus and Ruca Malén bodegas, recently moved his tiny 743 Bistro out of a family house and into the Clos de Chacras winery. He is also the creative force behind the new restaurant in the Melipal winery. Two noteworthy Uco Valley newcomers are the French-owned Atamisque and Tupungato Divino.

chile

Chile is still best known for producing vast quantities of high-quality affordable wines, though it is also an underrated source for premium reds. Its geography is ideal for grape-growing. Long and narrow, Chile is flanked to the east by the Andes range, which provides vineyard irrigation, and to the west by the Pacific, which moderates its warm, dry climate. Chile's geographical isolation has also protected its vines from the diseases that plague most wine regions.

Chile: An Overview

Vintners throughout Chile have worked for nearly a decade to improve their vineyards, eschewing sites on the valley floor in favor of lower-yielding hillsides that grow finer grapes. Most wine production still takes place in the Central Valley, where some well-known regions owe their reputations to a few star producers: the Rapel Valley with its important southern subregion of Colchagua is known for Casa Lapostolle and Los Vascos, while the Curicó Valley is the home of Miguel Torres. Notable emerging regions just north of the Central Valley include the valleys of San Antonio (home of the Leyda subregion), Aconcagua and Casablanca (see map, p. 234).

Chilean Wine Labels

Chilean labels list grape and often a proprietary name for blends. Single-vineyard designations are increasingly used, and the term *Reserva* is found on some quality wines.

chilean whites

Cool regions like Casablanca and San Antonio have broadened the scope of Chile's white production, primarily with
Sauvignon Blancs that recall Loire Valley whites in their
elegance and minerality. Wineries in southern regions have
had success with Chardonnay and occasionally Riesling.

chilean white recommendations

Apaltagua Reserva Chardonnay | 2008 | **CASABLANCA VALLEY**
★ $ The Casablanca Valley is particularly well suited for white wine.
This Chardonnay is marked by butterscotch-infused tropical fruit
flavors, a creamy mouthfeel and a lingering finish.

Arboleda Sauvignon Blanc | 2007 | **LEYDA VALLEY**
★ ★ $ Bright acidity and complex layers of grapefruit, lime and grass
make this Sauvignon Blanc worth seeking out.

Hacienda Araucano Sauvignon Blanc | 2008 |
CENTRAL VALLEY
★ ★ $ This Sauvignon Blanc displays an enticing mix of lime, aspara-
gus and straw notes balanced by good acidity and a citrusy finish.

Kingston Family Vineyards Cariblanco Sauvignon Blanc
| 2007 | **CASABLANCA VALLEY**
★ ★ $ Carl John Kingston's dreams of mining gold in Chile never
panned out, but they did result in amazing wines like this: nettle and
lime zest aromas are followed by a fruity, juicy, well-balanced palate.

Los Vascos Domaines Barons de Rothschild (Lafite)
Chardonnay | 2008 | **COLCHAGUA VALLEY**
★ $ The Basque Echenique family planted vines in Chile around 1750,
beginning a tradition of fine winemaking that continues today under
the leadership of the Rothschilds. This Chardonnay has a creamy
mouthfeel with flavors of pineapple, pear, citrus, vanilla and spice.

Montes Limited Selection Sauvignon Blanc | 2008 |
LEYDA VALLEY
★ ★ $ Montes's excellent Sauvignon is refreshing, with gooseberry
and grapefruit flavors rounded out with herbs and acidity.

MontGras Reserva Sauvignon Blanc | 2008 |
CASABLANCA VALLEY

★★ $ Brothers Hernán and Eduardo Gras created one of Chile's most modern wineries, where they craft this likable Sauvignon. Lime, melon, white pepper and grass give way to a slightly creamy palate.

Morandé Gran Reserva Chardonnay | 2006 |
CASABLANCA VALLEY

★★ $ Cool temperatures, sandy soils and 12 months in oak barrels combine to give this wine a rich complexity of flavors that range from white peach and citrus to yogurt and spicy oak. A refreshing acidity nicely offsets the long, creamy finish.

Quintay Sauvignon Blanc | 2007 | CASABLANCA VALLEY

★★ $ Nine producers with 617 acres among them formed this winery, and their second vintage shows the great potential of their collaboration. Concentrated grapefruit, lime, asparagus and white-flower notes are balanced by acidity and show a long, juicy finish.

Santa Ema Reserve Chardonnay | 2007 | CASABLANCA VALLEY

★ $ Santa Ema was founded by an Italian immigrant to Chile who began producing grapes in the 1930s. Their 2007 Chardonnay is mouth-filling and lush, with notes of mango, papaya, cream and oak.

Veramonte Reserva Sauvignon Blanc | 2008 |
CASABLANCA VALLEY

★ $ Grown alongside a creek, Veramonte's Sauvignon Blanc vines benefit from cool temperatures and good airflow that help the grapes retain acidity and fresh flavors of lime, melon and gardenia.

Viu Manent Reserva Sauvignon Blanc | 2007 | LEYDA VALLEY

★★ $ Cooling coastal breezes make Leyda a spectacular Sauvignon Blanc region. Marked by flavors of white peach and lilies, this well-priced bottling achieves a round, rich mouthfeel (a result of time spent on lees) balanced by crisp acidity.

chilean reds

Chile, sometimes called the Bordeaux of South America, produces primarily fruit-driven reds such as Cabernet Sauvignon and Merlot, though the country's most distinctive grape is Carmenère, a spicy French variety officially identified here in 1994. Emerging reds such as Pinot Noir and Syrah, especially from coastal regions like Casablanca and San Antonio, are also getting attention.

chilean red recommendations

Antiyal | 2006 | MAIPO VALLEY

★ ★ ★ $ $ $ Considered by many to be Chile's first small-lot "garage wine," Antiyal is made with an organic blend of Carmenère, Cabernet Sauvignon and Syrah. Aromas of black currant, cedar and tobacco are followed by spiced blueberry flavors and a perfectly balanced finish.

Casa Silva Los Lingues Gran Reserva Carmenère | 2006 | COLCHAGUA VALLEY

★ ★ $ $ Working with vines transplanted from Bordeaux a century ago, the Silva family continues a rich winemaking tradition with this Carmenère, defined by berry and toast flavors and a lush, full body.

Chono Reserva Carmenère/Syrah | 2007 | ELQUI VALLEY

★ $ Bright cherry and fig flavors are highlighted by vanilla notes and soft tannins in this vibrant blend.

Concha y Toro Don Melchor Cabernet Sauvignon | 2006 | PUENTE ALTO

★ ★ ★ ★ $ $ $ $ Don Melchor Concha y Toro's 1883 vision of crafting Bordeaux-style wines in Chile continues with this wonderfully intriguing Cabernet, which combines great complexity—fig, tobacco, blackberry and cigar box flavors—with a powerful, full-bodied palate.

Cousiño Macul Antiguas Reservas Cabernet Sauvignon | 2006 | MAIPO VALLEY

★ ★ $ Founder Matías Cousiño's sixth-generation descendants continue to improve wine quality and earn international recognition for this brand. Made with 100 percent Cabernet, their red is dominated by black fruit that is laced with an appealing savory quality all the way through the soft, delicious finish.

Domus Aurea Cabernet Sauvignon | 2005 | UPPER MAIPO VALLEY

★ ★ ★ ★ $ $ $ This well-structured wine, made with grapes grown in one of Maipo's finest subregions, offers a big nose of black currants and earth and flavors of cured meats held up by firm tannins.

Errazuriz Single Vineyard Carmenère | 2005 | ACONCAGUA VALLEY

★ ★ $ This nicely built Carmenère is rich and soft, thanks to 12 months in 80 percent new French and American oak barrels. There is a wonderful spiciness in the nose, joined with toast, blueberry and blackberry flavors on the palate and supported by mellow tannins.

Kuyen | 2006 | MAIPO VALLEY
★★ $ $ Celebrated biodynamic winemaker Álvaro Espinoza makes this Syrah-dominated red with organic grapes; it delivers blueberry flavors and accents of meat and sage.

Los Vascos Domaines Barons de Rothschild (Lafite) Cabernet Sauvignon | 2007 | COLCHAGUA VALLEY
★ $ Here's a lovely red wine with a Bordeaux pedigree at a fraction of the price; perfumed with red currant, cherry and cedar aromas, it reveals mouthwatering dark berry flavors and sweet tannins.

Miguel Torres Conde de Superunda | 2003 | CURICÓ VALLEY
★★★ $ $ $ Spanish icon Torres demonstrates its muscle with this powerhouse red blend: layers of blackberry, currant and cherry flavors are framed by massive tannins and spicy oak.

Montes Folly Syrah | 2006 | SANTA CRUZ
★★★★ $ $ $ $ A dark, dense, nearly black Syrah, this is one of Chile's finest reds, marked by complex flavors of licorice, fig, blackberry, plum, coffee, violet and meat and a plush, powerful texture.

MontGras Reserva Carmenère | 2007 | COLCHAGUA VALLEY
★★ $ From the rustic Colchagua Valley comes this great value Carmenère, with intense flavors of prune, blackberry and cherry highlighted by a hint of tobacco.

Morandé Reserva Carmenère | 2007 | MAIPO VALLEY
★★ $ Employing a delicate approach to winemaking, Morandé crafts wines that are elegant and unique. This bright, cherry-flavored red has notes of currants, a silky mouthfeel and a very fair price.

Odfjell Aliara | 2005 | CENTRAL VALLEY
★★★ $ $ $ Named after the tin measuring cups that once held a sailor's daily ration of wine, Aliara is a small-production wine that offers flavors of rich berries, earth, violet and spicy sage held up by muscular tannins.

Odfjell Orzada Malbec | 2005 | LONTUÉ
★★ $ Odfjell insists on low yields and handpicking in order to achieve purity in its wines. This plum-scented Malbec starts out soft, then opens up to show bold blackberry flavors and supple tannins.

Palin Carmenère | 2007 | RAPEL VALLEY
★★ $ Interest in this label spiked in 2008 thanks to its shared name with vice presidential candidate Sarah Palin. Regardless of one's political ideology, this Carmenère is worth seeking out for its elegant flavors of ripe berries, vanilla and toast.

Peñalolen Cabernet Sauvignon | 2007 | MAIPO VALLEY

★ ★ $ Maipo's gravelly slopes give Peñalolen's Cabernet firm structure and bold flavors, including blackberry and espresso. Earth tones and soft tannins round out the profile.

Root: 1 Cabernet Sauvignon | 2007 | COLCHAGUA VALLEY

★ $ Here is a great everyday Cabernet, with mint and blackberry aromas, a spicy vanilla richness in the mouth and an elegant finish.

Santa Ema Reserve Merlot | 2006 | MAIPO VALLEY

★ ★ $ Founded in 1955 by Pedro Pavone, the son of Italian winemakers from Piedmont, and his son, Felix, Santa Ema is a long-standing go-to for quality and value. The 2006 Merlot weaves together cocoa, mint and dried fig flavors on the full-bodied yet velvety palate.

Santa Rita Medalla Real Cabernet Sauvignon | 2006 | MAIPO VALLEY

★ ★ ★ $ An excellent value, this Santa Rita Cabernet has a complex profile of fig, blackberry, tobacco and earth, offset by good acidity and big tannins. Enjoy now or cellar for ten years.

Tabalí Reserva Especial | 2006 | LIMARÍ VALLEY

★ ★ $ $ The Limarí Valley's winemaking history dates back to the 16th century. Today the region produces intriguing wines, like this blend of Syrah, Cabernet and Merlot, which shows thick blueberry, smoke, prune and vanilla flavors and silky tannins.

Tabalí Reserva Syrah | 2007 | LIMARÍ VALLEY

★ ★ $ The cooling ocean influence and dry climate in Limarí Valley, one of Chile's northernmost wine regions, contribute to this plump Syrah's nose of dark fruit, prune and fig, while oak aging provides a toast-accented finish.

Ventisquero Grey Cabernet Sauvignon | 2006 | MAIPO VALLEY

★ ★ ★ $ $ Part of Ventisquero's premium line, the Grey Cabernet is still nicely priced. It shows powerful aromas of currant, blueberry and earth, which are echoed on the medium-bodied palate.

Veramonte Reserva Pinot Noir | 2007 | CASABLANCA VALLEY

★ ★ $ This beautifully made, medium-bodied Pinot is full of smooth, bright cherry, spice and cocoa notes.

Viu 1 | 2006 | COLCHAGUA VALLEY

★ ★ ★ ★ $ $ $ $ Malbec dominates in this premium blend from Viu Manent, oozing with blackberry, cherry and blueberry, highlighted by notes of plum, pencil shavings and smoked meat. The palate is plush and the finish long in this outstanding wine.

south africa

The Dutch brought grapevines to South Africa as early as the 1650s, but the country's modern wine industry is still considered young and in flux. Great strides have been made over the past two decades toward fully realizing the potential of South Africa's stellar terroir. Right now, two grapes in particular seem poised to redefine South African winemaking and earn it the international attention it deserves: Chenin Blanc and Syrah.

Coastal Region

Atlantic Ocean

Paarl

Cape Town

Constantia

Stellenbosch

Robertson

Elgin

Walker Bay

Indian Ocean

Principal Wine Region

South Africa: An Overview

Most of the wine that South Africa exports is made in the Coastal Region and surrounding areas of the Western Cape. Cabernet Sauvignon–based Bordeaux-style blends excel in the Coastal Region's Stellenbosch area, while Sauvignon Blanc, Chardonnay and Pinot Noir do better in the region's cooler area of Constantia, as well as in Overberg, Walker Bay and Cape Agulhas to the southeast. While many of these Cape wines are excellent, none has managed to create a truly distinctive style for South Africa. The minerally, tropical-scented Chenin Blancs and fruit-forward Syrahs that winemakers are creating in the Coastal Region, however, may well be on their way to becoming South Africa's defining wines.

South African Wine Labels

The straightforward labels used by South African winemakers list the winery name, variety, region and vintage. Blends may be given proprietary names, but the varieties that went into them will usually appear on the back label.

south african whites

South African Chenin Blanc, sometimes referred to as "Steen," is lighter in body and has more citrusy and tropical flavors than the traditional Chenin Blanc wines of France's Loire Valley. The other main varieties, Sauvignon Blanc and Chardonnay, generally yield medium-bodied wines with pronounced mineral flavors; Sauvignon Blancs sometimes stray into herbal and exotic fruit flavors as well. The remaining white wine production is less significant, consisting mostly of examples made from Colombard (sometimes referred to as Colombar in South Africa), Cape Riesling (also known as Crouchen, an obscure French grape with no relation at all to Riesling), Semillon, Gewürztraminer and various Muscats.

south african white recommendations

Beyond Sauvignon Blanc | 2008 | COASTAL REGION

★ ★ $ This low-priced wine exceeds expectations, offering classic Sauvignon Blanc aromas of asparagus and lime, a vibrant acidity and a lasting, flavorful finish.

Brampton Unoaked Chardonnay | 2008 | COASTAL REGION

★ $ Rustenberg makes this wine, named after their champion Jersey bull, Brampton. It's a well-structured, refreshing and crisp style of Chardonnay, with ample tropical fruit and red apple flavors, bright acidity and a clean finish.

Durbanville Hills Sauvignon Blanc | 2007 | DURBANVILLE

★ ★ $ Durbanville's locale, in a cooler area of the Cape, is ideal for white grape varieties, since the slower ripening helps concentrate flavors. This Sauvignon shows a mix of lime, asparagus and white pepper and a crisp acidity.

Fleur du Cap Sauvignon Blanc | 2008 | WESTERN CAPE

★ $ Bright and well balanced, this easy-drinking wine offers pink grapefruit and fresh-cut grass flavors with a solid backbone of acidity and a round mouthfeel.

Glen Carlou Chardonnay | 2007 | PAARL

★ ★ $ This lovely Paarl white has a whiff of butter on the nose, followed by pronounced mango and rich butterscotch flavors that linger on a creamy palate.

Goats do Roam | 2008 | WESTERN CAPE

★ $ This fragrant white blend is packed with juicy, mouth-filling flavors of honeysuckle, ripe white peach, lemon verbena and a touch of butter and spice.

Graham Beck Gamekeeper's Reserve Chenin Blanc | 2008 | COASTAL REGION

★ ★ $ Here's a delightful example of South African Chenin Blanc more nuanced than most. Melon, apple and citrus notes on the nose and palate are balanced by firm acidity and a slight, honeyed sweetness on the palate.

Mulderbosch Chenin Blanc | 2008 | WESTERN CAPE

★ ★ ★ $ Winemaker Mike Dobrovic inspires a cultlike following for his wines, and this excellent Chenin Blanc helps explain why: complex layers of honeydew, overripe apples, white flowers and pepper are supported by a refreshing acidity.

Neil Ellis Chardonnay | 2007 | ELGIN
★★ $ $ Elgin is one of the Cape's cooler areas, yet this Chardonnay is very ripe and spicy, with generous tropical fruit flavors like mango, pineapple and ginger. Notes of vanilla and creamy oak complete the long, complex finish.

Rustenberg Chardonnay | 2007 | STELLENBOSCH
★★ $ Lees-stirring lends richness to this peach- and mango-flavored white. Spicy oak and a hint of tangy yogurt carry through on the balanced finish.

Sutherland Chardonnay | 2007 | ELGIN
★★ $ Made by Thelema Mountain Vineyards with Chardonnay grapes grown along the first biodiversity wine route, this tastes like sunshine in a bottle. Meyer lemon and juicy pineapple aromas are followed by butter and spiced vanilla flavors on the palate and a citrus kiss at the end.

Vergelegen Sauvignon Blanc | 2007 | STELLENBOSCH
★★ $ This unique and interesting Sauvignon Blanc has flavors of kaffir lime, tomatillo, asparagus and nuts—and a whiff of brine—spiked with high acidity and a citric bite.

south african reds

For better or for worse, South Africa's preeminent local grape is Pinotage, a cross between native French grapes Cinsault and Pinot Noir. With its pungent aromas and decidedly eccentric, earthy taste profile, Pinotage is far from a crowd-pleaser, though carefully made, full-bodied, smooth versions have their admirers. Vintners have more commercial success with international grape varieties such as Cabernet Sauvignon, Merlot, Pinot Noir and Cabernet Franc, which are often blended together to produce complex, enjoyable red wines. South Africa's Merlots and Pinot Noirs are somewhat comparable in style to those wines from America's Pacific Northwest, but for the country's most exciting reds, look to Syrah (Shiraz). Many South African Syrahs show assertive, concentrated jammy fruit flavors in the Australian style, while others possess an earthier, more French-like refinement—the best are superb wines regardless of style.

south african red recommendations

Cirrus Syrah | 2006 | STELLENBOSCH

★ ★ ★ $ $ $ South African winemaking partners Jean Engelbrecht of Rust en Vrede and Ernie Els teamed up with Californian Ray Duncan of Silver Oak to craft this gorgeously layered, coffee-scented beauty packed with licorice, fig compote and cocoa. A whiff of pepper on the finish makes for the perfect ending.

De Toren Z | 2006 | STELLENBOSCH

★ ★ ★ $ $ Plump and approachable now, this Bordeaux-style wine balances strong, dark plum flavors, baking spices and hints of cedar with lively acidity and soft tannins. The finish is plush and velvety.

Ernie Els | 2004 | STELLENBOSCH

★ ★ ★ $ $ $ $ This beautiful Bordeaux-style blend is crafted with grapes grown on the granite slopes of Helderberg Mountain. Blackberry, prune and smoky, sweet spice aromas give way to a soft palate with mellowed tannins and notes of cigar box and hickory.

Fleur du Cap Cabernet Sauvignon | 2007 | COASTAL REGION

★ ★ $ This simply delicious Cabernet is produced by winemakers at the Bergkelder, one of the most advanced underground cellars in the Southern Hemisphere. It shows dark fruit, cedar and sweet spice and has a finish that lingers.

Glen Carlou Grand Classique | 2005 | PAARL

★ ★ $ Made with the same blend as the wines from Bordeaux's Left Bank, this wine was then matured two years in new and old French oak. The nose reveals black currants, herbs and meat notes; the palate offers black pepper, ripe tannins and a perfect balance.

Guardian Peak SMG | 2005 | WESTERN CAPE

★ ★ $ $ The classic triumvirate of Grenache, Syrah and Mourvèdre is rearranged in this Western Cape wine to great success. The nose and palate—rich with blackberry, dried currant, vanilla and licorice flavors—are balanced by lively acidity and supple tannins.

Indaba Shiraz | 2008 | WESTERN CAPE

★ $ "Indaba" is a traditional Zulu term for a gathering, and this is indeed a perfect wine for sharing, redolent of spiced blueberry jam.

Kanonkop Pinotage | 2006 | SIMONSBERG-STELLENBOSCH

★ ★ ★ $ $ $ From the Simonsberg foothills comes this standout, complex Pinotage, with black, spicy fruit, licorice, cedar and mint flavors and big, firm tannins that will see it through a decade.

Meerlust Rubicon | 2004 | STELLENBOSCH

★ ★ ★ $ $ This estate has been owned by the Myburgh family since the 1750s, and their 2004 red blend shows an intriguing and fragrant bouquet of dried cherry, prune, violet, rosemary, meat and sage.

Rust en Vrede Cabernet Sauvignon | 2004 | STELLENBOSCH

★ ★ $ $ Over the course of 30 years, Rust en Vrede has appointed only two winemakers, who have earned the estate a reputation for impressive wines, like this gorgeous Cabernet. Dried cherry and prune flavors are highlighted by subtle licorice, spice and meat notes.

Sizanani Pinotage | 2008 | STELLENBOSCH

★ $ Sizanani is dedicated to social empowerment, and its wines represent extraordinary value. Handpicked grapes yield a spicy, black plum–flavored wine with a soft finish.

Vilafonté Series M | 2004 | PAARL

★ ★ $ $ $ The product of a joint venture between South African and American winemakers, this Bordeaux blend offers spicy blackberry aromas and a palate well balanced with tannins, medium acidity and hints of dried fruit, leather and cocoa.

Warwick Estate Reserve | 2002 | STELLENBOSCH

★ ★ ★ $ $ $ Warwick's land was once a farm named Good Success, and this wonderful wine lives up to the former moniker. Fresh fruit and complex flavors of sweet spice, dried rose petals and meat are backed by firm tannins and good acidity.

The Wolftrap Syrah/Mourvèdre/Viognier | 2007 |
WESTERN CAPE

★ ★ $ This lush ménage à trois is an amazing value for the price, exhibiting the structure of a more expensive wine. Spicy berry, sweet oak, vanilla and herb notes couple with soft tannins, medium acidity and black licorice on the velvety finish.

other new world wines

Canada is the world's largest producer of ice wine, but Canadian vintners are also crafting fine dry wines from grapes like Pinot Noir and Riesling. Mexican wines continue to improve, although very few are exported. In South America, Brazil and Uruguay are taking on their neighbors Chile and Argentina with increasingly well-crafted wines that are reaching U.S. wine shops with greater frequency.

Canada, Mexico, Brazil, Uruguay: An Overview

Nothing about making wine in Canada is easy. Still, the country's vintners manage to produce quality red and white wines despite extreme winters and early frosts. The Canadian winemaking industry is centered in Ontario and British Columbia. Ontario's Niagara Peninsula and Pelee Island regions benefit from the moderating influences of the Great Lakes (Ontario and Erie), which allow winemakers here to succeed with Riesling, both as a dry wine and in the regions' famous ice wines (see p. 274). The Okanagan Valley, British Columbia's preeminent region, produces elegant wines primarily with Chardonnay, Pinot Noir and Bordeaux varieties.

Farther south, Mediterranean-like conditions in Mexico's Baja California regions result in full-bodied reds from Petite Sirah, Zinfandel, Nebbiolo and Tempranillo. About 90 percent of Brazil's wine comes from Serra Gaúcha, the main appellation in the state of Rio Grande do Sul, where the temperate climate and hillside vineyards are ideal for growing Tannat and other French transplants like Cabernet Sauvignon and Merlot. Tannat is even more important in Uruguay, where it thrives near Montevideo, the capital. All of these Latin American countries produce white wines as well.

other new world whites

Riesling is grown successfully in Ontario and British Columbia, along with Gewürztraminer, Chardonnay and Pinot Gris. Canada is also the world's largest producer of sweet ice wine, made from Riesling or Vidal Blanc grapes that are left to freeze on the vine before they are harvested. Mexico produces Sauvignon Blanc, Chenin Blanc and Semillon, while Brazil's cooler regions support Chardonnay, Muscat, Semillon and Sauvignon Blanc. Uruguay makes a few nice whites from Chardonnay, Albariño and Torrontés.

other new world white recommendations

Bouza Albariño | 2008 | **LAS VIOLETAS, URUGUAY**
★★ $ $ Bouza's take on Spain's fragrant white grape is bright and flavorful, with notes of lemon, herbs and yogurt underscored by an intense minerality. Oak aging lends a creamy roundness that balances out the refreshing acidity.

Cave Spring CSV Riesling | 2007 |
BEAMSVILLE BENCH, CANADA
★★★ $ $ Parts of Ontario have the perfect latitude and soil composition to produce great Rieslings. This off-dry version is mineral-laden and displays concentrated flavors of peach, mango, tangerine and honey, upheld by a searing acidity.

Marson Famiglia Chardonnay | 2005 | **SERRA GAÚCHA, BRAZIL**
★★ $ The Marson winery pays tribute to its family winemaking heritage with this Famiglia Chardonnay. Bright apple, pear and yogurt aromas take on a spicy, round quality on the palate.

**Mission Hill Family Estate S.L.C. Sauvignon Blanc/
Semillon** | 2006 | OKANAGAN VALLEY, CANADA
★★ **$ $** The Okanagan Valley enjoyed a banner year in 2006, with a
cool start but a warm ripening season that is reflected in this rich
wine: citrus, pear, apple and stone flavors are balanced by acidity.

Monte Xanic Chenin/Colombard | 2007 |
VALLE DE GUADALUPE, MEXICO
★ **$** This sophisticated, value-priced white from Baja California,
Mexico, displays lively notes of tart apple, ginger, and bitter honey: a
perfect choice for grilled chicken and seafood.

Stratus White | 2006 | NIAGARA PENINSULA, CANADA
★★★ **$ $ $** Stratus's winemaker, J-L Groux, believes strongly that
blending yields the most complex wines. This white achieves a wonderful array of apple, wet wool, melon, pear, cherry, pineapple, oak,
spice and flower flavors, integrated with a lush, creamy texture.

other new world reds

In Ontario, the hybrid grape Baco Noir produces rustic
reds. British Columbia's Bordeaux blends resemble Washington State reds and are some of the region's best wines.
Most Mexican reds are made from Tempranillo, Cabernet,
Petite Sirah and Nebbiolo. In Brazil, France's Tannat grape
makes quality reds, as do Cabernets Sauvignon and Franc,
Merlot and Pinot Noir. But it's in Uruguay that Tannat
reigns supreme, yielding dark, tannic wines that are softer
than most French examples yet have the same full body.

other new world red recommendations

Bouza Monte Vide EU Tannat/Merlot/Tempranillo | 2006 |
MONTEVIDEO, URUGUAY
★★★★ **$ $ $** Bouza's standout blend is reminiscent of a late-
summer garden. Notes of rose-hip tea, blackberries, black cherries,
flowers and wet leaves culminate in a lingering, balanced finish.

Don Adelio Ariano Reserve Oak Barrel Tannat | 2004 |
CANELONES, URUGUAY
★★★ **$** The combination of a coastal climate and barrel aging have
endowed this Tannat with intriguing flavors—cherry, cranberry, dried
meat, sweet spices, bay leaf and vanilla—balanced by high acidity,
firm tannins and a fruity finish.

Familia Deicas 1er Cru Garage Tannat | 2000 |
JUANICO, URUGUAY

★ ★ ★ ★ $ $ $ $ Aiming to be the Grand Cru of Uruguay, and priced accordingly, this Tannat stands above its peers with a sophisticated, complex and beautifully woven palate of dark fruit, dried fruit, nuts, spice, leaves, firm tannins and good acidity. Cellar another ten years.

Fausto by Pizzato Cabernet Sauvignon | 2005 |
SERRA GAÚCHA, BRAZIL

★ $ In 1880 the Italian Fausto family immigrated to Brazil, where they began producing great-value wines with an Old World sensibility. Dark fruit notes are scented with bay leaf, eucalyptus, black pepper and mushroom in this interesting Cabernet.

Henry of Pelham Family Estate Reserve Baco Noir | 2006 |
ONTARIO, CANADA

★ ★ ★ $ $ Ontario specializes in Baco Noir, and Henry of Pelham makes some of the finest in the province. With a well-layered nose of bright red berries, earth, wet leaves and mushrooms, this one is medium-bodied and flavorful.

L.A. Cetto Private Reserve Nebbiolo | 2004 |
VALLE DE GUADALUPE, MEXICO

★ ★ $ A surprising amount of fresh fruit—rich plums and cherries—comes forward on this older Nebbiolo, along with layers of wet leaves, vanilla, cinnamon and spice. Good acidity and strong tannins balance it out and carry through the long finish.

Le Clos Jordanne Le Clos Jordanne Vineyard Pinot Noir
| 2006 | **NIAGARA PENINSULA, CANADA**

★ ★ ★ ★ $ $ $ This gorgeous Pinot from Niagara's Jordan Bench is the result of a partnership between Vincor Canada and Boisset of France. Complex flavors of raspberry, earth, tea leaves, smoked meat and sweet spice are offset by good acidity and soft tannins.

Marson Gran Reserve Cabernet Sauvignon | 2002 |
SERRA GAÚCHA, BRAZIL

★ ★ $ $ In southern Brazil, the Marson family produces beautifully balanced wines like this richly flavorful Cabernet, with notes of black currant, dried fruit, cedar and eucalyptus.

Megalomaniac Vainglorious Merlot/Cabernet Sauvignon
| 2004 | **NIAGARA PENINSULA, CANADA**

★ ★ ★ $ $ This well-crafted blend shows ripe and juicy dark fruit flavors spiced with notes of sage, cayenne, herbs and cured meats and framed by soft tannins.

champagne & other sparkling wines

It is perhaps one of the wine world's greatest ironies that its most food-friendly bottles—Champagne and other sparkling wines—are almost always reserved for formal occasions. And yet, a good sparkling wine can cost as little as $10 a bottle. With their refreshing acidity, these wines are perfect for everyday drinking.

Sparkling Wine: An Overview

There are several ways to make sparkling wine, but the finest is the traditional method—*méthode traditionnelle*—in which vintners create and trap carbon dioxide bubbles in a still wine by activating a second fermentation in sealed bottles. Sparkling wines vary in the strength of their effervescence, and are produced in styles that range from very dry to very sweet. Many regions produce them, but the best versions come from cool regions with mineral-rich soils. The pinnacle of sparkling wine regions is Champagne in northern France, but exceptional sparklers are also made in France's Loire Valley, northern Italy and Spain, and California's Anderson Valley and Carneros regions.

champagne

Champagne is undeniably the world's greatest sparkling wine. Only wines made in northern France's Champagne region are entitled to be called "Champagne," yet the word is often incorrectly used to refer to any wine with bubbles, regardless of origin, and those that falsely bear the name are invariably of inferior quality.

Champagne Grapes & Styles

Champagne vintners blend grapes from various vintages and villages using only three permitted grapes: Chardonnay, Pinot Noir and Pinot Meunier. *Blanc de Blancs* are made from 100 percent Chardonnay, whereas *Blanc de Noirs* are sparkling whites produced with red grapes Pinot Noir and/or Pinot Meunier. Rosés are created by either blending some red wine into white sparkling wine or by soaking pigment-rich red grape skins in pressed juice to "bleed" in some color.

Champagne Labels

Look for the word "Champagne" on the wine label to make sure it is the real thing. Most Champagnes are "NV," or non-vintage, meaning they are blends of wines produced in different years, a practice that allows each Champagne house to create a distinctive and consistent taste profile from year to year. Vintage Champagnes are made only in exceptional years and usually aged for a longer period of time before release. Top Champagnes are labeled with unofficial terms such as *Tête de Cuvée* and are often given proprietary names such as Moët's Dom Pérignon. Sweetness levels are categorized as follows, from driest to sweetest: *Brut Nature* (also known as *Brut Zéro, Pas Dosé* or *Sans-Dosage*), *Extra Brut, Brut, Extra Dry* (or *Extra Sec*), *Sec* (or *Dry*), *Demi-Sec* and *Doux*. Brut is the most common style on the market.

champagne recommendations

WHITES

Alfred Gratien Blanc de Blancs Brut | NV |

★ ★ ★ **$ $ $ $** Founded in 1864, Alfred Gratien is a very traditional house that eschews modern techniques in favor of old-fashioned methods. The excellent Blanc de Blancs is bright and citrus-driven, underscored by notes of white peach, apricot and mineral, with a vanilla-flavored finish.

Besserat de Bellefon Cuvée des Moines Blanc de Blancs Brut | NV |

★ ★ ★ **$ $ $ $** This 100 percent Chardonnay made by a small *négociant* house starts off with a savory, mushroomy quality on the nose, which blows off after a bit of time in the glass to reveal honey-coated orange and toast flavors. Its slight brininess and a lemon-kissed finish make it a perfect wine for oysters.

star producers
champagne

Alfred Gratien
Among the most traditional Champagnes available, Gratien's vintage cuvées remain fresh for decades.

Dom Pérignon
These long-lived, complex cuvées live up to their namesake, Pérignon, a monk who is credited with perfecting the art of Champagne production in the 1600s.

Gosset
This storied producer consistently receives rave reviews, particularly for its Excellence Brut and vintage prestige cuvées Célebris and Grand Millésime.

Henriot
This family-owned house was established in the early 1800s and has cultivated a devoted following for its rich, distinctive, biscuit-flavored wines.

Laurent-Perrier
For nearly two centuries Laurent-Perrier has been making elegant Champagnes that today are among the most highly sought after.

Ruinart
Although this is the oldest house dedicated exclusively to Champagne, Ruinart is not as well known as many others. That is changing, as word of its excellence spreads.

Gosset Excellence Brut | NV |

★ ★ ★ $ $ $ Gosset Champagnes are made without the acid-softening effects of malolactic fermentation, which preserves their fresh flavors. Yet, this golden-hued wine is still rich, with notes of almond, sweet butter and a hint of marshmallow on the dry, balanced finish.

Henriot Souverain Brut | NV |

★ ★ ★ ★ $ $ $ Made with 60 percent Pinot Noir and 40 percent Chardonnay, this shows incredible depth and character for a non-vintage Champagne. Notes of earth, cream and chalky mineral infuse a base of nectarine and citrus flavors in this exquisite, brisk wine.

Krug Brut | 1998 |

★ ★ ★ ★ $ $ $ $ Produced after an unusually hot late summer in Champagne, this 1998 was the fourth vintage Krug declared in the decade. A blend of Chardonnay and Pinots Noir and Meunier, it is elegant and beautifully textured, with layers of honey, citrus and toast.

Louis Roederer Premier Brut | NV |

★ ★ ★ $ $ $ Steely acidity provides a firm backbone for flavors of fresh peach, flower, citrus and subtle red berry in this rich, toast-accented brut. Mostly Pinot Noir, filled out with Chardonnay and Pinot Meunier, it has an intriguing petrol quality laced throughout.

Nicolas Feuillatte Brut | NV |

★ ★ $ $ $ Consistently well made and relatively low-priced, this is as close as you can get to a bargain from Champagne. It displays equal parts mineral and zesty fruit—green apples and citrus—and is refreshingly delicious.

Pol Roger Extra Cuvée de Réserve Rich Demi-Sec | NV |

★ ★ $ $ $ This demi-sec balances its sweetness well with a racy acidity that supports creamy flavors of honey-coated apples.

Ruinart Blanc de Blancs Brut | NV |

★ ★ ★ ★ $ $ $ $ Founded in 1729, Ruinart is the oldest Champagne house and sources nearly all its fruit from Premier Cru vineyards. The Blanc de Blancs shows amazing depth and finesse, with intriguing notes of woodsy earth and coffee highlighting expressive ripe citrus and brioche flavors.

Tribaut L'authentique Brut | NV |

★ ★ ★ $ $ $ Fastened with a rustic string closure, this Champagne has a taste as unique as its package. Pronounced aromas of buttered toast—the result of two years fermenting and aging in oak barrels—are complemented by peach and melon flavors and a refreshing acidity.

ROSÉS

Laurent-Perrier Cuvée Rosé Brut | NV |

★ ★ ★ ★ $ $ $ $ An outstanding rosé made from 100 percent Pinot Noir, this is fresh yet decadent, with lush flavors of black cherry, strawberry and orange and a thread of chalky minerals woven throughout. The ultrafine bead creates a creamy-textured mousse in the mouth, further augmenting the opulent profile.

Perrier-Jouët Blason Rosé Brut | NV |

★ ★ ★ $ $ $ $ This rosé Champagne from Perrier-Jouët is a serious yet festive wine, marked by bright and fruity flavors of strawberry, dried flowers, herbs and cotton candy, all upheld by bubbles that are especially lively.

news from a wine insider
champagne by Tom Stevenson, author of the *Champagne and Sparkling Wine Guide*

In the News

The state of affairs in Champagne has changed dramatically in a relatively short period of time. Global wine sales had been increasing every year since 2000, and exporters were seeing huge potential for sales in countries like China, Russia and India. The Champagne region was even debating a controversial expansion of the region in order to meet the overwhelming demand. In 2007, the U.S. was the first major market to experience a sales decline for Champagne. The decline became worldwide in 2008, and Champagne sales continued to decrease in 2009.

Some Champagne producers have planned accordingly. Luc Montaudon of the Montaudon Champagne house, for one, sold his business in 2008. Others used the years of insatiable demand to increase prices; these producers can now lower prices and still make money.

Significant Trend

The good news for Champagne lovers is that there has never been a better time to step up to vintage Champagne. A vintage Champagne is made from the best grapes from an outstanding year. Though more expensive, vintage Champagne is a great bargain for those who can afford it, particularly now that prices have fallen.

other sparkling wines

Champagne will always be the benchmark by which all sparkling wines are measured. Still, countless regions around the world produce a wide range of quality sparklers, many of them selling at a fraction of Champagne's cost.

france

Beyond the region of Champagne, France abounds with sparkling wines, most notably from the Loire Valley, Alsace and Languedoc's Limoux subregion. Most versions are made with grapes typical to each region and are labeled *méthode traditionnelle, méthode classique* or *Crémant* if made the same way as Champagne. Others are labeled *Brut* or *Mousseux.*

other french sparkling wine recommendations

Baumard Carte Turquoise Brut | NV | CRÉMANT DE LOIRE
★★ $ The Baumard family has been a benchmark producer in the Loire for several generations and now leads the way in adopting screw-cap closures on all still wines. This gorgeous Crémant displays baking spice and Granny Smith apple aromas, a delicate mousse and an almond-accented finish.

La Taille aux Loups Triple Zéro | NV | MONTLOUIS-SUR-LOIRE
★★ $ $ This is the finest wine from one of the top domaines in Montlouis in the Loire Valley. It is crisp, dry and mineral-infused, with apple flavors balanced by mouthwatering acidity and chalky softness in the finish. The "triple zéro" refers to the fact that no sugar was added at any of the three possible times during fermentation.

Robert & Bernard Plageoles Mauzac Nature | NV | GAILLAC
★★ $ $ Bernard Plageoles makes this unique sparkling wine with the Gaillac region's native Mauzac grape. It is vinified dry and yields amazingly ripe pear flavors that are balanced beautifully with waves of citrus and minerals.

italy

Italian *spumante* (sparkling) wines are made primarily in the country's northern regions. One of Italy's best sparkling wines comes from Lombardy's Franciacorta zone, with its mineral-rich soil and cool nights. Made by the *méthode traditionnelle* (or *metodo classico,* as it is known locally), Franciacorta sparklers often taste similar to Champagne. The Piedmont region's flowery and fresh Moscato d'Asti and the light red, berry-scented Brachetto d'Acqui are also worth noting. An increasingly popular sparkler from Veneto, Prosecco provides an affordable and tasty alternative to many pricier sparkling wines made elsewhere.

italian sparkling wine recommendations

Banfi Rosa Regale | 2007 | BRACCHETTO D'ACQUI
★★ $ $ True to its name, this festive red sparkler smells like roses with ample notes of raspberry. Juicy, sweet fruit flavors throughout make it a perfect partner for another Italian delight: Gianduiotti—hazelnut-spiked chocolates.

Bellavista Gran Cuvée Satèn Brut | NV | FRANCIACORTA
★★★ $ $ $ $ Winemaking started as a hobby for vintner Vittorio Moretti more than 30 years ago, yet today he makes some of the finest sparklers in Franciacorta. This 100 percent Chardonnay is all about finesse, with toasted almond aromas and ripe apple flavors on a creamy, medium-bodied palate.

Michele Chiarlo Nivole | 2008 | MOSCATO D'ASTI
★★ $ (375 ml) Fresh and clean, this melon-flavored gem is blessed with both delicious fruit flavors and a great price.

Mionetto Sergio | NV | PROSECCO DI VALDOBBIADENE
★★ $ Tied with a little string—an homage to Mionetto's hand-tied bottles of Prosecco made back in the 1880s—this sparkler is marked by honey, pear and apple aromas layered with baking spices.

Vignaioli di S. Stefano | 2008 | MOSCATO D'ASTI
★★★ $ $ This tastes like a summer day, complete with ripe melon and sweet peach flavors wrapped in a subtle fizz (it is a *frizzante,* less bubbly than a *spumante*) that uplifts the round, mouth-filling nectar.

spain

Spanish Cavas by law must be made using the traditional method and have historically been marketed as less-costly substitutes for Champagne. The vast majority come from the Catalonia region near Barcelona and are made mostly from Macabeo, northern Spain's most planted white grape. In general, the best Cavas come from larger firms that control their own vinification, though some small vintners are producing high-quality examples.

spanish sparkling wine recommendations

WHITES

Cuvee Henri Brut | 2005 | CAVA
★ $ Notes of citrus, spice and biscuit infuse lush fruit flavors in this full-bodied blend of native Spanish grapes.

Huguet Gran Cava Reserva Brut Nature | 2005 | PENEDÈS
★ ★ ★ $ $ $ This sparkling wine is proof-positive that Champagne isn't the only game in town. It has a zesty acidity—as a *brut nature*, there's no sugar added in the second fermentation—classic apple and citrus flavors with a hint of spice and a mineral-laden, creamy finish that lingers beautifully on the palate.

Mont Marçal Brut Reserva | 2006 | CAVA
★ $ Toasty aromas of fresh bread dominate the nose on this Catalonian charmer. A blend of Spanish grapes Xarel-lo, Macabeo and Parellada, as well as a bit of Chardonnay, it offers nicely balanced lemon curd and herb flavors and a great acidity.

Segura Viudas Brut Heredad Reserva | NV | CAVA
★ $ Inside this hand-blown glass bottle is a refreshing, clean and vibrant Cava with a pleasant mouthfeel and a biscuit-flavored finish—all for a great price.

ROSÉS

Conde de Subirats Brut Rosé | NV | CAVA
★ $ Named for the landmark castle that was attached to these vineyards, Conde de Subirats crafts this rosé sparkler. It has aromas and flavors of pear and apple blossoms and a welcome hint of spice on the candied cherry finish.

united states

The quality of American sparkling wine has been rising in recent years. Northern California is still the best source, especially the cooler-climate appellations such as Carneros and the Anderson and Green valleys. Yet Washington, Oregon, New York and New Mexico are making a growing number of flavorful, complex and vibrant sparkling wines.

u.s. sparkling wine recommendations

WHITES

Domaine Carneros by Taittinger Le Rêve | 2003 | **CARNEROS, CALIFORNIA**
★★★★ $ $ $ $ This California sparkler has a Champagne pedigree and flavors to match. A spectacular nose of citrus, tropical fruit and toast leads into beautiful ripe pear and apple in the mouth, with notes of spice, yeast and nuts on the lingering finish.

Gruet Blanc de Blancs | 2004 | **NEW MEXICO**
★★ $ $ Although this hails from the unlikely location of New Mexico, it is made in the *méthode champenoise* and is simply delicious. Yeasty bread aromas are filled out with apple and spice notes, all layered with green apple and citrus on the palate and ginger notes on the finish.

Roederer Estate L'Ermitage Brut | 2002 | **ANDERSON VALLEY, CALIFORNIA**
★★★ $ $ $ The *tête de cuvée,* or top-tier wine, of Roederer's California winery is brimming with sweet aromas of toast, cinnamon and tart apple jelly. With a weighty mouthfeel and crisp, lime-flavored acidity that comes on mid-palate, it has a long, spicy finish.

Schramsberg J. Schram | 2001 | **NORTH COAST, CALIFORNIA**
★★★★ $ $ $ $ Schramsberg's current owners of 45 years, Jack and Jamie Davies, honor the winery's 1862 founder, Jacob Schram, with this wine. A perfect combination of New World boldness and Old World elegance, this wine boasts yeasty cinnamon roll and Red Delicious apple flavors, bolstered by pear, ginger and lime on the palate.

ROSÉS

Soter Beacon Hill Brut Rosé | 2004 | **OREGON**
★★★ $ $ $ Pinot Noir master Tony Soter made his name in Napa. Here, in Oregon, he crafts a great wine with flavors of strawberries, pears and apples that are concentrated and creamy in the mouth.

other countries

Vintners in many other corners of the world craft sparkling wines, ranging from countless average examples to a few great ones. German and Austrian winemakers use Riesling and Pinot Blanc to make some fine (and a lot of mediocre) sparkling wine, called *Sekt*. Portugal and Greece offer middling sparklers at fair prices, as do Georgia, Armenia and Moldova. South Africa, Argentina, Australia and New Zealand produce sparkling wines modeled after Champagne, some of them excellent. Australia makes many good examples, including dark red and tannic sparkling Shirazes.

other countries sparkling wine recommendations

WHITES

Ernesto Catena Siesta en el Tahuantinsuyu Extra Brut
| 2007 | MENDOZA, ARGENTINA

★★ $ The name might be nearly unpronounceable (ta-HWAN-tin-SOO-yoo), but the wine is remarkably easy to drink. Made by Ernesto Catena—son of Argentinean wine legend Nicolás Catena—this fresh sparkling wine combines flavors of peach, brioche and butter.

Movia Puro | 2001 | GORISKA BRDA, SLOVENIA
★★ $ $ $ Winemaker Ales Kristancic crafts this blend of Chardonnay, Ribolla and Pinot Nero in the traditional method for maximum flavor, and it is on a par with good Champagne. Crisp and dry, it offers honeysuckle aromas and honeyed flavors that are balanced with a lovely, chalky minerality.

Vértice Reserva Bruto | 2004 | DOURO, PORTUGAL
★★ $ This refreshing *vinho espumante* is made by American sparkling wine giant Schramsberg with traditional Douro grapes. Its enticing biscuit and apple aromas lead to flavors of citrus and minerals and an invigorating acidity in the mouth.

ROSÉS

Simonsig Kaapse Vonkel Rosé Brut | 2007 | STELLENBOSCH, SOUTH AFRICA
★★ $ $ Cherry and pear aromas make a big first impression in this South African wine made with the country's signature Pinotage grape. Bold acidity offsets its creamy texture and sweet fruit flavors.

fortified & dessert wines

Fortified and sweet wines typically serve as the bookends of a meal, enjoyed as aperitifs or as a delectable finale. Despite the immense versatility of these wines, with styles ranging from dry, palate-stimulating Sherries to intensely sweet red and white dessert wines, they remain unknown to many wine lovers. Luckily, this makes it possible to find true bargains on high-quality examples from countries around the world.

fortified wines

The practice of fortifying wines—by adding a neutral spirit, such as clear grape brandy, before bottling—began as a way to ensure the wines' stability over long ocean voyages. Traditional fortified wines include Sherry, Port, Madeira and Marsala, although variations abound. The alcohol content of these wines is higher than that of most unfortified wines, usually between 16 and 20 percent. A fortified wine's style depends largely on when the spirit is added during its production. Adding it during fermentation, as in most Port and Madeira, halts the process, and the resulting wines retain a good deal of natural grape sugar. When brandy is added after fermentation to fully fermented dry wine, the result is much drier, a good example being Fino Sherry.

sherry

Sherry (a.k.a. Jerez or Xérès) has the unfortunate reputation in America of being a "little old lady" drink. In truth, this distinctive wine has a noble heritage. Made in southern Spain's Jerez region, Sherry gains its complex flavors from the area's chalky soils and a peculiar indigenous yeast that appears on the wine's surface after fermentation. Sherry's many styles range from utterly dry to incredibly sweet.

Sherry Grapes & Styles

Most Sherries are blends of wines from different years. The dominant grape is Palomino, though sweeter styles often contain Pedro Ximénez or Moscatel. Vintners employ a fractional blending system called "solera," which combines barrel-aged liquids from different vintages in such a way that all Sherries bottled contain a portion of the oldest wine in that specific solera. Sherry comes in two basic varieties, *Fino* and *Oloroso*, both of which have subcategories.

• **FINO SHERRY** gets its unusual flavors from a yeast called *flor* that grows on the wine's surface and protects it from oxygen. There are two basic Fino types, both dry. **Manzanilla Sherry** displays notes of chamomile (*manzanilla* in Spanish) and a salty tang. **Amontillado Sherry** is a Fino that has lost its *flor* while aging; it shows nutty qualities and mineral flavors. **Pale Cream Sherry** is a Fino sweetened by the addition of Pedro Ximénez wine or grape juice concentrate.

• **OLOROSO** sherry does not develop flor, so the presence of oxygen during aging creates a nutty, smoky, earthy flavor and a darker hue. Most Olorosos are sweet, though some are sweetened further by adding Pedro Ximénez, creating **Cream Sherry**. **Palo Cortado** is a chestnut-colored Sherry that begins to develop flor but then backtracks, ending up somewhere between Oloroso and Amontillado in style.

• **PEDRO XIMÉNEZ** (often called PX for short) is produced in many Sherry houses even though, technically, it is not considered to be a true Sherry. Crafted from grapes of the same name grown primarily in the Montilla-Moriles region located just outside of Jerez, Pedro Ximénez wines tend to be rich and sweet, with a thick texture and pronounced flavors of dried fruit.

sherry recommendations

Bodegas Dios Baco Imperial Oloroso 30 Years
★ ★ ★ ★ $ $ $ $ This boutique bodega showcases the Palomino grape's capabilities. Its stunning, dry Oloroso enchants with a dazzling mix of caramel, cashew and toffee flavors that show impressive length on the palate.

Emilio Hidalgo Gobernador Oloroso Seco
★ $ $ While this intensely aromatic Sherry smells of raisin, prune and caramel, it is surprisingly dry on the palate, with flavors of dried orange peel and nuts. It is best served at room temperature.

Lustau East India Solera
★ ★ ★ $ $ What is now the Emilio Lustau company was founded in 1896. Today, Lustau is a benchmark producer in the region, with a wide range of offerings. This sweet Sherry has a nose of sultana, fig and nut. Full-bodied, with a smooth and round mouthfeel, it displays a delightful combination of prune, toffee and candied apricot flavors.

Osborne Pedro Ximénez
★ ★ ★ $ A truly special wine, this Pedro Ximénez is unctuous, sweet and viscous, with a concentrated honey character. Flavors of raisin and other dried fruits make it ideal for sipping or pouring on top of vanilla ice cream.

Sandeman Royal Esmeralda Fine Dry Amontillado 20 Years
★ ★ ★ $ $ (500 ml) Aged for a minimum of 20 years, this exquisite Sherry is deserving of its "royal" name. Concentrated and dry on the palate, it exhibits a wide range of flavors, from nuts and toffee to caramel and roasted fruit.

Toro Albalá Fino Eléctrico | MONTILLA-MORILES
★ ★ $ (500 ml) Eléctrico delivers a jolt of nutty, briny and mineral aromas followed by subtle citrus flavors. Served chilled, this bone-dry Fino is delicious with olives and almonds.

port

Portugal's second-largest city, Oporto, gave its name to the country's emblematic wine. Made in the Douro Valley and fortified with brandy to arrest fermentation, Port is a dark, sweet wine with a high alcohol content.

Port Grapes & Styles

The grapes most often used in Port production are Touriga Nacional, Touriga Franca and Tinta Roriz (Tempranillo). Categorized by style, Port comes in three basic types: White, Ruby and Tawny (the last two have subcategories).

• **WHITE PORT** exhibits the slightly sweet, citrusy flavors of the white grapes from which it is produced. Some houses make oak-aged, subtly oxidized, orange-hued versions.

• **RUBY PORT** is the most common style of Port. Inexpensive and straightforward, Rubies are blended from a variety of young wines. **Ruby Reserve Ports** (formerly known as Vintage Character Ports) are more complex blends, often carrying proprietary names like Graham's Six Grapes. **Late Bottled Vintage (LBV) Ports** are single-vintage Rubies that have been aged four to six years in barrel and are drinkable upon release, unlike most Vintage Ports. Made from the best grapes in the finest years and aged in oak for several years, **Vintage Ports** require decades of bottle aging to reach their maximum potential. **Single Quinta Vintage Ports** are produced with grapes from a single vineyard.

• **TAWNY PORTS** are wines that, in theory, have been aged in wood longer than a Ruby and thus take on a tawny hue. In reality, many of today's Tawny Ports are the same age as most Rubies; they're just made with lighter wines. Aged Tawny Port is authentic, however, made from blends of the highest-quality Ports that might otherwise have been bottled as Vintage Port. Tawny Port labels indicate the average age of the blend's components (10, 20 or 30 years old, for example). Tawnies are ready to drink upon release and usually exhibit delicate nutty aromas and dried fruit flavors.

port recommendations

Churchill's 10 Year Tawny

★ ★ ★ $ $ $ Ten years in oak casks have endowed this Port with many secondary aromas, like toasted nut and mocha, that complement gorgeous flavors of caramelized orange. Its mellowed tannins give it a satiny texture.

Ferreira White

★ ★ $ Founded by a family of Douro Valley winegrowers, Ferreira is the only *Porto* company not of British origin. Serve this amber-colored white Port with a slight chill to best showcase its intense fig flavors and golden raisin and sweet spice highlights.

Niepoort Tawny

★ ★ $ Niepoort provides a perfect introduction to Tawny Port with this fig-scented wine. Prune, spice, dried fruit and berry flavors have a long finish and make this a natural pour alongside Stilton cheese.

star producers
port

Croft

Founded over 300 years ago on exceptional Douro Valley terroir, Croft remains one of the highest-quality Port producers in the region.

Ramos Pinto

Noted for its important research into Port varieties, Ramos Pinto has been instrumental in the Douro's recent history of progress.

Sandeman

The first Port company to brand its wines—in 1805—Sandeman has a long history of smart marketing.

Taylor Fladgate

The long-lived Vintage Ports produced at this iconic Port house consistently fetch the highest prices at auctions.

Warre's

William Warre took over this Port house in the 1700s and traded dried cod in return for wine. This Port empire is still one of the finest today.

W. & J. Graham's

Scottish brothers William and John Graham established one of the first Port houses on the upper Douro; it is now owned by the Symington family.

Quinta do Crasto LBV | 2002 |

★ ★ ★ $ $ Because this is a traditional-style LBV, it is unfiltered, so decanting is recommended. Oxygen exposure will also allow the tannins of this full-bodied, ripe wine to soften and aromas of plum and dark cherry to develop.

Ramos Pinto Quinta do Bom Retiro 20 Year Tawny

★ ★ ★ ★ $ $ $ $ This single-quinta Tawny hails from the Douro sub-region Cima Corgo. Aromas of hazelnuts, vanilla, baking spices and apricot yield to a velvety mouthfeel invigorated by lively fruit flavors that linger on the palate.

Taylor Fladgate 40 Year Tawny

★ ★ ★ ★ $ $ $ $ An exceptionally complex Tawny, this delivers layers of molasses, toffee and pecan pie flavors that are balanced and harmonious on the rich, textured palate.

Warre's Vintage | 2003 |

★ ★ ★ ★ $ $ $ $ Dark chocolate, bold spice and sweet wild raspberry dominate the nose of Warre's 2003. It is ink-colored, tooth-staining and dense, but not clumsy, and will continue to improve for the next 20 years.

W. & J. Graham's Six Grapes Reserve

★ ★ ★ $ $ This is an exceptional Ruby, opulent and sweet. Raspberry and spice flavors are complemented by dark cherry and plum on a full-bodied palate.

FORTIFIED WINES

madeira

An iconic American drink in the 19th century, Madeira, like other fortified wines, has fallen out of fashion. Named for the Portuguese island off the coast of Morocco where it's produced, Madeira comes in a variety of styles suitable for drinking before, during and after meals.

Madeira Grapes & Styles

Most Madeiras are a blend of grapes, but the best carry the name of one of four: Sercial, Verdelho, Bual or Malmsey (Malvasia). Sercial Madeira is the driest, while Verdelho, Bual and Malmsey are progressively sweeter. Most age designations indicate the youngest wine in the blend.

madeira recommendations

Barbeito Bual | 1978 |
★★★ $ $ $ Founded in 1946, Barbeito is one of Madeira's young-est firms, and also one of its best. This off-dry beauty offers a fabu-lous mélange of pomegranate, brandied cherry and nut flavors that show great length on the palate.

Broadbent Rainwater Medium Dry
★★ $ Bartholomew Broadbent, son of the famous wine personality Michael Broadbent, bottles this stellar, well-priced Madeira. Three years of aging in oak casks imparts intriguing oxidized aromas and flavors of nut, sultana, fig, vanilla and caramelized orange peel.

Cossart Gordon 5 Year Bual
★★★ $ $ Cossart Gordon—the oldest wine firm in Madeira—crafts this amber-colored gem. With a bouquet of cashews, sweet spice and Turkish delight, it boasts a silky-textured, off-dry palate full of rich flavors of citrus and fig.

D'Oliveira Verdelho | 1981 |
★★★★ $ $ $ $ Packed with heady aromas of candied almonds, walnuts and seductive hints of sweet brown sugar, D'Oliveira's excep-tionally elegant Madeira displays impressive depth, concentration and length.

The Rare Wine Co. Historic Series New York Malmsey
★★★ $ $ $ This unctuous, full-bodied Madeira is brimming with aromas of nut, fig and toffee. Flavors of citrus and spice brighten the sweet palate and make it a lively pairing for baklava.

dessert wines

As the name implies, dessert wines are typically enjoyed with or in place of dessert. Sauternes from France's Bor-deaux region has long held court as perhaps the most pres-tigious of all sweet wines and continues to command high prices. But wine drinkers today can experiment with many other reasonably priced and high-quality sweet wines, as interesting examples are being produced in Australia and Canada, brimming with sweet fruit, zippy acidity and even the addictive, honeyed aroma of botrytis (see below).

white dessert wines

The finest white dessert wines are intense nectars bursting with powerful flavors of flowers, spice, honey and smoke. All well-made examples possess high levels of acidity, which keeps them refreshing in spite of a high sugar content.

White Dessert Wines Grapes & Styles

• **LATE HARVEST WINES** are made from grapes left on the vine late into the season, allowing them to develop especially high sugar levels; any grape can be used to make them. The most famous examples come from Germany (marked *Spätlese,* which means "late," or *Auslese,* which is later and sweeter) and Alsace (where they're called *Vendanges Tardives*). California, Australia, South Africa, Chile and the Greek isle of Samos also make good versions.

• **PASSITO** wines are an Italian specialty made from grapes that have been dried before pressing. Tuscan vintners use Trebbiano to make the local version, *Vin Santo,* while Sicilian vintners use the Zibibbo grape for their passito wines.

• **BOTRYTIS** wines obtain their unique and highly praised flavors from *Botrytis cinerea,* a mold referred to as "noble rot," which concentrates the wine's fruit flavors while adding hints of smoke and truffle. Some of the best are made in the Sauternes region of Bordeaux, where Sémillon, Sauvignon Blanc and Muscadelle are blended to craft wines of exceptional flavor and longevity. Bordeaux's Barsac subregion makes outstanding examples, while neighboring Loupiac and Cadillac yield similar, though less expensive, versions. The Loire subregions of Quarts de Chaume, Vouvray, Coteaux du Layon, Montlouis and Bonnezeaux use Chenin Blanc to produce their generally outstanding sweet wines. Alsace vintners utilize the region's finest grapes for their *Sélection de Grains Nobles* wines, and German and Austrian vintners produce sublime botrytized wines from Riesling and other grapes, which they designate *Beerenauslese* (BA) or *Trockenbeerenauslese* (TBA) according to sugar levels (see p. 134). California, Australia and South Africa also make wines from botrytis-affected grapes.

- **ICE WINE/EISWEIN** is made from grapes that have been left on the vine until after the first freeze. The grapes are pressed while frozen, which yields small amounts of sweet, concentrated juice. The finest ice wines are crafted in Germany and Austria with Riesling, though almost any grape can be used. Some beautifully made versions come from Canada, New York and Washington State. In warmer regions some vintners simply put extra-ripe grapes in a freezer and then press them for the same effect.

- **VIN DOUX NATUREL** is fortified with brandy during fermentation, which retains the grape's sugars. These wines are made mainly in southern France, with the two most noteworthy examples being Muscat de Beaumes-de-Venise from the Rhône and Muscat de Rivesaltes from Roussillon.

- **TOKAJI** is a unique wine infused with a mash of botrytis-affected grapes (*aszú*). Produced mainly in Hungary, Tokaji is graded by the amount of crushed grapes added to the base, on a scale measured by *puttonyos*; the more puttonyos, the more intense the wine. All tend to exhibit delicious apricot, orange and almond flavors and high acidity.

white dessert wine recommendations

Bacalhôa | 2001 | **MOSCATEL DE SETÚBAL, PORTUGAL**
★ ★ **$** Aged for more than three years in oak, this fascinating wine showcases complex aromas of eucalyptus, fresh peppercorn and golden raisins. The palate is equally expressive, with the addition of black tea, sage and dried apricot notes.

Bonny Doon Vineyard Le Vol des Anges | 2007 |
ARROYO SECO, CALIFORNIA
★ ★ ★ **$ $** (375 ml) Founder Randall Grahm started out trying to craft the perfect American Pinot Noir but fell for Rhône grapes instead. This Roussanne drips with oolong, hibiscus, rose hip and peach aromas that lead into a black tea– and apple-dominated palate.

Chambers Rosewood Vineyards Muscat | NV |
RUTHERGLEN, AUSTRALIA
★ ★ **$** (375 ml) Produced in a solera-type system that contains wines 100 years old, this is an unctuous and decadent wine. Nose and palate abound with notes of apricots, raisins, caramel and walnut.

Château de Jau | 2006 | MUSCAT DE RIVESALTES, FRANCE
★ ★ ★ $ $ (500 ml) The Dauré family has tended vineyards here since 1974, focusing specifically on Mediterranean varieties. Their Muscat is lively and bright, yet also rich, with flavors of cream custard, lemon sorbet and orange blossom.

Château Les Justices | 2005 | SAUTERNES, FRANCE
★ ★ $ $ $ Aromas of honey, beeswax, apple and marzipan precede a ripe, creamy, stone fruit–flavored palate layered with waves of candied orange peel—making this a perfect choice to serve with pâté topped with slightly sweet fig preserves.

Château Les Tuileries | 2005 | SAUTERNES, FRANCE
★ ★ $ $ $ The botrytized grapes for this wine—a blend of 85 percent Sémillon, 10 percent Sauvignon Blanc and 5 percent Muscadelle— were hand-selected in a multistep process. They were then aged in vats, which imparts notes of oak and vanilla to flavors of honey, beeswax and fresh hay.

C.H. Berres Erdener Treppchen Riesling Auslese | 2006 |
MOSEL-SAAR-RUWER, GERMANY
★ ★ $ $ $ (375 ml) The Berres family has been in the Riesling business since 1510, and the winery is currently led by 21st-generation wunderkind Markus. This 2006 is a delicious Auslese, layered with wet slate, fresh herb and pear aromas, while the palate tends toward ripe stone fruit.

Disznoko Tokaji Aszú 5 Puttonyos | 2000 | TOKAJ, HUNGARY
★ ★ $ $ $ (500 ml) This historic winery was resuscitated 16 years ago, and it is now back to producing outstanding wines. The 2000 vintage offers aromas of apricot and honey followed by flavors of peach tart, custard and vanilla pound cake.

Dolce Toscolo | 2007 | SICILY, ITALY
★ ★ $ (500 ml) Pair this refreshing Moscato d'Alessandria with warm chocolate chip cookies. Packed with dessert-friendly flavors of honey, apple, fennel and candied violet, it finishes with an intriguing bitter almond note.

Domaine des Baumard | 2004 | QUARTS DE CHAUME, FRANCE
★ ★ ★ $ $ $ $ Established in 1634, this winery is currently run by descendant Florent Baumard, who takes a traditional approach to winemaking but incorporates modern innovations. His classic-style dessert wine is made from Chenin Blanc and displays mineral, wildflower, honey and sea salt on the palate.

Ernst Bretz Riesling Eiswein Prädikat | 2003 |
RHEINHESSEN, GERMANY

★ ★ **$ $** (375 ml) The Bretz family has produced wine in the Rheinhessen since 1721 and has earned a reputation for well-priced, stellar wines. This well-balanced Eiswein boasts ripe Fuji apples up front, sticky caramel on the mid-palate and a hint of citrus on the finish.

Feiler-Artinger Ruster Ausbruch Pinot Cuvée | 2006 |
BURGENLAND, AUSTRIA

★ ★ ★ ★ **$ $ $** (375 ml) Blended from Pinot Blanc, Neuburger and Chardonnay, this Austrian sweet wine is matured in 50 percent new French oak, which lends vanilla notes to highly concentrated, complex flavors of honey, apricot and candied citrus.

Georg Breuer Auslese | 2007 | **RHEINGAU, GERMANY**

★ ★ **$ $ $** (375 ml) Lighter than many *Auslesen*, this is a vibrant white, with flavors of grapefruit, lemon, green apple and honeydew.

star producers
white dessert wines

Château de Jau
Estelle and Simon Dauré run this estate in French Catalonia, home to 330 cultivated acres of hillside vineyards responsible for some of the region's best wines.

Château Haut-Bergeron
The Lamothe family has been at the helm of this French estate since the late 18th century, and is still crafting fine dessert wines in Sauternes and Barsac.

Clos des Camuzeilles
This Languedoc producer is a dependable source for delicious, earthy sweet wines from old-vine Muscat.

Gunderloch
On 30 acres of sun-baked slopes in Nackenheim, along Germany's Rhine River, this vintner has grown Riesling, Pinot Gris and Silvaner for more than 100 years.

Inniskillin
The international market for Canadian ice wine might not exist were it not for the efforts of Inniskillin and the quality of its world-class wines.

Kracher
Considered one of the world's best dessert-wine makers, this Austrian producer works with Chardonnay, Gewürztraminer, Zweigelt, Muscat and more.

Hess Su'skol Vineyard Late Harvest Chardonnay | 2006 |
NAPA VALLEY, CALIFORNIA

★ ★ $ $ (375 ml) Produced from botrytized grapes, this is a dense dessert wine with aromas of brandied peach, dried apricot and honey. Baked apple, candied pear, honey, clove and nutmeg flavors come together on the palate.

Inniskillin Vidal Icewine | 2006 |
NIAGARA PENINSULA, CANADA

★ ★ ★ $ $ $ $ (375 ml) The most important name in Canadian ice wine, Inniskillin crafts a range of stunning sweet wines. The 2006 Vidal is opulent and mouth-filling, oozing ripe, honeyed fruit flavors held up by a backbone of strong acidity.

Jackson-Triggs Proprietors' Reserve Vidal Icewine | 2007 |
NIAGARA PENINSULA, CANADA

★ ★ $ $ (187 ml) Equally suited to fresh fruit and foie gras, this is a relatively light ice wine that presents a range of aromas from peach and apricot to cantaloupe and mango, all balanced by good acidity.

Kanu Kia-Ora Noble Late Harvest | 2005 |
STELLENBOSCH, SOUTH AFRICA

★ ★ ★ $ $ (375 ml) This late-harvest wine speaks to its origins, with intriguing animal and earth notes distinctive to the region. Honey, pineapple and candied fruit flavors round out the palate, punctuated by notes of roasted nuts.

Kiona Ice Wine | 2007 | YAKIMA VALLEY, WASHINGTON

★ ★ $ $ (375 ml) Planting vines and building their winery on land that lacked road access and electricity when they bought it, John and Ann Williams set out to make world-class wines in the Yakima Valley— and they have succeeded. This wine entices with an irresistible array of tropical aromas and flavors.

Louis Guntrum "Penguin" Eiswein | 2007 |
RHEINHESSEN, GERMANY

★ ★ ★ $ $ $ $ (375 ml) More subdued than the average ice wine, this German Eiswein hints at lilies and succulent white peaches on the nose. The palate remains subtle yet resonant with clover honey, honeysuckle and apricot.

Lucien Albrecht Vendanges Tardives Pinot Gris | 2001 |
ALSACE, FRANCE

★ ★ ★ ★ $ $ $ (375 ml) This indulgent wine evokes a freshly baked pineapple upside-down cake dripping with tropical fruit, vanilla, baking spice, almond and cream flavors.

Nobility Late Harvest Semillon/Sauvignon Blanc | 2006 |
SONOMA AND NAPA COUNTIES, CALIFORNIA
★ ★ ★ $ $ $ $ (375 ml) After years of winemaking at Beringer Vineyards, Roger Harrison decided to strike out on his own, specializing in
botrytized dessert wines. This blend offers richly layered flavors of
mango, melon, apricot, peach and vanilla, ending with a honey note.

Oremus Late Harvest Tokaji | 2005 | TOKAJ, HUNGARY
★ ★ $ $ (375 ml) By some accounts, Tokaj produced botrytized
wines two centuries before Sauternes figured out what to do with
those rotten grapes. Oremus's 2005 version boasts a peach preserves
and baking spice bouquet, while the palate is defined by fresh apricot,
great acidity and an incredibly long finish.

Pieropan Le Colombare | 2004 | RECIOTO DI SOAVE, ITALY
★ ★ ★ $ $ $ (500 ml) Made from air-dried Garganega grapes and
aged in oak for two years, this Soave sweet wine engages from start to
finish. Generous pineapple, honey, star fruit, spring flower and caramel flavors are penetrated by a refreshing acidity.

Rudolf Müller Eiswein | 2007 | PFALZ, GERMANY
★ ★ ★ $ $ (375 ml) This surprisingly complex wine is expansive,
with a captivating mélange of honeysuckle, agave, stone fruit, apple
blossom and spring rain aromatics. There is a hint of *dulce de leche* in
the mouth, which adds stunning depth and a long finish.

red dessert wines

The renown of Port and Madeira (see pp. 269 and 271)
should not overshadow the red dessert wine contributions
of Italy, France, California and Australia, all of which produce intriguing versions ranging in style from light, bubbly
and refreshing to dark and intensely rich.

Red Dessert Wines Grapes & Styles

Red dessert wines vary greatly from region to region. From
northern Italy comes Recioto della Valpolicella, the sweet
sibling of bittersweet Amarone (see p. 89), as well as pink
Muscat (Moscato Rosa) and the lightly sparkling Brachetto
d'Acqui. France's Roussillon region offers the fortified
wines of Banyuls and Maury, both made with Grenache.
California and Australia produce sweet late-harvest and
Port-style wines from many different grape varieties.

red dessert wine recommendations

Daniel Gehrs Fireside Port | 2006 |
AMADOR COUNTY, CALIFORNIA
★★ $ $ $ Unlike many similar offerings from California, this fortified wine is made with Portuguese varieties, resulting in a striking likeness to *Porto*. Loads of dense blackberry, plum, violet and mocha flavors fill out the rich palate.

Dashe Late Harvest Zinfandel | 2007 |
DRY CREEK VALLEY, CALIFORNIA
★★ $ $ (375 ml) This bold, earthy red tempts with robust aromas of blueberry, cassis and lavender. Full-bodied flavors of dark berry, herbs and eucalyptus are supported by assertive tannins.

Domaine de la Casa Blanca | 2006 | **BANYULS, FRANCE**
★★ $ $ This traditional French fortified wine is made from Grenache and aged in Bordeaux barrels. The result is a clean palate full of plum, blackberry, black currant, chocolate and baking spice flavors.

Felsner Hesperia Zweigelt Eiswein | 2007 |
KREMSTAL, AUSTRIA
★★ $ $ $ (375 ml) Named for one of the nymphs that lived in the mythical garden where Hercules sought the golden apples, this red Eiswein offers remarkably bright fruit flavors—cranberry, raspberry, peach and grapefruit—balanced by gentle acidity.

Kracher Nouvelle Vague Nummer 1 Zweigelt Trockenbeeren Auslese | 2006 | **BURGENLAND, AUSTRIA**
★★★★ $ $ $ $ (375 ml) From one of Austria's most renowned winemaking families comes this stunner with excellent varietal character. It is saturated with honey, vanilla and clove flavors and features highlights of currants, plums, black tea and fresh herbs.

Pillitteri Estates Winery Sticky Beak Red Icewine | 2007 |
NIAGARA PENINSULA, CANADA
★★★ $ $ $ (200 ml) This is a decadent, concentrated red sweet wine with remarkable depth of fruit. Strawberry, raspberry, honey and pepper flavors show highlights of dark chocolate and fresh herbs.

Stratus Icewine | 2007 | **NIAGARA PENINSULA, CANADA**
★★ $ $ $ (200 ml) This Cabernet Sauvignon–Cabernet Franc beauty would be ideal alongside chocolate torte. Straightforward aromas of raspberry, strawberry and blackberry are echoed on the palate, supported by bright acidity and hints of cinnamon, nutmeg, toffee, cranberry and candied tangerine.

how to pair wine & food

The old adage "White wine with fish and red with meat" has been replaced with "Drink whatever you like with whatever you want." Both approaches have advantages, but you're bound to encounter pitfalls by adhering too closely to either. The trick is to pair food and wine so that neither distorts or overwhelms the other. Ideally, you want to bring together dishes and wines that highlight each other's best qualities. In the next three sections, you'll find general matching rules, a host of ideas for pairing by grape variety and a pairing "cheat sheet."

general rules for matching

be body-conscious Delicately flavored food goes best with a light and delicate wine; heavy, full-flavored dishes call for heftier wines. The subtle flavors of sole meunière are going to get lost if paired with a big, oaky Chardonnay, and a light Beaujolais will seem like water if served with braised short ribs.

balance extremes If a dish is rich and creamy, you need a tart, high-acid wine to cut through the fat and to cleanse your palate. A bit of sweetness in wine balances salty or spicy foods. If you can't wait to drink those young and astringent Bordeaux, Barolos or California Cabernet Sauvignons, the protein and fat of a rich cut of meat will help moderate their tannins.

pair likes Peppery meat dishes work well with spicy red wines like those from the Rhône Valley. Play fruit sauces off rich and fruity wines. Grassy, herbal whites tend to go beautifully with green vegetables.

look to the locals Wines from a particular region often match well with foods from the same place.

mix & match The "red with meat, white with fish" rule is a good fallback when you're unsure what to pair with a dish, but it's a rule made to be broken. Try a light, acidic red such as a Burgundy with a rich fish like salmon; or pair a rich Chardonnay with grilled chicken.

bridge the gap If your table has ordered steak, salmon and sea scallops, and you have to pick the wine, choose one that offers a bit of something for each dish. Full-bodied rosés such as those from Bandol or Tavel or lighter-bodied reds like non-Riserva Chianti Classico or a light-style Oregon Pinot Noir have the subtlety not to overwhelm delicate dishes and the substance to stand up to a hearty steak.

pairing by grape

Of the thousands of different grape varieties in the world, only about 20 are regularly represented on American wine shelves. Each variety has its own particular characteristics that yield different styles of wine and result in a greater affinity with certain foods than others. Here is a guide to the most common varieties, with suggestions for dishes that pair especially well with each and a selection of wines that express each grape's typical qualities.

cabernet franc

Cabernet Franc adds spicy pepper and bright red cherry flavors to Bordeaux red wines, but it stars in France's Loire Valley, where it makes light, spicy reds. California and Long Island also make some good examples.

BEST PAIRINGS Cabernet Franc tends to be a bit lighter and more herbal than Cabernet Sauvignon, so pair it with dishes like herb-rubbed roast chicken (or any light meat involving a lot of herbs), roast pork loin or veal chops. Earthier, more structured Old World versions—for instance, those from the Chinon region of the Loire Valley—are ideal with roast duck or other game birds.

Clos Cristal Hospices de Saumur | 2006 | ★ ★ $ $ | P. 56
Domaine du Mortier Graviers | 2007 | ★ $ | P. 56
Jean-Maurice Raffault Clos des Capucins | 2006 | ★ ★ ★ $ $ | P. 56
Macari | 2004 | ★ ★ ★ $ $ | P. 211

cabernet sauvignon

Cabernet Sauvignon is revered for cedary black currant and blackberry flavors bolstered by tannins, which endow it with great aging potential. The best expressions come from Bordeaux, where the variety is blended with Merlot, Cabernet Franc and Petit Verdot, as well as from California's Napa Valley, Chile's Upper Maipo Valley and Tuscany, where the grape appears on its own in some Super-Tuscans.

BEST PAIRINGS Cabernets from California, Australia and South America, with their rich fruit and substantial tannins, pair best with meat—well-marbled steaks, braised short ribs, hearty roasts. European Cabernets and Bordeaux blends tend to have higher acidity and less overtly ripe flavors; lamb is a great match for them, or game of any kind.

Carpe Diem | 2006 | ★ ★ $ $ | P. 172
Château Cantemerle Grand Cru | 2006 | ★ ★ ★ $ $ | P. 32
Château Villa Bel-Air | 2004 | ★ ★ ★ $ $ | P. 36
Henry's Drive Vignerons The Trial of John Montford | 2006 | ★ ★ ★ $ $ | P. 218
Peñalolen | 2007 | ★ ★ $ | P. 245

chardonnay

Chardonnay grows almost everywhere. It reaches its apex in France's Burgundy, where it produces elegant, mineral-laden whites. Elsewhere it is responsible for full-bodied, fruit-driven wines, toasty Champagnes and dessert wines.

BEST PAIRINGS Lighter, unoaked Chardonnay and Chablis pair well with fish, shellfish and salads. Oakier versions (most California Chardonnays, for instance) are better with more substantial dishes like roast chicken, pork tenderloin or richer fish or shellfish such as salmon or lobster.

Byron | 2007 | ★ ★ ★ $ $ | P. 161
Clos du Bois Calcaire | 2007 | ★ ★ ★ $ $ | P. 162
Joseph Burrier Château de Beauregard Classique | 2006 | ★ ★ ★ $ $ | P. 48
Marc Brocot Les Champs Salomon | 2006 | ★ ★ ★ $ $ | P. 42
Yalumba Wild Ferment | 2008 | ★ ★ ★ $ | P. 215

chenin blanc

Full of fruit and high acidity, Chenin Blanc produces some of France's best wines, like the Loire Valley's full-bodied, long-aging, dry whites, dessert elixirs and sparklers. South Africa and California also produce enjoyable examples.

BEST PAIRINGS Dry Chenin Blanc is a good partner for white-fleshed fish, chicken or even light veal or pork dishes. Off-dry (lightly sweet) versions pair better with spicy foods such as Indian or other Asian dishes.

Château de Chamboureau | 2005 | ★ ★ ★ $ $ | P. 52
Domaine des Baumard | 2005 | ★ ★ $ $ | P. 52
Domaine du Vieux Pressoir Elégance | 2006 |
★ ★ $ | P. 52
Mulderbosch | 2008 | ★ ★ ★ $ | P. 248
Sauvion | 2007 | ★ ★ $ | P. 53

gewürztraminer

Pink-skinned Gewürztraminer offers exuberant aromas and flamboyant flavors ranging from honeysuckle to lychee, candied apricot, mineral and Asian spice. It is an especially important grape in the white wines of Alsace and Germany. New York and California are also home to some excellent Gewürztraminer-based wines.

BEST PAIRINGS Gewürztraminer almost always pairs well with Asian and Indian food—for spicy dishes, choose an off-dry (lightly sweet) bottling; for less spicy dishes, dry Gewürztraminer is the better match. Gewürztraminer is also good with strong cheeses like Époisses or Muenster.

Fitz-Ritter Spätlese | 2007 | ★ ★ ★ $ $ | P. 138
Handley | 2007 | ★ ★ $ | P. 169
Hugel & Fils Hugel | 2007 | ★ ★ $ | P. 26
J. Hofstätter Kolbenhof | 2006 | ★ ★ ★ ★ $ $ $ | P. 88
Pierre Sparr Mambourg Grand Cru | 2007 |
★ ★ ★ $ $ $ | P. 27

grenache/garnacha

The fresh, spicy cherry flavors of the Grenache grape are essential to many of the red wines of southern France, such as Châteauneuf-du-Pape and Côtes-du-Rhône. Spanish winemakers rely heavily on Grenache (called Garnacha in Spanish), particularly in Priorat. The variety is also impor-tant in Sardinia (where it is known as Cannonau) and shows up in wines from California and Australia.

BEST PAIRINGS Grenache, with its warm, quintessentially Mediterranean flavors, pairs well with hearty dishes like grilled sausages, lamb chops and rustic stews.

Château Mont-Redon | 2006 | ★ ★ $ | P. 65
Domaine Rabasse Charavin | 2005 | ★ ★ $ $ | P. 66
Elix | 2006 | ★ ★ ★ $ $ $ | P. 120
Muret Old Vines | 2007 | ★ ★ ★ $ $ | P. 124
Sella & Mosca Riserva | 2005 | ★ ★ $ | P. 111

malbec

Malbec is the signature red wine grape of Argentina, where it yields wines that are bursting with lush, dark berry fruits and rich chocolate flavors. It is no longer important in Bordeaux, its place of origin, but dominates red wine production in the French region of Cahors, where it goes by the name Auxerrois, and shows up in the Loire Valley, California, Australia and Chile.

BEST PAIRINGS Malbec's full-bodied dark fruit flavors and light, peppery spiciness make it a natural partner for beef, lamb, venison and other substantial meats.

Château Lagrézette Cuvée Dame Honneur | 2003 | ★ ★ ★ $ $ $ $ | P. 77
Kaiken | 2007 | ★ ★ ★ $ | P. 238
Odfjell Orzada | 2005 | ★ ★ $ | P. 244
Viña Cobos Felino | 2007 | ★ ★ ★ $ | P. 239
Zette | 2003 | ★ $ | P. 77

marsanne

Most at home in France's Rhône Valley, the white wine grape Marsanne is prized for its succulent honey flavors and full body. Good versions are found throughout California and Australia as well. Marsanne often appears as part of a blend, usually with the Roussanne grape, but also with Viognier and other grapes.

BEST PAIRINGS Marsanne's gentle stone fruit and melon flavors and moderate acidity make it a good all-around white wine for pairing with chicken, white-fleshed fish and main-course salads.

Domaine Romaneaux-Destezet | 2007 | ★ ★ $ $ $ | P. 59
La Vieille Ferme | 2008 | ★ ★ $ | P. 63
Les Vignerons d'Estézargues From the Tank Vin Blanc
| 2007 | ★ ★ $ $ $ | P. 63
M. Chapoutier Les Meysonniers | 2007 | ★ ★ $ $ $ | P. 59

merlot

With its plum and chocolate flavors, Merlot is one of the most popular grapes in the world and is responsible for some of the greatest red wines, such as those from Bordeaux's Pomerol and Washington State. Terrific examples are also produced in California and northeastern Italy.

BEST PAIRINGS Merlot's plummy, spicy notes and full-bodied texture make it a good match for everything from pork chops and roasts to pasta in meat sauce and sausages off the grill.

Arceno PrimaVoce | 2005 | ★ ★ $ | P. 101
Château Clinet | 2006 | ★ ★ ★ ★ $ $ $ $ | P. 32
Chateau Ste. Michelle Ethos | 2005 |
★ ★ $ $ $ | P. 205
Ehlers Estate | 2006 | ★ ★ ★ $ $ $ | P. 180
Markham Vineyards | 2006 | ★ ★ $ $ | P. 180

muscat

All Muscat, both red and white, bursts with fragrant flavors such as honeysuckle, orange blossom and musk. It's grown throughout the world, most famously in Italy as Moscato and in Spain as Moscatel, as well as in Alsace, southern France, Greece, California and Australia.

BEST PAIRINGS Most Muscat bottlings are lightly sweet; that, together with the grape's tangerine-scented fruitiness, makes it a natural partner for fresh fruit desserts.

Bacalhôa | 2001 | ★ ★ $ | P. 274
Michele Chiarlo Nivole | 2008 | ★ ★ $ | P. 262
Torres Viña Esmeralda Moscato/Gewürztraminer | 2008 |
★ ★ $ | P. 119
Vignaioli di S. Stefano | 2008 | ★ ★ ★ $ $ | P. 262

nebbiolo

Nebbiolo achieves its greatest glory in Italy's Piedmont region, where the variety's cherry, tar and tobacco flavors define the elegant, long-lived reds of Barolo and Barbaresco. A small number of winemakers outside of Italy work with Nebbiolo, too, particularly in California and Australia, although away from its home turf the grape tends to express different characteristics.

BEST PAIRINGS This structured, aromatic red grape pairs particularly well with any dish involving mushrooms, but it is also good with lamb, venison and beef (beef braised in Barolo is a classic Piedmontese dish). Older vintages go perfectly with truffles.

Gaja Barbaresco | 2005 | ★★★★ $ $ $ $ | P. 83
L.A. Cetto Private Reserve Nebbiolo | 2004 | ★★ $ | P. 255
Michele Chiarlo Reyna Barbaresco | 2006 |
★★★ $ $ $ | P. 83
Produttori del Barbaresco Nebbiolo delle Langhe | 2007 |
★★ $ $ | P. 85
Serradenari Nebbiolo | 2005 | ★★★ $ $ | P. 86
Vietti Castiglione Barolo | 2005 | ★★★ $ $ $ | P. 83

petite sirah

Petite Sirah (not to be confused with Syrah) yields wines that are lusty and dark, with chewy tannins. Originally from France's Rhône Valley, the grape is believed to be a cross between the Peloursin variety and Syrah, and grows well in California, Mexico, South America, Australia and parts of the Middle East.

BEST PAIRINGS Almost invariably full-bodied and bursting with blackberry and spice flavors, Petite Sirah is ideal with saucy barbecued meats or rich braised short ribs prepared with an array of sweet or savory spices.

Big House The Prodigal Son | 2006 | ★ $ | P. 193
Earthquake | 2006 | ★★ $ $ | P. 194
Ravenswood Vintners Blend | 2007 | ★ $ | P. 195
Stags' Leap Winery | 2006 | ★★ $ $ $ | P. 196

pinot blanc

Winemakers in Alsace, California and Italy craft wines from Pinot Blanc (also called Pinot Bianco) that tend to be medium-bodied and mildly fruity. Sometimes referred to as "the poor man's Chardonnay," Pinot Blanc goes by the name Weissburgunder ("white Burgundy") in Austria, where the variety expresses richer, more concentrated flavors and greater overall character than in typical Pinot Blanc styles found elsewhere.

BEST PAIRINGS Pair Pinot Blanc with delicate freshwater fish like trout or perch, or light meat dishes involving chicken breasts or veal scallops. Italian Pinot Biancos tend to be leaner and are best with raw shellfish or fresh green salads lightly dressed.

Byron | 2007 | ★ ★ **$** | P. 169
Domaine Mittnacht Freres | 2007 | ★ ★ ★ **$** | P. 24
Domaine Weinbach Clos des Capucins Réserve | 2007 | ★ ★ ★ **$ $** | P. 24
Erath | 2007 | ★ **$** | P. 198
Josmeyer Mise du Printemps | 2006 | ★ ★ **$ $** | P. 24

pinot gris/pinot grigio

In Alsace and Oregon, Pinot Gris produces full-bodied, nutty white wines. In Italy, where it is called Pinot Grigio, the grape makes light, brisk whites. It also has success in California's cooler regions.

BEST PAIRINGS Light and simple Pinot Grigios make a good match for equally light fish dishes and green salads. Alsace-style Pinot Gris tends to be richer and goes better with flavorful pasta dishes or chicken in cream-based sauces; it also pairs well with modestly spiced Asian and Indian dishes.

Anne Amie | 2007 | ★ ★ ★ **$** | P. 197
Brigl Sielo Blu | 2007 | ★ **$** | P. 87
Domaine Paul Blanck | 2007 | ★ ★ **$** | P. 25
Kracher Illmitz | 2007 | ★ ★ **$** | P. 144
RoxyAnn | 2007 | ★ ★ ★ **$** | P. 198

pinot noir

Called the heartbreak grape, Pinot Noir is difficult to grow and vinify. At its best, Pinot Noir is incredibly seductive, with aromas of roses, smoke, red fruits and earth. The red wines of Burgundy are regarded as the variety's ultimate expression, but excellent examples are also made in Australia, California, the Loire Valley, New York, New Zealand and Oregon.

BEST PAIRINGS Old World Pinot Noir (Burgundy, for instance) goes best with simple, flavorful dishes such as steaks, lamb chops or wild game birds. Fruitier, more straightforward New World bottlings are good matches for duck, richer fish, particularly salmon, and dishes involving mushrooms.

DeLoach | 2007 | ★ ★ ★ $ $ | P. 182
Domaine Bruno Clair Les Longeroies | 2006 | ★ ★ ★ $ $ $ | P. 44
Handley | 2007 | ★ ★ ★ $ $ | P. 184
Poderi Colla Campo Romano | 2006 | ★ ★ $ $ | P. 85
René Favre & Fils | 2005 | ★ ★ $ $ | P. 147

riesling

Riesling can make white wines of incredible complexity, with high acidity and plenty of mineral flavors, in styles that range from bone-dry to sumptuously sweet. Riesling is made all around the world, but the best versions come from Alsace, Germany, Austria, Australia and New York. Many can age for decades.

BEST PAIRINGS Off-dry (lightly sweet) Rieslings pair very well with Asian cuisines, especially Thai and Vietnamese. Dry Riesling is a good accompaniment to freshwater fish such as trout, as well as dishes with citrus flavors.

Daniel Gehrs | 2007 | ★ ★ $ | P. 169
Domaine Mittnacht Freres | 2007 | ★ ★ $ $ | P. 26
Egon Müller Scharzhof | 2007 | ★ ★ ★ $ $ | P. 135
Högl Loibner Vision Smaragd | 2007 | ★ ★ ★ $ $ $ | P. 144
Peter Lehmann of the Barossa | 2008 | ★ ★ $ | P. 216

roussanne

The white wine grape Roussanne is most at home in France's northern Rhône Valley, where it yields wines with nutty, unctuous flavors. Often blended with Marsanne for the esteemed white wines of Crozes-Hermitage, Hermitage and St-Joseph, Roussane also appears with Viognier and other grapes. California grows Roussanne, too, with good results.

BEST PAIRINGS With its mineral notes and hints of melon and herbs, Roussanne makes an ideal partner for herb-based sauces on lighter meats and more substantial fish. It's also good with simple roast chicken and with vegetables like parsnips, fennel and celery root.

Château de Beaucastel | 2006 | ★ ★ ★ ★ $ $ $ $ | P. 63
Domaine de Lancyre | 2007 | ★ ★ $ $ | P. 69
Domaine Romaneaux-Destezet | 2007 | ★ ★ $ $ $ | P. 59
La Vieille Ferme | 2008 | ★ ★ $ | P. 63
Les Vignerons d'Estézargues From the Tank Vin Blanc
| 2007 | ★ ★ $ $ $ | P. 63

sangiovese

Sangiovese is an important grape in Italy, where it is prized for its red cherry and leather flavors and high acidity. It is most common in Tuscany, where it makes most of the red wines of Chianti and many of the exalted Super-Tuscans. The grape is also grown in California.

BEST PAIRINGS Sangiovese's bright cherry-berry flavors, firm acidity and moderate tannins are all characteristics that make it ideal for pastas with tomato-based sauces as well as pizza. Rich, starchy dishes such as risotto and full-flavored, dry-cured sausages are other good partners.

Altamura Sangiovese | 2005 | ★ ★ ★ $ $ $ | P. 193
Angelini Estate Sangiovese | 2006 | ★ ★ $ | P. 105
Antinori Pèppoli Chianti Classico | 2006 | ★ ★ ★ $ $ | P. 94
Barone Ricasoli Brolio Chianti Classico | 2006 |
★ ★ ★ $ $ | P. 94
Mazzei Fonterutoli Chianti Classico | 2006 |
★ ★ ★ $ $ | P. 95

sauvignon blanc

Sauvignon Blanc's finest expressions are the lemony, herbaceous white wines of the Sancerre and Pouilly-Fumé regions of France's Loire Valley, but many New Zealand examples, with flavors of zingy grapefruit and fresh-cut grass, are also outstanding. Winemakers in parts of California, Austria and South Africa produce excellent Sauvignon Blancs as well.

BEST PAIRINGS With its bright acidity, mixed citrus (most commonly grapefruit) flavors and herbal notes, Sauvignon Blanc makes an ideal partner for raw shellfish, light fish dishes, salads and fresh vegetable dishes; it's also a classic partner for anything involving goat cheese.

Beckmen Vineyards Purisima Mountain Vineyard | 2007 | ★ ★ ★ $ $ | P. 165
Comte Lafond | 2006 | ★ ★ ★ $ $ | P. 54
Craggy Range Te Muna Road Vineyard | 2008 | ★ ★ ★ $ $ | P. 228
Domaine Michel Thomas Silex | 2006 | ★ ★ ★ $ $ | P. 55
Spy Valley | 2008 | ★ ★ ★ $ | P. 229

sémillon

The second of Bordeaux's great white wine grapes after Sauvignon Blanc, Sémillon is the primary component of the region's luxurious, sweet Sauternes wines. The variety also appears on its own or blended with Sauvignon Blanc to make some delicious, full-bodied dry wines in Bordeaux and Australia.

BEST PAIRINGS Sémillon's notes of lemon and honey are an ideal complement to light fish in butter-based sauces, as well as simple baked or roast fish; it's also good with light chicken dishes.

Château Bonnet | 2008 | ★ $ | P. 31
Château Haut Rian | 2007 | ★ $ | P. 31
Château Lamothe de Haux | 2008 | ★ ★ ★ $ | P. 31
Château Nicot | 2007 | ★ ★ $ | P. 31
Les Arums de Lagrange | 2007 | ★ ★ $ $ | P. 31

syrah/shiraz

Typically rich, round, full-bodied and tannic, with berry, pepper and smoke aromas and flavors, Syrah is capable of producing wines that show both power and finesse and can age for decades. Its most renowned domains are the Hermitage and Côte-Rôtie appellations in France's Rhône Valley, but California's Central Coast, Washington State and Australia, where the grape is called Shiraz, also make impressive versions.

BEST PAIRINGS Pair spicy, structured Old World Syrahs with big steaks or game such as venison and lamb. Fruitier New World bottlings, like most examples from Australia, also work well with lamb and can go with rich, cheesy dishes like eggplant Parmesan or hamburgers topped with blue cheese.

Cimicky Trumps | 2007 | ★ ★ ★ $ | P. 219
Concannon Selected Vineyards | 2006 | ★ ★ $ | P. 187
M. Chapoutier Petite Ruche | 2007 | ★ ★ $ $ | P. 61
Perbruno | 2006 | ★ ★ ★ $ $ $ | P. 102
S.C. Pannell | 2006 | ★ ★ ★ ★ $ $ $ | P. 221

tempranillo

Grown throughout Spain, Tempranillo is best known as the variety responsible for the red wines of Rioja. Tempranillo-based wines tend to give spicy aromas, red fruit flavors and medium body.

BEST PAIRINGS Lamb in almost any form is a classic pairing for Tempranillo. Other good partners include hard sheep cheeses like Manchego and lighter roast meats like pork or veal. Tempranillo's typically cherrylike fruit also makes it nice with duck.

Bodegas Bilbaínas Viña Zaco | 2006 | ★ ★ ★ $ | P. 115
Bodegas Ondarre Ursa Maior Crianza | 2005 | ★ ★ $ | P. 115
Condado de Haza | 2006 | ★ ★ ★ $ $ | P. 117
Coto de Imaz Reserva | 2004 | ★ ★ $ $ | P. 115
Legaris Crianza | 2005 | ★ ★ ★ $ $ | P. 118

293 PAIRING BY GRAPE

viognier

The basis of many of the famed white wines of France's northern Rhône Valley, Viognier has become a favorite in California for its lush peach, citrus and floral flavors.

BEST PAIRINGS Pair low-acid, lush Viognier with fruits such as apples, pears and peaches, richer shellfish such as scallops or lobster and white-fleshed fish with butter or cream sauces. French versions, which tend to be leaner and spicier, are also good partners for guinea hen, quail, rabbit or sweetbreads.

Bridlewood Estate Winery Reserve | 2007 | ★★ $ $ | P. 168
E. Guigal | 2007 | ★★★ $ $ $ | P. 59
Jean-Luc Colombo La Violette | 2007 | ★ $ | P. 70
Paul Jaboulet Aîné Les Cassines | 2007 | ★★★ $ $ $ | P. 59
Routas Coquelicot | 2007 | ★★ $ | P. 74

zinfandel

California's own red grape (by way of Croatia), Zinfandel assumes many forms, from off-dry pale rosés and simple reds to full-bodied, tannic wines with blackberry and spice flavors. Zinfandel also makes thick Port-style dessert wines.

BEST PAIRINGS Zinfandel's robust, dark berry flavors, spice notes and moderate tannins make it an ideal partner for simple, hearty meat dishes like hamburgers, sausages or lamb chops. It's also a great match for barbecue, as the wine's sweet-spicy flavors complement the sweet, spicy sauce, and for Mexican food.

Dashe | 2007 | ★★★ $ $ | P. 189
Haywood Estate Los Chamizal Vineyard | 2006 | ★★★ $ $ | P. 191
Kendall-Jackson Vintner's Reserve | 2006 | ★★★ $ | P. 191
Terra d'Oro Home Vineyard | 2006 | ★★★ $ $ | P. 192
Windmill Old Vine | 2006 | ★★ $ | P. 192

wine & food pairing cheat sheet

CLASSIC DISHES	THE WINES
RAW OYSTERS	Muscadet
TUNA STEAK	Rosé
GRILLED SALMON	Pinot Gris
CRAB CAKES	Sauvignon Blanc
LOBSTER	Chardonnay
SALAD WITH VINAIGRETTE	Pinot Grigio
ROAST CHICKEN	Pinot Noir
PORK TENDERLOIN	Merlot
HAMBURGERS/SAUSAGES	Zinfandel
SPAGHETTI WITH RED SAUCE	Sangiovese
STEAK	Cabernet Sauvignon
PIZZA	Barbera
INDIAN CURRIES	Gewürztraminer
SPICY ASIAN FOOD	Off-dry Riesling

WHY THE MATCH WORKS	BOTTLE TO TRY
This white has an almost briny note that's great with raw shellfish.	**Marc Pesnot La Bohème** | **2007** | ★★ **$** | **P. 54**
Rosés have the fruit to stand up to meaty fish, but lack tannins that can make fish taste metallic.	**Château d'Aqueria** | **2008** | ★★ **$** | **P. 63**
Salmon and other rich fish can pair with either full-bodied whites or lighter reds.	**Domaine Ostertag Fronholz** | **2006** | ★★★ **$ $ $** | **P. 25**
Tangy, high-acid whites cut through the fat of pan-fried or deep-fried seafood.	**Spy Valley** | **2008** | ★★★ **$** | **P. 229**
Lobster's luscious, sweet flavor calls for a substantial white.	**Catena Chardonnay** | **2007** | ★★ **$** | **P. 236**
A salad with a tangy dressing will overwhelm low-acid whites but not tart whites.	**Fantinel Vigneti Sant' Helena** | **2006** | ★★ **$ $** | **P. 88**
Pinot Noir is light enough for white meat, yet flavorful enough for dark.	**Handley** | **2007** | ★★★ **$ $** | **P. 184**
Medium-bodied Merlot is a good red wine for lighter meats like pork or veal.	**Markham Vineyards** | **2006** | ★★ **$ $** | **P. 180**
Big, juicy reds have the substance to match robust meats.	**Dashe** | **2007** | ★★★ **$ $** | **P. 189**
Red wines with bright acidity complement tomato-based pasta sauces.	**Barone Ricasoli Brolio** | **2006** | ★★★ **$ $** | **P. 94**
The tannins in Cabernets balance the richness of well-marbled beef.	**Hill of Content** | **2005** | ★★ **$** | **P. 218**
This Italian red has enough acidity to cut through cheesy pizza slices.	**Vietti Tre Vigne** | **2006** | ★★ **$ $** | **P. 85**
Gewürztraminer's exotic aromas complement Indian spices like cumin and coriander.	**Fitz-Ritter Spätlese** | **2007** | ★★★ **$ $** | **P. 138**
Light sweetness can help cool the heat of spicy foods.	**Egon Müller Scharzhof** | **2007** | ★★★ **$ $** | **P. 135**

bargain wine finder

Great wine does not have to be expensive. Good value for money was an important consideration in the process of selecting the wines recommended in this guide. Following is an index of many different wines whose quality (★) to price ($) ratio makes them exceptional values and well worth stocking up on.

Whites

★ ★ ★ ★ $ $

R. López de Heredia Viña Gravonia, Rioja, Spain, p. 114

★ ★ ★ ★ $

Willamette Valley Vineyards Pinot Gris, Willamette Valley, Oregon, p. 198

★ ★ ★ $

Anne Amie Pinot Gris, Willamette Valley, Oregon, p. 197

Becquer, Rioja, Spain, p. 114

Château Lamothe de Haux, Bordeaux, France, p. 31

Covey Run Riesling, Columbia Valley, Washington, p. 203

The Crossings Sauvignon Blanc, Marlborough, New Zealand, p. 228

Domaine La Haute Févrie Le Fief du Pégatine Muscadet sur Lie, Muscadet Sèvre et Maine, France, p. 53

Domaine Mittnacht Freres Pinot Blanc, Alsace, France, p. 24

Domaine Spiropoulos, Mantinia, Greece, p. 150

Giesen Sauvignon Blanc, Marlborough, New Zealand, p. 229

Glatzer Grüner Veltliner, Carnuntum, Austria, p. 142

Hellfire White, Columbia Gorge, Oregon, p. 198

Hermann J. Wiemer Dry Riesling, Finger Lakes, New York, p. 210

Manni Nössing Kerner, Valle Isarco, Alto Adige, Italy, p. 88

Millbrook Tocai Friulano, Hudson River Region, New York, p. 210

Mulderbosch Chenin Blanc, Western Cape, South Africa, p. 248

Nautilus Pinot Gris, Marlborough, New Zealand, p. 230

Omaka Springs Estates Pinot Gris, Marlborough, New Zealand, p. 230

Omaka Springs Estates Sauvignon Blanc, Marlborough, New Zealand, p. 229

RoxyAnn Pinot Gris, Rogue Valley, Oregon, p. 198

Soellner Hengstberg Grüner Veltliner, Wagram, Austria, p. 143

Spy Valley Sauvignon Blanc, Marlborough, New Zealand, p. 229

Umani Ronchi Casal di Serra, Verdicchio dei Castelli di Jesi Classico Superiore, Italy, p. 105

Valmiñor Albariño, Rías Baixas, Spain, p. 123

Vavasour Sauvignon Blanc, Awatere Valley, New Zealand, p. 230

Villa Matilde Rocca dei Leoni Falanghina, Campania, Italy, p. 109

Villa Sparina, Gavi di Gavi, Italy, p. 81

Vinosia, Fiano di Avellino, Italy, p. 109

Wairau River Riesling, Marlborough, New Zealand, p. 230

Yalumba Wild Ferment Chardonnay, Eden Valley, Australia, p. 215

Rosés

★ ★ ★ $

Bieler Père et Fils Sabine, Coteaux d'Aix-en-Provence, France, p. 74

Reds

★ ★ ★ $

Ambra, Barco Reale di Carmignano, Italy, p. 99

Baron d'Ardeuil Vieilles Vignes, Buzet, France, p. 77

The Black Chook Shiraz/Viognier, South Australia, p. 222

Bodegas Bilbaínas Viña Zaco Tempranillo, Rioja, Spain, p. 115

Ca' Montini Cabernet Sauvignon, Umbria, Italy, p. 105

Cimicky Trumps Shiraz, Barossa Valley, Australia, p. 219

Clos de los Siete, Mendoza, Argentina, p. 237

Domaine Cabirau Serge & Tony Grenache, Vin de Pays des Côtes Catalanes, France, p. 71

Don Adelio Ariano Reserve Oak Barrel Tannat, Canelones, Uruguay. p. 254

Esporão Reserva, Alentejo, Portugal, p. 130

Fontanafredda Briccotondo Barbera, Piedmont, Italy, p. 84

Kaiken Malbec, Luján de Cuyo, Argentina, p. 238

Kendall-Jackson Vintner's Reserve Zinfandel, California, p. 191

Layer Cake Shiraz, South Australia, p. 221

Llano Estacado Signature Mélange, Texas, p. 211

Loriñon Crianza, Rioja, Spain, p. 116

Marchiori & Barraud Malbec, Perdriel, Argentina, p. 238

Mas Belles Eaux Les Coteaux, Languedoc, France, p. 72

Opawa Pinot Noir, Marlborough, New Zealand, p. 232

Red Red Wine, Oregon, p. 201

Santa Rita Medalla Real Cabernet Sauvignon, Maipo Valley, Chile, p. 245

Sasso al Poggio, Tuscany, Italy, p. 102

Slipstream Shiraz/Grenache, McLaren Vale, Australia, p. 224

Viña Cobos Felino Malbec, Mendoza, Argentina, p. 239

Vista Hills Treehouse Pinot Noir, Dundee Hills, Oregon, p. 202

Weinert Carrascal, Mendoza, Argentina, p. 239

Woop Woop Shiraz, South Eastern Australia, p. 222

Fortified Wines

★ ★ ★ $

Osborne Pedro Ximénez, Jerez, Spain, p. 268

top wine websites

The ever-increasing number of wine websites and blogs is making it easier to learn about wine and find great bottles. Here are a dozen of the most informative sites for both beginner oenophiles and connoisseurs.

burgundy-report.com & burghound.com
Two fonts of wisdom and opinion for Burgundy lovers.

cellartracker.com
An interactive site for sharing tasting notes, with a virtual wine cellar for tracking purchases and consumption.

drvino.com
Tyler Colman's wine-centric PhD dissertation spawned a scholarly website written for everyone.

erobertparker.com
A website and chat forum devoted to in-depth discussion of wine and events in the wine world.

foodandwine.com
Expert advice on bottles to buy and perfect food pairings from America's premier culinary magazine, FOOD & WINE, plus wine editor Ray Isle's lively Tasting Room blog.

jancisrobinson.com
One of the world's most admired wine critics offers her insights as well as the complete text of her invaluable Oxford Companion to Wine.

localwineevents.com & wineevents-calendar.com
Find a local wine tasting or plan a wine-oriented vacation.

snooth.com
An ever-growing wine community where you can research, shop and interact with fellow wine lovers.

winezap.com & wine-searcher.com
Find obscure bottles and compare prices in the U.S. (winezap.com) and worldwide (wine-searcher.com).

reliable importers

Not sure which bottle to choose? Look for the importer's name on the label. These importers, grouped by specialty, offer excellent wines that are among the best of their type.

Australia The Australian Premium Wine Collection, Epicurean Wines, Epic Wines, The Grateful Palate, Old Bridge Cellars, Pasternak Wine Imports

Austria Domaine Select Wine Estates, Monika Caha Selections, Terry Theise Estate Selections, Vin Divino, Winemonger

France Bourgeois Family Selections, European Cellars, Jenny & François Selections, Kermit Lynch Wine Merchant, Kysela Père et Fils, Louis/Dressner Selections, North Berkeley Imports, Robert Chadderdon, Robert Kacher Selections, Rosenthal Wine Merchant, Vineyard Brands, VOS Selections, Wilson Daniels

Germany Classical Wines, Rudi Wiest Selections, Terry Theise Estate Selections, Valckenberg

Greece Athena Importing, Athenee Importers

Italy Angelini Wine, Ltd., Dalla Terra, Domaine Select Wine Estates, Empson USA, John Given Wines, Kobrand, Marc de Grazia Selections, Montecastelli Selections, Panebianco, Summa Vitis, Terlato Wines International, Vias Imports, Vin Divino, Vinifera, Winebow

Portugal Aidil Wines & Liquors, Broadbent Selections, Signature Imports, Tri-Vin Imports

South Africa Cape Classics, Vineyard Brands

South America Billington Wines (Argentina & Chile), Brazilian Wine Connection, Vine Connections (Argentina)

Spain Classical Wines, De Maison Selections, European Cellars, Europvin, Fine Estates from Spain

index of wines

a

Abadal Picapoll, Pla de Bages, 119

Abeja Chardonnay, Washington State, 203

Abtei Muri Riserva Lagrein, Alto Adige, 90

Accornero Bricco Battista, Barbera del Monferrato Superiore, 84

Adega Eidos Viticultores Eidos de Padriñán Albariño, Rías Baixas, 121

Alfred Gratien Blanc de Blancs Brut, Champagne, 258

Alphonse Mellot La Moussière, Sancerre, 56

Altamura Cabernet Sauvignon, Napa Valley, 172

Altamura Sangiovese, Napa Valley, 193

Altamura Sauvignon Blanc, Napa Valley, 165

Ambra, Barco Reale di Carmignano, 99

Amisfield Pinot Noir, Central Otago, 231

Andrew Will Champoux Vineyard, Horse Heaven Hills, 205

Angelini Estate Sangiovese, Colli Pesaresi, 105

Angelini Pinot Noir, Veneto, 90

Angel Juice Pinot Grigio, California, 168

Anna Maria Syrah, Rogue Valley, 199

Anne Amie Pinot Gris, Willamette Valley, 197

Anne Amie Winemaker's Selection Pinot Noir, Willamette Valley, 199

Antinori Pèppoli, Chianti Classico, 94

Antiyal, Maipo Valley, 243

Apaltagua Reserva Chardonnay, Casablanca Valley, 241

Aramis Vineyards (Black Label) Cabernet Sauvignon, McLaren Vale, 218

Arboleda Sauvignon Blanc, Leyda Valley, 241

Arbor Crest Wine Cellars Merlot, Columbia Valley, 205

Arceno PrimaVoce, Tuscany, 101

Archery Summit Red Hills Estate Pinot Noir, Dundee Hills, 199

Argyros Atlantis, Santorini, 151

Argyros Estate Argyros, Santorini, 150

Arrogant Frog Lily Pad White Chardonnay/Viognier, Vin de Pays d'Oc, 69

Arrowood Saralee's Vineyard Syrah, Russian River Valley, 186

Artesa Pinot Noir, Carneros, 181

Artezin Zinfandel, Mendocino County, 189

Atlas Peak Cabernet Sauvignon, Napa Valley, 172

A.T. Richardson Chockstone Riesling, Grampians, 216

Austin Hope Hope Family Vineyard Grenache, Paso Robles, 193

Austin Hope Hope Family Vineyard Syrah, Paso Robles, 186

AutoMoto Riesling, California, 168

b

Bacalhôa, Moscatel de Setúbal, 274

Banfi Rosa Regale, Brachetto d'Acqui, 262

Barbeito Bual Madeira, 272

Barboursville Vineyards Pinot Grigio, Virginia, 210

Barda Pinot Noir, Río Negro, 237

Barefoot Chardonnay, California, 161

Baron d'Ardeuil Vieilles Vignes, Buzet, 77

Baron de Ley 7 Viñas Reserva, Rioja, 115

Barone Ricasoli Brolio, Chianti Classico, 94

U

V

W

X

Y

Z